P9-DOC-566

More

POWER to

YA

Céleste perrino Walker

REVIEW AND HERALD® PUBLISHING ASSOCIATION
HAGERSTOWN, MD 21740

Copyright © 2001 by
Review and Herald® Publishing Association
All rights reserved

The author assumes full responsibility for the accuracy of all facts
and quotations as cited in this book.

Unless otherwise noted, all texts cited are from the *Holy Bible, New International
Version.* Copyright © 1973, 1978, 1984, International Bible Society. Used by
permission of Zondervan Bible Publishers.
    Texts credited to Message are from *The Message.* Copyright © 1993, 1994, 1995,
1996. Used by permission of NavPress Publishing Group.
    Verses marked TLB are taken from *The Living Bible,* copyright © 1971 by
Tyndale House Publishers, Wheaton, Ill. Used by permission.

This book was
Edited by Helen Lee
Copyedited by Lori Halvorsen and James Cavil
Designed by Trent Truman
Electronic makeup by Shirley M. Bolivar
Cover art by Greg Winters
Typeset: 11.5/13.5 Kandal Book

PRINTED IN U.S.A.

05 04 03 02 01   5 4 3 2 1

R&H Cataloging Service
Walker, Céleste perrino, 1965-
    More power to ya, by Céleste perrino Walker.

    1. Teenagers—Prayer—books and devotions—English.
2. Devotional calendars—Juvenile literature.   1. Title.

242.6

ISBN 0-8280-1573-2

Dedication

his book is dedicated to my friend Michele Deppe, who patiently fed me devotional ideas when I was slamming my forehead against the Wall of Desperation to see if anything else would drop out. Together we have walked and talked with Jesus, and I have learned the value of a true Proverbs 27:6 friend. *Merci, mon amie. Je t'aime.*

Introduction

eaven is one of those things we think of as in the hazy future. *Someday we'll get to heaven.* But heaven is more than a someday fantasy. It can be a right now reality. Jesus came here to hand it over to us.

Sure, heaven is a physical place, but it's also a relationship with God. When Adam and Eve sinned, they separated themselves from God and lost their home in the Garden of Eden.

God has been working to restore them to Himself ever since. That's why Jesus came. That's why He did everything He did while He was here. That's why He died. And that's why He rose again.

We may not be living in the physical heaven right now, but we can have heaven in our hearts this very minute and every minute of every day. All we have to do is let go of sin and grab on to Jesus.

That doesn't mean you'll be living in a bed of roses. Stuff happens, after all. This world is *not* heaven. But when Jesus is in our hearts and we are connected with Him, then heaven happens for us every moment no matter what else is going on.

Life is all about relationships. Our relationship with God. Our relationship with our parents or guardians. Our relationships with friends, relatives, sisters and brothers, teachers, pastors, youth directors, everyone. Even the bus driver. To some extent we have relationships with everyone in our lives.

And that's where it all starts. Our most important relationship is with God. But our other relationships are important too. And if they are messed up, life can be a lot harder than it needs to be.

You've probably had misunderstandings or fights with your parents or friends. You know how it can make you feel. Your stomach gets upset, and you feel depressed and don't want to do anything. You mope around and everything is just *raunchy*.

But it doesn't have to be that way. God specializes in *restoration*. In other words, He wants to fix the relationship between us and Him. He can also help us take care of our other relationships, help them grow, and show us how to fix them when bad things happen.

Jesus wants to help you strengthen your relationships. He's got unlimited power. What are you waiting for? Come on! Let's go!

— Céleste

Start at the Very Beginning

nce upon a time. That's how all stories start, isn't it? It's always best to start at the beginning. And in our beginning was God. God was always there, had always been there, would always be there. Nothing that happened at Creation could have happened without God.

In the beginning God. God was always there. He had always been there, and He would always be there. Nothing that happened at Creation could have happened without God.

Genesis tells us how everything started. It tells us the mistakes people made and the opportunities they had. And it shows us clearly that God's way is the best way. Anything other than God's way involves pain and consequences.

Not too long after she was created, Eve found herself in a bad situation. She was where she shouldn't have been. We all end up in bad situations now and then. But whenever you find yourself in a similar situation as Eve, ask yourself, "What is God's best for me?"

God's best for Eve was that she obey Him and not eat the fruit from the tree of the knowledge of good and evil. But she said, "No way," and found herself living outside the garden. Eve changed the whole course of her life with one decision. And we can too.

Let's make good decisions and choose God's best way. Remember, God doesn't abandon us to make our own choices. Ask Him what to do, and He'll tell you.

■ ■ ■ ■

In the beginning God. Genesis 1:1.

The Devil Made Me Do It

ne of the hardest things to do is to accept responsibility for something we've done wrong. Have you ever done something you shouldn't have and then blamed the devil for it?

"It's not my fault that I dinged the car, Dad. I was sure I could get my bike out of the garage without hitting it. The devil must have made me do it."

Eve made a bad choice. But instead of owning up to it, she blamed the devil without batting an eye. "The devil made me do it," she told God.

But you know what? The truth is that the devil can't make us do anything. Oh, he can suggest plenty of things. He can wheedle and bribe and make it sound so wonderful that you have a hard time turning it down. But he can never force you to do something.

It's always your choice to obey God or to give in to the devil. The most powerful weapon God gave us against the devil is prayer. Use it the next time you're tempted. It will send the devil running in the other direction.

Then the Lord God said to the woman, "What is this you have done?" The woman said, "The serpent deceived me, and I ate."
Genesis 3:13.

Lose-Lose Situation

ave you ever been in a lose-lose situation? When you know that no matter what you do, you're going to lose in the end? That's how Hagar must have felt. After she ran away from Sarai and Abram, she sat down beside a desert spring, unsure of what to do next. That's when an angel appeared.

"Go back to Sarai," the angel said.

Go back to Sarai? Great, either wander aimlessly around in the scorching desert until she died, or go back and be beaten by a mistress who hated her. What a choice! It looked bad for Hagar either way.

But God cared about Hagar. He cares for everyone, even those who are rejected and abused. Hagar must have felt as though she had to choose between death and abuse, but God was in one of the choices. "Go back," He said. "I will so increase your descendants that they will be too numerous to count."

In the end Hagar obeyed God, and His promise was fulfilled. Today God promises us, "I will never leave you nor forsake you," (Joshua 1:5). Remember that promise the next time you face a lose, lose situation.

"Your servant is in your hands," Abram said.
"Do with her whatever you think best." Then Sarai mistreated
Hagar; so she fled from her. Genesis 16:6.

The "I" in SIN

he "I" in sin is there for a reason. When we start thinking about ourselves, we stop thinking about God. We might think we've got it all together, but we're only fooling ourselves. It's what gets us into trouble, just as it got Samson into such a mess.

Samson had a big problem in the way he related to women—Delilah, in particular. He wanted to be with her, so he ignored the problems. *Three times* she tried to turn him over to the Philistines. Some friend, huh?

Samson refused to admit that there was a problem. *I can take care of myself,* he thought. And finally he told Delilah what she wanted to know. The fourth time the Philistines came they captured him. Samson had been so busy thinking about what he wanted (being with Delilah) that he forgot to look at the bigger picture (where it was going to lead him in the end).

We have to admit every day that we have no power over sin. Only God does. After all, when we take the "I" out of sin, it's not even a word anymore.

He awoke from his sleep and thought, "I'll go out as before and shake myself free." But he did not know that the Lord had left him. Judges 16:20.

Humble Beginning

I t's very uncomfortable to admit that we are powerless. I mean, who wants to admit that something is out of his or her control? That's like being a failure, right? Nope. Not at all.

Naaman was the kind of guy who had it all together. He was a big shot. Then he got leprosy. He couldn't cure it. He couldn't ignore it. He couldn't even command it to leave. Poor Naaman. Here he was with a big problem, and there was nothing he could do about it. On top of that, he faced the humiliation of jumping into the Jordan and taking seven baths. He didn't want to do it. He wanted something more spectacular.

But there is no spectacular cure for the bad stuff. There is no easy way to forgive people. There is no fantastic way not to take drugs. There is no nifty way to keep yourself pure while you're dating. The only way to be strong in tough situations is to admit that by yourself you can do nothing. Then ask God to give you the strength to do it His way.

■ ■ ■ ■

So he went down and dipped himself in the Jordan seven times, as the man of God had told him, and his flesh was restored and became clean like that of a young boy. 2 Kings 5:14.

The Sand of a Thousand Seashores

and is neat stuff, especially real beach sand. It's so fine that you can pick it up, sift it through your fingers, and the wind will just carry it away. But what if the same sand were wet? You'd probably break your back trying to lift a shovelful of it to toss over your shoulder.

Job's sadness and troubles felt as heavy to him as the sand of a thousand seashores. That's pretty heavy, even if it wasn't wet!

Have you ever felt as though you'd lost everything? Life can change in ways we don't like. Maybe you have to move to another state. Maybe you want, more than anything, to play basketball—but you're too short.

God never promised us that we'd have fantastic, happy, fun-filled lives. It doesn't mean we won't. He just never promised that. So if you find yourself feeling bummed out, keep in mind that what He *did* promise us is even better.

He promised that He would always be with us. He promised to help us in all circumstances. He promised He'd never send us more than we could bear *with His help.* That's the key. Lean on God through prayer, through Bible study, through the support of godly people. His help is only a prayer away.

■ ■ ■ ■

Oh, that my sadness and troubles were weighed. For they are heavier than the sand of a thousand seashores. Job 6:2, 3, TLB.

The Braggy King of Babylon

e was walking. Well, maybe swaggering would be a better description. King Nebuchadnezzar was swaggering along on the rooftop (it was flat) of his house. Actually, it was a palace, a really big royal palace. And as he looked out on Babylon, bathed in the glow of a sunset untouched by pollution, he couldn't help the swelling of his chest as he glowed with pride.

"I built all this, by *myself*, for *my* glory," he said to himself.

And just like that, God took it all away from him. For the next seven years he wandered in the fields like a wild animal, nuttier than a tree full of acorns. It wasn't until he admitted his sin of pride that God restored him.

Until we admit our sin to God and look to Him for help, we can't be healed of it. We must submit to God's will. *Then* we will receive His power. Sometimes it takes a real tumble to bring us to our knees where we belong. But when you get there, you'll know you're in the right place.

Now I, Nebuchadnezzar, praise and exalt and glorify the King of heaven, because everything he does is right and all his ways are just. And those who walk in pride he is able to humble. Daniel 4:37.

Yeahbut

ave you got yeahbuts? They're handy when you don't want to be responsible for something you did. Someone says "But you said" and you say "Yeah, but" and come up with an excuse. Or you don't do your homework, and you use a yeahbut to explain why. "Yeah, but a comet crashed through the roof of my house."

The biggest problem with yeahbuts is that we think they release us from responsibility. But they don't. An excuse doesn't really excuse anything. When we throw up our hands and say "It's not my fault," what we're really saying is "OK, it *was* my fault, but I refuse to admit it because I don't want to learn anything from this experience."

We pass up a lot of learning that way, and it always leads to problems later on. When you get to be old like me and graduate from high school and get a job, your boss isn't going to care what crashed through your house. He's going to want your work done anyway.

Two words will rid you of yeahbuts. They are: "I'm sorry." If you did it, own up to it and apologize. Learn something from it. And the yeahbuts will never bother you again.

*The lips of the righteous nourish many, but fools
die for lack of judgment. Proverbs 10:21.*

In the Garden

As Jesus knelt in the Garden of Gethsemane, it seemed as though the very darkness were pressing in on Him. Calvary loomed in front of Him like a rock about to crash down off a mountainside and smash the very breath out of Him. He could see no way around it, over it, or past it without going *through* it.

Jesus prayed that night for God's will to be done. Even though He was God Himself, He submitted Himself to the will of God the Father. He prayed *so that He would be willing.*

Bad things happen to all of us. We can either yell and scream and kick our feet like a toddler having a temper tantrum, or we can pray and ask God to help us to be *willing* to go through it. When we do that, when we're willing, we learn things. It's how He teaches us.

Sometimes it hurts, but we can be sure that if we're walking with God, His way is the best way. Jesus could have skipped town that night instead of going through with Calvary. But we will be forever grateful that He didn't. God's way may not always be the easiest way, but it's always the *best* way.

And being in anguish, he prayed more earnestly, and his sweat was like drops of blood falling to the ground. Luke 22:44.

And Then There Were None

dam and Eve huddled together as the night grew cold. They shivered. They had never felt cold before. Around them they noticed the rustle of leaves in the nearby woods. The animals were no longer friendly, and they were afraid. From the direction of the garden they heard a strange sound. Like the sound of a wounded animal.

But no, it wasn't an animal. In wonder they listened as the voice became clearer through the still night air. They recognized it. The voice of the One who had spoken so kindly to them. The voice of the One who had walked and talked with them on the garden paths. It was God's voice. But He wasn't laughing or singing or calling them to come see something new. This was a sound they had never heard before.

God was crying.

He missed them, and He had a plan to bring them back. Not to the garden, but to a place even more wonderful. Adam and Eve had said no to God's best plan. But there was a way back for them. And for all of us who want to take it.

All we have to do is believe in Jesus.

So the Lord God banished him from the Garden of Eden to work the ground from which he had been taken. Genesis 3:23.

Self-help Is No Help

here was a man who was great working with computers, but he had a problem with a pipe under his kitchen sink. He thought about calling a plumber and then changed his mind. *I can do this,* he thought. So he rolled up his shirtsleeves and crawled under the sink. He took a big ole wrench and started yanking on the coupling that held the pipes together.

Know what happened? The whole pipe broke off, and water gushed out. The man got very, very wet. And then his kitchen got very wet. And he *still* had to call a plumber.

That man thought he could do it himself even though he didn't have the knowledge or resources to do the job right. He had no idea what he was doing, and he ended up making a big mess.

The same thing can happen to us when we try to fix ourselves up instead of letting God do it. Only God knows what we need in order to grow. Trying to do it ourselves is a big mistake. Salvation isn't a do-it-yourself job. Let God fix what's wrong. He's got the stuff to do the job right.

Anyone who intends to come with me has to let me lead. You're not in the driver's seat; I am. Mark 8:34, Message.

And Then He Sank

The water whipped up a misty spray. Peter could feel it lashing across his face and dribbling down his beard. Beneath him the waves felt, well, squishy under his bare feet. The water around the Master seemed calmer somehow. Maybe it was just because Jesus didn't have a panic-stricken look on his face that Peter knew was on his own.

Everything had been going well—until he took his eyes off Jesus. Peter stared fearfully at the water beneath his feet. The boat was behind him, and Jesus was in front of him. There was nothing holding him up on the water but his faith.

And then he sank.

Glug, glug.

Well, OK, he didn't *really* sink. He only started to. Jesus reached out, and Peter had a choice: drown or take Jesus' hand. He could have listened to his pride and said, "No way! If I accept help, it shows that I'm weak. I can't do that. I'll look bad." But instead he chose to accept help from God.

To accept help, even to admit you need help, requires a certain amount of humility. Pray that God will make you humble enough to ask for and accept help when you need it. Because there *will* be times when you'll need it.

But when he saw the wind, he was afraid and, beginning to sink, cried out, "Lord, save me!" Matthew 14:30.

The Hole in Your Soul

icole didn't have a very good relationship with her father. Most of the time he was too busy to pay any attention to her. When he did notice, it was to tell her what she was doing wrong. He never hugged her or was affectionate in any way. What do you suppose Nicole did?

When you don't get what you need from the person you should get it from, you look somewhere else. And that's what Nicole did. She started dating early. Boys pressured her to do things she didn't want to do and usually she caved in, terrified that she'd lose even their limited affection if she said no.

Are you growing up with a big empty hole in your soul for reasons you'd rather not share? If you are, you don't have to use temporary "Band-Aids" you'll regret later. You'll see other kids using "Band-Aids," such as drugs, alcohol, pre-marital sex, cigarettes, and joining gangs. But you don't have to.

You have a God who is bigger than the hole in your soul. If you ask Him, He will fill it up for you. He will fill you with joy!

May the God of hope fill you with all joy and peace as you trust in him, so that you may overflow with hope by the power of the Holy Spirit. Romans 15:13.

Like a Little Child

hen you're big *[bump, bump, bump],* you can do anything you want *[bump, bump, bump]."* So sang a 5-year-old boy to his own tune, at the top of his lungs, while he stomped around the house. To him, being grown up was the goal. When he was finally big, he could do anything he wanted. Then his mother informed him that even adults have to do things they don't especially like to do. Such as work. And pay bills. And work. (She mentioned work more than once.)

Chances are you can think of at least 10 things you'll be able to do when you're officially "grown up" that you can't do right now. But there is one thing you can't grow up to do. In fact, you have to stay a child.

Jesus said that we must be like little children when we go to God. That's because little children are so innocent. They believe you. They trust you. They rely on you. We have to approach God that way—trusting, relying, letting Him lead us. We may not be able to do everything we want, but we'll sure be going in the right direction!

■ ■ ■ ■

I tell you as seriously as I know how that anyone who refuses to come to God as a little child will never be allowed into his Kingdom. Mark 10:15, TLB.

Multitude of Sins

ave you ever thought that your sins couldn't possibly be forgiven? That you were such a horrible person that God couldn't possibly love you? One of Jesus' best friends also thought that.

Peter. Poor, loud, impetuous Peter. Only opening his mouth to change feet. Hot one minute, cold the next. He chopped the ear off the high priest's servant to defend Jesus and only hours later denied ever knowing Him.

When that cock crowed, he was sure it was laughing at his cowardice. No way could he look Jesus in the eye again. What Peter and you and I and every other person on the planet has a hard time realizing is that *God loves us all the time.* No matter how horrible we've been. No matter what rotten things we've done. God loves us.

When you're sinning, He doesn't like what you're doing, but He still loves you. More than anything on earth. He wants you to stop because you're hurting yourself, and no one wants to see someone they love being hurt. He doesn't want to zap you with a thunderbolt. He wants to give you a great, big hug. He wants to tell you that He loves you. That He always has. That He always will.

■ ■ ■ ■

Whoever turns a sinner from the error of his way will save him from death and cover over a multitude of sins. James 5:20.

Head of the Class

I think Paul got straight A's in school. I think he passed his SAT with flying colors. I think he actually read all the books for his book reports. I think he went to banquets with the most popular girls. I think he wore robes with the "right" labels.

Paul had it all. He was on his way up. He wanted to work for God. He was a "Hebrew of the Hebrews" (Philippians 3:5). The order of the day was serve God first, ask questions later. And really, looking at him, you have to admit that God couldn't have found a more likely looking candidate for His work.

But Paul had to learn one important lesson first. He had to learn that everything he was, all he had done, and the sum total of his knowledge didn't amount to a hill of beans as far as God was concerned. God wanted one important thing before Paul was ready to work for Him.

He wanted Paul.

He wanted to be first with Paul. He wanted Paul to follow Him instead of trying to lead Him. We sometimes get those two confused. We're the followers, not the leaders in our relationship with God. So what did Paul do? Look up Acts 9:1-31 to find out.

■ ■ ■ ■

*But whatever was to my profit I now consider loss
for the sake of Christ. Philippians 3:7.*

The Ogre

he Ogre was my sister, and I would have rather been caught picking my nose than hanging around with her. It was irritating how she was always copying me.

"We don't want her around," my friends would whine.

And I was afraid they'd stop being my friends. So I snarled at the Ogre and ignored her and wished she'd been born into any family but mine.

Peer pressure can help us to do good things (such as participate in sports) or bad things (such as experiment with drugs). It's about what other people think of us. Their opinion is important to us. And it should be. But what people think of us is not as important as God's opinion.

When your friends pressure you to do something, run it past God first and see what He thinks of it. If I hadn't done that, I might never have found out what a great person the Ogre—I mean my sister, Faith—really was.

If any of you are embarrassed over me and the way I'm leading you when you get around your fickle and unfocused friends, know that you'll be an even greater embarrassment to the Son of Man when he arrives in all the splendor of God, his Father, with an army of the holy angels. Mark 8:38, Message.

Use Your Head

bram thought he'd pull a fast one. When he and his wife, Sarai, pulled into Egypt, Abe checked out the situation and thought the Egyptians might be tempted to bump him off so they could have his wife. He talked her into saying she was his sister instead.

Even though God had led him from his country, Abram didn't trust God to keep him and his wife safe in Egypt. He took matters into his own hands. And that's when the trouble started.

The king thought Sarai was very pretty and took her into his house, intending to marry her. But God sent serious diseases on Pharaoh and his household. Pharaoh was mad when he figured out what was going on.

"Why didn't you tell me she was your wife?" he demanded (Genesis 12:18).

Why indeed?

Because Abe looked around and got nervous. Instead of asking God to protect them and *trusting Him to do it,* he took charge.

Wrong answer.

God expects us to use the brains He's given us. But He also wants us to use them as we *follow Him.*

Say you are my sister, so that I will be treated well for your sake and my life will be spared because of you. Genesis 12:13.

Graded

I can still remember how nervous I was when report cards were handed out. And when tests were passed back. Isn't it great when the teacher hands it to the kid at the front of the row and it's passed back (so everyone can see it) until it reaches you—at the back of the row? That always made me want to crawl under the carpet.

Grades are important. But they aren't everything. God doesn't love us or not love us based on our performance. Don't forget that the next time you open your report card and feel as though you're looking in a mirror:

B, C+, D, A, A–, C

What a reflection, huh?

But really, grades only reflect what we know. That's only one part of us. An A or a D is only a reflection of one subject. We have to take *all* of us into account when we measure our worth. And then we have to know, really know, that God loves *all the parts of us.* He loves the D's and even the F's. But more than that, if we let Him tutor us, He can help us turn them all into A's.

Consider the ravens: They do not sow or reap, they have no storeroom or barn; yet God feeds them. And how much more valuable you are than birds! Luke 12:24.

Bananarama

hen I was 10, my best friend was a boy named Michael. He came to my school from St. Joseph's Orphanage. He had a face like an elf and a mop of brown hair that was always in his eyes. He was shorter than I was, and he had this game he called bananarama. During recess he would come up to me and yell "bananarama" as he jumped up and slammed his forehead into mine.

It hurt. But I pretended to like it because Michael was one of my only friends. And I felt sorry for him and his brother and sister. They stuck together with a fierce loyalty. I'm not actually sure if both their parents were dead, but whatever the situation was, they were all they had.

Jesus wants us to think of others first. It's what He calls us to do. But He doesn't want us to be doormats. My desire to be friends with Michael was good, but not at the expense of a headache. I never told Michael I didn't like bananarama. Now I wish I had. We might have invented a different game that we both liked, and saved my aching head.

You, my brothers, were called to be free. But do not use your freedom to indulge the sinful nature; rather, serve one another in love. Galatians 5:13.

Don't Worry, Be Happy

The disciples were first-class worriers at times. They worried about what they were going to wear, what they were going to eat, who was going to sit next to Jesus in heaven, how they were going to feed a hungry crowd, whether their boat was going to capsize in storms. Yep, they were worriers all right.

And maybe from a human, earthly perspective it looked as though they had something to worry about. I mean, I've been in a boat during a stretch of rough water, and it's hard not to get a little paralyzed with fear and doubt and start worrying. And since worry hangs out with fear and doubt, it's also hard not to worry.

The thing is that when we let ourselves worry about *anything,* it's like admitting that we don't trust God to take care of it. Jesus said, "Look, God takes care of *flowers;* He'll take care of you. He loves you more than He loves them."

Your job isn't to worry. Your job is to get close to God. If you do, you will have nothing to worry about.

And do not set your heart on what you will eat or drink; do not worry about it. For the pagan world runs after all such things, and your Father knows that you need them. But seek his kingdom, and these things will be given to you as well. Luke 12:29-31.

Some Things Never Change

ome things never change." Have you ever heard that expression? It can be a major pain, right? I mean, if it's your allowance that never changes or rules you don't like. That kind of stuff. And sometimes change is a good thing. Of course there are things you don't want to ever change, such as how much your parents love you or that you have food to eat every day and a warm bed to sleep in at night.

See, change can be good or it can be bad. The problem with change is that it's so unpredictable. One minute everything is the same and the next minute it's, well, changed. And sometimes when something changes, it won't change back. As you get older some things will change for you and no matter how hard you wish for them you won't be able to get them back.

But one thing will never, ever change. And that's how much God loves us. And the fact that He will be there for us no matter what happens. One of God's statements about Himself is that He will never change. So whenever you experience change in your life that makes you uncomfortable, lean on God, who never changes. He will comfort and guide you.

■ ■ ■ ■

I the Lord do not change. Malachi 3:6.

Power Full

aul was on a mission. From mild-mannered citizen he became—ta-dah!—Super Scourge. Out to rid the galaxy of Christians. And he did well. The Christians were scared of him. His reputation was developing nicely. He was moving up in the world.

The only problem was that he wasn't moving in the right direction, God's direction. When Jesus appeared to him on the road to Damascus, he was traveling there to capture more Christians. Jesus sent Saul to Damascus, all right—blind as a bat. Saul stayed there for three days unable to see anything.

Have you ever had a "Saul" moment? When you thought everything was going great and then something happened that made you realize that you're not really in control of your own life after all? Sooner or later we all have those moments.

The important thing to do when you have one is to admit that yeah, maybe you were headed in the wrong direction. And then ask God to lead you in the right direction.

Saul thought he was powerful. But after his conversion he realized that being "power full" means that you are full of God's power. And that only happens when you stop leading God and start following Him instead.

■ ■ ■ ■

For three days he was blind, and did not eat or drink anything. Acts 9:9.

The Family of God

ave you ever wondered if you were "good enough" to go to heaven? I mean, it's only natural, right? I don't think any of us would deny that we are sinful human beings.

Think of it this way. If someone asked you if you were part of your family, would you answer, "I don't know. I *think* so." Do you say, "Let's see, I have to take out the trash, sweep the floors, help with the grocery shopping, do my homework, feed the dog, and make my bed. I hope that's enough to belong to the family."

No way! You belong to your family because you're part of it. Those are things you *should do* because you are part of your family and because you *like* being part of your family. But not one of those things will *make* you a part of your family.

We're part of God's family, right? And it's the same way. God "saves" us (makes us part of His family), and everything we do *for* Him should be out of gratitude as family members. Be glad today that you're part of the family of God.

"Then who has any chance at all?" they asked. Jesus was blunt: "No chance at all if you think you can pull it off by yourself. Every chance in the world if you let God do it." Mark 10:26, 27, Message.

As You Will

 ometimes doing God's will is hard. Such as when He wants us to do one thing and we'd rather do another. That's kind of what Jesus experienced in the garden of Gethsemane. He asked God to take Calvary away, but if God wouldn't, He was willing to go through with it.

Doesn't that seem kind of odd? I mean, Jesus came to earth to die for us. He knew that before He came. Did He think God would change that at the last minute?

No, Jesus knew that God didn't want Him to die any more than He wanted to climb Calvary the next day. But they both knew that's what had to happen. God's will is what is *best*, not what is *easiest*. Many times we wish it was the other way around.

Of course, as humans, we are drawn to the easy road. That's why we need to pray before we make decisions and pray that God will show us His will. God's will may not be the easiest choice, but it will always be the choice that leads us into heaven. And He will always give us the strength to do His will. Just as He did for Jesus.

My Father, if it is possible, may this cup be taken from me.
Yet not as I will, but as you will. Matthew 26:39.

De Nile

enial, it ain't just a river in Egypt. Get it? Denial, De Nile (the Nile)? I'm so funny.

Of course, what isn't funny is our short-sightedness when it comes to facing problems. "Problem? Who, me? I don't have a problem." Even when people we trust point it out or even though something happens that shows us beyond a shadow of a doubt that we have a problem, it is still hard to admit it.

But living in denial is living dishonestly, pretending to be perfect when we know we're not. You may think that hiding your problems protects you, but that isn't true. It just makes you a slave to your problem. You have to lie about it and be aware of it all the time.

It's when we admit the truth that we become free to work on our problems. Hiding them only makes them worse. Jesus doesn't want us to be enslaved to our problems. He wants to help us get rid of them. If you need help admitting your problems, talk to an adult you trust. And be sure to take the problem to your heavenly Father, who is always worthy of your trust.

■ ■ ■ ■

If you hold to my teaching, you are really my disciples. Then you will know the truth, and the truth will set you free. John 8:31, 32.

Church Fix

Shara loves going to church. She's in the choir (which practices every Friday night and sometimes even more during the week). She's in Pathfinders. She's a junior deaconess. She's in the youth group, and they go on *lots* of trips every year. Oh, and she helps feed the homeless and visits the nursing homes with her folks.

The only problem is that Shara is so busy doing wonderful things in God's name that she's neglecting Him in the process. She never has time to read her Bible. Studying her Sabbath school lesson consists of skimming through it Friday night after choir practice before she passes out from exhaustion. And prayer? Well, there's no time for prayer.

Jesus wants us to enjoy Christian fellowship and service to others. But He wants a *relationship* with us even more. Sometimes we can get so caught up doing good that we forget the One who is good. Church activities, as fun as they are, should come *after* spending time with Jesus. Our relationship with Him should be our number one priority.

If He's not first on your list, you'd better take some time to rearrange your list before He slips away altogether.

■ ■ ■ ■

I know my sheep and my sheep know me. John 10:14.

Jars of Clay

I tried pottery for the first time last week. It was awesome. I took a lump of wet clay and put it on the pottery wheel. As the wheel turned, I created a bowl—not a perfect bowl, but a bowl. Then after the bowl was fired in a kiln, I painted it with a glaze. Now it's on my table full of apples.

The only problem is that it's fragile. If I dropped it on the floor, it would shatter.

Each of us is like that bowl. We're fragile. We break easily. And life knocks us around pretty hard sometimes. My clay bowl can't do anything to protect itself from being broken, and neither can we. We can't take ourselves out of the game or call time-out. We just have to trust our Creator to protect us.

And because He loves us so much, He doesn't just protect us. He fills us up with Himself and makes us unbreakable. Even though we're not strong, He gives us the power to rise above our circumstances and to keep going when life gets hard. He won't let anything break us. And the world will be amazed at our strength, *His* strength, that turns ordinary clay into steel.

■ ■ ■ ■

But we have this treasure in jars of clay to show that this all-surpassing power is from God and not from us. 2 Corinthians 4:7.

Pure Joy

hen Brian's best friend started teasing him about going to church, he didn't react with joy. And when he missed out on a class picnic because it was on a Saturday, he didn't feel joy. And when he messed up on his Pathfinder badge and ended up being the only one not to receive it, well, he wasn't a bit joyful about that either.

It's pretty hard to be joyful when bad things happen to us. But God doesn't want us to be grumpy just because things don't go our way. Tough times help us grow and become stronger Christians. When bad things happen, it's a chance for us to lean harder on God and to make sure we're still heading His way. If we are, then we should be thankful and even joyful.

Jesus never said life on earth would be easy or that it would be fun most of the time. But He *did* promise to help us through all the difficulties. And when He does that, we can be joyful even during the bad times because we know that He's helping us become strong.

Consider it pure joy, my brothers, whenever you face trials of many kinds, because you know that the testing of your faith develops perseverance. James 1:2, 3.

The End of the Line

Poor Hagar. She'd run away, but had returned and had borne Abraham a son. And she was probably pretty happy until Sarah gave birth to a son as well.

Sarah was angry when Ishmael picked on her son, Isaac. She demanded that Abraham send them away. So he did.

Hagar and Ishmael wandered in the desert of Beersheba until they ran out of water. Then Hagar set her son down under a bush and sat down a little way from him to watch him die. She began to sob. She'd done all she could. She was at the end of the line.

That's when God sent an angel to comfort her. He opened her eyes and showed her a well. Saved! By God Himself! You can be sure she was thankful. Are you?

God saves us from much more than death by thirst or starvation. He saves us from eternal death. But like Hagar, we have to give up everything. We have to come to the end of the line. We have to say, "God, I can do nothing. Be everything for me."

He will open our eyes to show us where the water of life is. The water that fills us so that we "will never thirst" (John 4:14). Drink up; it's free!

■ ■ ■ ■

And as she sat there nearby, she began to sob. Genesis 21:16.

Meet Maria

aria was tired. She had stayed up late to watch a movie, and now she stifled a yawn as she sat down. The words "pop quiz" woke her up fast, though. As the teacher passed out the papers she slunk down in her seat and started to sweat. She couldn't afford a bad grade, but she hadn't studied. She was going to have to cheat. Again.

She had promised herself that she wouldn't do it any more. But she didn't want to fail either. She looked at her neighbor's answers and began to copy them. Ten minutes later she was finished with the quiz, and she felt awful.

As she sat in her chair waiting for the class to be over, her thoughts were far away. "Dear God," she prayed silently, "I'm out of control. I can't stop cheating. Please help me."

When she got home that night she read her Bible and prayed. Then she looked at her stack of homework. And she remembered her friend Julie's invitation to play video games. She wanted to play video games, but she didn't want to have to cheat anymore. Sighing, she took out her books and settled down to study.

■ ■ ■ ■

The heart is deceitful above all things and beyond cure.
Who can understand it? Jeremiah 17:9.

Highway to Salvation

rrrr! It's getting pretty cold here now. I'm wishing for summer days and heat. So let's say I decide to head from snowy Vermont to Bermuda to warm my bones. What do you think would happen if I hiked down through the snow to the road and started walking?

Well, if you know anything at all about geography, you'd know that the cold must have affected my brain. It's a long way from Vermont (way up in the northeastern corner of the United States) to Bermuda (plunk out in the middle of the Atlantic—well, practically). Even if I could walk that far, I'd get pretty wet doing it. No, about the only way I could hope to make it to Bermuda is to rely on the generosity of people willing to pick up a slightly frozen hitchhiker, first by car and then by boat.

Believe it or not, this scenario is very similar to salvation. We often think we can get to heaven on our own, but really we can't. We have to stick out our thumbs and let Jesus give us a lift. It's the only way we'll get there because it's *much* too far to walk.

For it is by grace you have been saved, through faith—and this not from yourselves, it is the gift of God—not by works, so that no one can boast. Ephesians 2:8, 9.

Goddy Rains

L ittle kids don't always understand what they hear. Such as the child who thought God's name was Howard because he heard people pray, "Our Father, who art in heaven, Howard be thy name."

My 3-year-old daughter, Rachel, insisted that she wanted to listen to "Goddy Rains." I finally figured out that she was referring to Rich Mullins' song "Awesome God," which goes, "Our God is an awesome *God, He reigns.*"

I like that song myself because in the middle of life on a sin-sick planet it's easy to forget just how awesome God is. Cars crash, planes drop out of the sky, and storms destroy homes. But still God is here. He isn't powerless over these things. Think about it. He hung the worlds in space. Surely He can keep our families from splitting up and our friends from hurting us.

But that's not God's priority. He knows we're never going to be completely happy on this side of heaven. He knows that our lives won't be beds of roses. But He wants to save us for something much more important: eternity with Him. *That's* awesome.

■ ■ ■ ■

Hallelujah! For our Lord God Almighty reigns. Let us rejoice and be glad and give him glory! Revelation 19:6, 7.

Please Love Me

fter Ruth's husband died she followed her mother-in-law to a strange land. She picked up grain in the fields just so that they could have something to eat. Even though Ruth was sad about losing her husband, she must have wanted someone to love her again. Naomi, her mother-in-law, told her how to ask their kinsman Boaz to take care of her. All she had to do was curl up at his feet while he was asleep. It was like pleading, "Please, love me!" Ruth did just that, and Boaz responded to her cry.

It's hard to ask for love. Especially if someone has hurt you in the past. People often say that they love us, but their actions don't match their words. (And you know which one speaks louder.)

We all crave love. Being loved is important, and we need healthy relationships with people who will give us love. We can always be sure that God loves us, no matter who else does or doesn't. Any time we "curl up at His feet" He will be glad to take care of us.

■ ■ ■ ■

May you be richly rewarded by the Lord, the God of Israel, under whose wings you have come to take refuge. Ruth 2:12.

The Power of His Might

ver look at a problem and think, *Hey, I can lick that. No problem.* That's what Gideon must have thought. After all, he had 32,000 men to take with him into battle. Yep, he felt pretty safe. But God made him send 31,700 of them home! Can you hear Gideon's knees knocking together?

What would you have done? Gideon was scared, all right. But God told him to bust it down to the Midianites' camp and hear what they were saying about him. Sure enough, one of them had had a dream that the camp was crushed by Gideon. That made Gideon pretty happy.

God always knows what's coming up next. He doesn't always share that information with us, though. He asks us to trust Him. Gideon wasn't happy about letting all those men go. And I bet he wasn't too keen on sneaking into the enemy's camp, either. But he trusted God, and everything came out all right in the end. We have to remember that it's the destination that's important, not how we get there.

The Lord said to Gideon, "With the three hundred men that lapped I will save you and give the Midianites into your hands." Judges 7:7.

Put on a _____ Face

ou know that little yellow happy face you see people wearing on pins or sticking on their notebooks? That happy face makes my teeth hurt. I mean, what is it trying to say anyway? That you should be happy all the time? 'Cause I'm pretty sure that's impossible.

I know this because there have been times when I definitely wasn't happy. Such as today. While in a fabric store I stood in the wrong place to be checked out. A saleswoman rudely pointed out that there was only one line. I shuffled to where I should have been, but I wanted to hide in a fabric bolt instead. I wasn't happy.

But do you know what? God made us with emotions. And I think if He expected us only to be happy, He wouldn't have bothered making all the emotions, such as sadness and excitement. I think that God wants us to feel and express emotions, but He also wants us to know and rejoice in the fact that He is always our help and our salvation. Even against rude salespeople.

Rejoice in the Lord always. I will say it again:
Rejoice! Philippians 4:4.

Wake Up

Nebuchadnezzar thought he was really something. He was BMOC—Big Man on Campus. He was better than anyone else. He had it all. The best name brands? He had 'em. Popular people? He knew 'em. Everyone looked up to him. Well, they had to—he was the king. But believe you me, he also *knew* he was the king.

But when pride puffed him up and he took credit for everything he had, God sent Nebuchadnezzar into the wilderness to eat grass with the cows for seven years. He wasn't Big Man on Campus anymore; he was Big Mouth on Countryside. How humiliating!

How many times have you caught yourself doing the same thing? Everyone likes to be important, to be popular, to have friends. We think, *I have it all. I have arrived.* And then something goes wrong. God is giving us a chance to change our ways.

Like Nebuchadnezzar we need to turn our eyes to heaven and give God the glory and honor He deserves. Only He can deliver us.

■ ■ ■ ■

At the end of that time, I, Nebuchadnezzar, raised my eyes toward heaven, and my sanity was restored. Then I praised the Most High; I honored and glorified him who lives forever. Daniel 4:34.

Bad Stuff Happens

Joseph didn't exactly have an easy life. His brothers hated his guts. His mother was dead. He was sold into slavery when he was just a kid. He worked hard for his master, but his master's wife accused him of assaulting her, and he was thrown into prison.

Life isn't fair. Bad stuff happens all the time, even to good people. Unless we have something higher than ourselves to believe in, it's easy to give up when the going gets tough. We can't change the fact that the world is not the way it should be. But we can choose what attitude to have and whom to follow.

We need help from God to get us through—day after day. We need courage to confront our world with optimism when life kicks us in the teeth. We need help from God to change our responses to bad circumstances. And we need wisdom to know when to fight injustice and when to make the best of a bad situation.

Joseph relied on God in all things, and he ended up saving thousands of people. Trust God with your problems today.

■ ■ ■ ■

Joseph's master took him and put him in prison, the place where the king's prisoners were confined. Genesis 39:20.

Under Pressure

Obedience is important. Adam and Eve disobeyed God in the Garden of Eden. The snake pressured Eve to eat the fruit, and then Eve pressured Adam. They got kicked out.

King Saul refused to obey God at Gilgal. He buckled under pressure and offered sacrifices he didn't have any business offering. God ended his dynasty, and his throne later passed to David.

It's easy to get sidetracked by pressure, especially peer pressure, into doing something we had no intention of doing. Eve didn't head to the tree of the knowledge of good and evil with the intention of eating the fruit. But that's what she did. Saul didn't plan to offer the sacrifice. But when Samuel was late and his men were deserting him, he went ahead and did it.

When we knuckle under pressure from others, we often find ourselves in trouble. We need strength from God and faith in His ultimate plan to keep us on track and to give us strength when the pressure is on.

"You acted foolishly," Samuel said. "You have not kept the command the Lord your God gave you; if you had, he would have established your kingdom over Israel for all time." 1 Samuel 13:13.

Looking Out for Number One

om's girlfriend, Leisha, was the brightest girl in school. She was pretty, smart, and wildly popular. He really enjoyed getting to know her. They dated in high school, then college, and then Tom popped the question. She said "Yes," and they were married.

One evening Tom got home and found Leisha getting ready to go out. He asked her where she was going. "I'm going out with Bill tonight," Leisha responded.

"Who's Bill?" Tom wanted to know. Leisha calmly explained that she was dating someone else even though she was married to him. Can you imagine how terrible Tom must have felt?

And can you imagine how God feels when we claim to be Christians but love other things more than Him? Keeping God first is important. It's also something that doesn't just happen. Satan is more than happy to distract us with something to take God's place.

We really have to work at having a relationship with God. We have to make time to spend with Him. And we have to realize that anything Satan offers is a poor substitute for the gifts God wants us to have.

Make God number one today. You'll be eternally grateful.

■ ■ ■ ■

And God spoke all these words: "I am the Lord your God, who brought you out of Egypt, out of the land of slavery. You shall have no other gods before me." Exodus 20:1-3.

May the Force Be With You

You're in command of the galaxy. You must save all the friendly planets from invading forces. Only you can prevent tragedy of universal proportions. You climb aboard your Supergalactic space fighter and enter the battle.

Bzzzzt! Not quite.

We're in a war, all right. But it's not the kind of star wars that comes immediately to mind. No, the war is fought every day. It's fought in math class when you're tempted to cheat because you didn't study. It's fought in the cafeteria when the cashier gives you back too much change. It's fought when your best friend spreads lies about you all over school.

The war we're in isn't glamorous or even exciting. It's hard and painful and takes a lot of effort. Don't think it's not a real war because there aren't any light sabers or starships. It's real, all right. And we fight it through the choices we make every day.

Our choices determine how the battles are won. The good news is that we're not fighting alone. You can have all the help you want. Just ask for it. God will give you the wisdom to choose right over wrong and the strength to do it.

■ ■ ■ ■

So give your servant a discerning heart to govern your people and to distinguish between right and wrong. 1 Kings 3:9.

Out of the Graveyard

I t was dark and cold, but the man didn't notice the temperature. He heard the wind howling, and prowled restlessly around the gravestones. Inside legions of demons fought to control him. The small part of him that was still sane struggled to fight back, but it was too hard.

In the morning he looked down and saw Jesus climbing out of a boat. Screaming with anger, he rushed at Jesus. But he couldn't stand before Him. He fell down at Jesus' feet.

The demons inside him begged to be allowed to enter a herd of pigs nearby. Jesus agreed, and they entered the pigs, driving them into the water, where they drowned. Jesus lifted the man to his feet. He was sane.

Have you ever felt as though something else was controlling you? We can get involved with all kinds of things that take over our lives. We use them to cover the sadness we feel, thinking we will be made happy. Even when we try to get away from them, it doesn't work. But Jesus can come into our graveyard and make us whole again. Let Him take full control of your life.

When Jesus stepped ashore, he was met by a demon-possessed man from the town. For a long time this man had not worn clothes or lived in a house, but had lived in the tombs. Luke 8:27.

Get Ready for Good News

**H**ave you ever looked at the headlines or listened to the news and wondered if anything good ever happens on earth? I don't think it should be called "the news." It should be called "the daily death and destruction report." Wouldn't that make more sense? When do you ever hear about anything good that happened? A year's worth of good news wouldn't fill a half hour report.

We have to face the fact that where there is sin there will never be complete peace or joy or real love. Not the perfect kind that God wants for us. When things are going badly for us, it's easy to look around and see all the terrible things. That's normal. This isn't heaven. It's not supposed to be.

But the wonderful news is that even though we're here in this dark place, we can have a little bit of heaven with us when Jesus lives in our heart, when He helps us through each day, when He takes our hand in the dark.

It's that light He wants us to share with others. Get out of the way, Satan! God's coming back. And when He does, "the news" will be out of business, because there won't be any more suffering to report.

■ ■ ■ ■

I bring you good news of great joy
that will be for all the people. Luke 2:10.

As Yourself

Jenny was busy. She was so busy that she didn't have any time for herself. She sang in the church choir, helped out in her youth group, gave Bible studies online to a teen in Korea, helped her folks make Dorcas baskets, worked on Sundays in the thrift store at her church . . . the list was endless. Sometimes Jenny felt so discouraged and overwhelmed that she just wanted to quit everything.

When Jesus gave us the commandment "Love your neighbor as yourself," He didn't mean for us to stop after the word "neighbor." We have to love ourselves, too. We're supposed to love our neighbor *as* ourselves. But how can we love our neighbor if we don't love ourselves?

It's not wrong to take care of your needs. Listen to your body. If you're tired, get some extra sleep. If you need to relax for a while with your family, go ahead and do it. Take time to enjoy the good things in life. If you don't take time to love yourself, how can you love your neighbor? You end up doing a lot of good things for the wrong reasons.

When Jesus and His disciples were tired, He taught them to get away. They rested, and God renewed their energies. He filled them so they could fill others. "Go and do likewise" (Luke 10:37).

■ ■ ■ ■

Love your neighbor as yourself. Leviticus 19:18.

I Have Sinned

avid really goofed up big-time. He slept with another man's wife. Then he had the poor guy killed so he wouldn't find out. Then he married the woman. He didn't even seem to have any pangs of conscience until God sent Nathan to point out his sin.

Then what did he do? Did he try to cover it up? "Who me? What? Married? Was she married? I didn't know that."

Did he try to justify what he'd done? "Well, you see, it was really hot out, and I must have lost my head."

Did he point his finger at Bathsheba and say, "It was all her fault! What was she doing taking a bath on the roof in the first place?"

These are all reactions we have when someone points out sin in our lives. But David didn't cop out and try to excuse or deny his sin. He admitted it. Flat out. "I sinned."

It's only when we take responsibility for our sins that we can be forgiven. Because even though God is willing to forgive our sins before we commit them, we have to ask for His forgiveness and accept it before He can heal the damage our sins have caused.

When we repent He says, "I forgive you. Go and sin no more."

■ ■ ■ ■

Then David said to Nathan, "I have sinned against the Lord." 2 Samuel 12:13.

Your Faith Has Healed You

aphael was waiting for the bus. He stood patiently at the bus stop. Soon a bus pulled up. The door opened. Raphael watched. The door closed. The bus drove off. This happened over and over all day long. In the evening Raphael went home. Tomorrow he would try again.

Pretty silly story, huh? If Raphael really wanted to get on the bus and go somewhere, do you think he would have? All he had to do was walk onto the bus. Maybe he was scared. Maybe he thought the bus wouldn't actually take him where he wanted to go. Maybe he thought it *would,* and he really didn't want to go there.

We're a lot like that sometimes. We want God to take us somewhere in our lives, but we're afraid to get on the bus. So we hang out, *saying* we want to go somewhere but not actually going. It's safer that way, isn't it?

In the book of Luke a woman who had been sick for a very long time grabbed onto Jesus. She had faith that He would heal her, and He did. We need the same kind of faith to grab onto God and to let Him take us where we need to go. It's time to get on the bus! Jesus wants to give us the ride of our lives.

■ ■ ■ ■

Then he said to her, "Daughter, your faith has healed you.
Go in peace." Luke 8:48.

One More Time

osea had a problem. His wife, Gomer, had been a prostitute before he married her and now she had returned to prostitution. He probably wouldn't have married her in the first place if God hadn't told him to. But God wanted to show the people of Israel that no matter how much they rejected God, He would still love them just as Hosea loved his wife.

If you're ever tempted to believe Satan's lie that God doesn't love you or that you've done something so terrible that God can't love you, read the whole story of Hosea. When his wife left him to become a prostitute again, he redeemed her and brought her home. In the same way Jesus redeemed us so that we can go home with God.

Hosea didn't wait until Gomer changed her mind and came back on her own. He went after her. God does too. He doesn't want to lose us because He loves us too much. But it's up to us to go home with God and to get to know Him even more.

■ ■ ■ ■

Then you will lie down in peace and safety, unafraid; and I will bind you to me forever with chains of righteousness and justice and love and mercy. I will betroth you to me in faithfulness and love, and you will really know me then as you never have before. Hosea 2:18-20, TLB.

Day by Day

an you imagine eating only once a week? How about just a couple times a year? How about just at Christmastime? We know that our bodies need to be fed every day, and we don't usually starve ourselves.

Then why do we starve our spiritual lives? We think we can go for a long time without connecting with God and getting filled up by Him. Sometimes we live off just going to church once a week and having a snack while we hang out with our friends.

When the going gets tough, we bug out because we don't have God living inside of us. We fall on our faces, and that's usually when it dawns on us how much we need God and just how long we've gone without Him.

We're starving to death spiritually. But there's no need to starve! God is more than willing to give us everything we need. He wants to renew us day by day. Not just now and then.

How long has it been since you last ate? Fall on your knees and get fed! The menu is out of this world.

Therefore we do not lose heart. Though outwardly we are wasting away, yet inwardly we are being renewed day by day. 2 Corinthians 4:16.

Not Me, Lord!

oses looked at the burning bush in ab-
solute astonishment. God—inside the
bush—was calling him. "Moses, Moses!"

And Moses says, "Who? Me? You sure
you have the right guy?" And he's looking
around and what do you know, there's
not another soul for miles. So he walks up
to the bush. "Yeah? I'm here. Can I help You with something?"

So God explains what He wants Moses to do, and Moses says, "I
am Your servant, Lord; Yours to command. Whatever You want me
to do, I'll do."

Right? Not a chance! What Moses really said was "You've got to
be kidding! Send somebody else. *Anybody* else! Please, I'm begging
You! Look at me! I'm not the guy you want. I stutter. I smell like
sheep. I'm a nobody. Pharaoh isn't going to listen to me."

Moses came up with countless excuses. In the end, of course, he
did what God asked him to do, which was to let God work through
him. But first he had to be willing to do it. God never goes anywhere
He's not invited. We have to invite Him and be willing for Him to
direct us.

We're not worthy—but He doesn't ask us to be worthy. Just willing. Are you willing?

■ ■ ■ ■

But Moses said, "O Lord, please send
someone else to do it." Exodus 4:13.

Lost and Found

r. Carpenter glanced out the window at the snow-covered surroundings and wondered how his son Jimmy was doing. He'd left home months before and had only sent them a postcard from Hawaii that said, "Wish you were here."

Mr. Carpenter's two sons, Jimmy and Nick, were supposed to take over the family business. But then Jimmy had asked for his half of the business in cash so he could leave. Mr. Carpenter felt his eyes fill up with tears at the thought of Jimmy and how much he missed him.

Nick was standing by his dad at the window. Mr. Carpenter laid a hand on his older son's shoulder as they stared out the window at the softly falling snow. They both saw him at the same time—a struggling, disheveled, dirty, pathetic figure.

"It's Jimmy!" Mr. Carpenter exclaimed happily. Before Nick could say a word, the old man was racing for the door. Nick watched the reunion through the window in stony silence.

Question: If God were Mr. Carpenter, would you be afraid to come home if *you* had wandered away? Why or why not?

But we had to celebrate and be glad, because this brother of yours was dead and is alive again; he was lost and is found. Luke 15:32.

Wise Up!

No offense or anything, but Balaam was a bit of a know-it-all. He fooled around entirely too much with the occult, and thought that made him an expert on everything. He was really good at assessing a situation. But he had less true knowledge than, say, his donkey.

That's right. His donkey knew more about what was going on than Balaam did. When an angel appeared in their path, the donkey did everything it could to stop or go around. And Balaam beat the donkey because *he didn't have a clue.*

If he'd really been as smart as he thought he was, he would have admitted that what he was doing was wrong. After all, he was on his way to curse the people of God. It doesn't take an Einstein to realize that that's not a good thing. But it didn't get through to Balaam until the angel revealed himself, flaming sword and all.

That opened Balaam's eyes, all right. He finally realized that relying on one's own wisdom often leads to spiritual blindness. We have to rely on God's wisdom if we really want to know what's what.

And Balaam? In the end he didn't curse the people. He blessed them.

He answered, "Must I not speak what the Lord
puts in my mouth?" Numbers 23:12.

Don't Wait

My son has what we affectionately call a one-track mind. That means that when he gets something into his head, he has to do it. Don't bother him about anything else until he's done. It's great with some things, but at times it can be very annoying. Such as when he's intent on building a puppet theater or a bridge and it's time for school.

The good thing about it, though, is that if he starts a bridge, you can be sure he's not going to rest until the bridge is finished. We need that kind of dedication when we search for God. Often we go in fits and spurts. We're hot one minute and cold the next. And while God would rather we were hot or cold instead of neither here nor there, He would definitely prefer us to be hot.

God tells us that if we look for Him, we'll find Him. But what if we're not looking? How can you find something you're not even looking for? It's impossible, unless you stumble across it. And you don't want to leave it up to chance to stumble on a relationship with God. You may never find it. And that's definitely not the kind of thing you want to ever leave home without.

■ ■ ■ ■

You will seek me and find me when you seek me
with all your heart. Jeremiah 29:13.

True Evidence

Do you believe that the earth is round? Why? People didn't believe it in the days of Christopher Columbus. They thought he'd sail right off the face of the earth, which they believed was as flat as a pizza.

Well, you might say, there's evidence, proof. But what makes you believe the evidence and proof that you haven't actually seen? You haven't walked all the way around our "round" earth on your own two feet, have you? So your belief isn't based on personal experience. You believe what other people have told you.

In a similar way people believe that there is a God, even if they've never seen Him. Why? Because there is proof. Nature is called God's second book because it points to God as our Creator. Then there is the Bible. And last, but most certainly not least, they see God in us.

People who don't believe in God are disproved by the evidence surrounding them, just as people who didn't believe that the earth was round were disproved by Columbus's ship. Remember, your life as a Christian can be part of that evidence.

■ ■ ■ ■

For the truth about God is known to them instinctively; God has put this knowledge in their hearts. Romans 1:19, TLB.

Not in the Wind

lijah was pretty upset. He had been working hard for God, but nothing was going right. The Israelites had rejected God, busted the altars, and killed the prophets. He was the only one left. And now Queen Jezebel wanted him killed. Elijah was tired and discouraged. Do you ever feel that way?

God decided to make a statement to Elijah. He sent a gale-force wind, an earthquake, and a fire, but He wasn't in any of those things. He was in the still small voice that followed them. God showed Elijah that it wasn't always the big demonstrations that are the most successful in His work.

Think about it. Maybe you can't be the featured guest speaker on a satellite program. But you can hug a friend who is having a hard time. Maybe you can't carry a tune and sing special music at your church. But you can visit the old people in a nursing home.

You don't have to make a huge statement for God. He just asks you to whisper when you get the chance. He'll do the rest.

■ ■ ■ ■

Then a great and powerful wind tore the mountains
apart and shattered the rocks before the Lord,
but the Lord was not in the wind. 1 Kings 19:11.

Be Honest

ave you ever seen the comedy skit where the kid decides to wash his own clothes? Junior puts the clothes into the washing machine. And since he doesn't know how much detergent to put in, he dumps in half the box. The machine starts chugging away, and junior goes whistling outside to play ball.

Soon the machine starts coughing out bubbles. Lots and lots of bubbles! They cover the top of the washing machine. They spill down onto the floor. They fill the room and begin to ooze out under the door into the rest of the house. When junior comes back in, you see his expression of surprise and dismay. And then he slips and is buried in the ocean of bubbles.

When it's just a comedy skit, it's funny. But the same thing happens to us when people are unfair to us or hurt us. If we bury the resentment inside, it festers there like the bubbles. Sooner or later it's going to come out. And when it does, it will ultimately hurt us.

We need to be honest about our feelings. After expressing them, we can ask God to help us work through them. He will help us so we won't be controlled by our hidden emotions.

God is our refuge and strength, an ever-present help in trouble. Psalm 46:1.

Trust Me

I like to think that I can manage things on my own, thank you very much. I can follow directions, get around an airport, and read a map. So it's hard for me to digest the fact that I can't do anything God wants me to do without, um, God.

Moses learned this lesson the hard way. He got so sick of the Israelites' complaints that when they wanted water he didn't do what God told him to do. He did what he felt like doing. Instead of just speaking to the rock, Moses gave it a couple good whacks. His words were also arrogant. "Must *we* . . ." he asked them. Not God, but we.

That would be like me getting stuck beside the road with a flat tire and some nice trucker stopping to help me and while he's sweating and changing the tire I say, "Why do *we* have to change our own tires?" I can see him handing me the tire iron and driving away.

God works *through* us. Our job is to let Him. That's why His burden is light.

■ ■ ■ ■

Moses said to them, "Listen, you rebels, must we bring you water out of this rock?" Then Moses raised his arm and struck the rock twice with his staff. Numbers 20:10, 11.

Anything Is Possible

hen I was in school I used to try to speed up the clocks. What kid doesn't? But I tried doing it a little differently. I sat at my desk, stared at the clock, and wished that it would speed up. And then I concentrated very hard with as much faith as I could, believing that the clock would speed up and get me out of school early.

Well, that's what I thought. After all, Jesus told His disciples that if they had the faith of a mustard seed, they could move mountains. I had faith *much bigger* than a mustard seed. I was quite sure of it. And a clock was much smaller than a mountain. It should have been a lot easier to move. But the clock hands didn't speed up even a second.

Even though "everything" is possible for someone who believes, that doesn't mean that it's the best or the wisest thing to happen. I wished for what I wanted. What if someone else was sitting beside a dying loved one, wanting the seconds to last forever, and my faith speeded them up? How awful! Everything is possible if we believe, but we must pray believing that God always knows best.

"'If you can'?" said Jesus. "Everything is possible for him who believes." Mark 9:23.

By Faith

nce I was in a skit written by a friend of mine. In the beginning one character asks another, "What is time?" The second character then tries to explain what time is and gets tongue-tied in the process. Now it's your turn. What is faith? See, it's not so easy describing things you can't see, is it?

Faith, the Bible tells us, is being sure of something that you hope for. For example, if you needed to go to band practice and I told you I'd give you a ride, faith would keep you standing on the curb, even if it was cold and I was late. You'd wait because you *believed* I would come. If you didn't have faith, you'd think, *Oh, she must have been lying or she changed her mind,* and you'd go back inside.

Faith works like this in our lives: we're sure that Jesus loves us and wants what's best for us, even when we fail our midterms or when our dog gets hit by a car or when we sprain an ankle just before the big track meet. No matter what life looks like, our faith will assure us of Jesus' love and the fact that it won't always be like this.

Now faith is being sure of what we hope for and certain of what we do not see. Hebrews 11:1.

By His Power

aria went for three weeks without cheating. She studied more than she ever had before. Her grades weren't perfect, but they were good. One night she went to Julie's house and got back a lot later than she had intended. She needed to study for a test the next day, but she was too tired, so she skipped it.

When the tests were passed out, Maria quickly saw that the information was on a section she didn't know very well. She was quite sure she would flunk the test. Inside her head her own voice screamed, "Cheat!"

Just once, Maria thought frantically. *Surely just one more time won't hurt.*

Then she remembered her decision not to cheat. "Please, God, help me not to cheat," she prayed, believing that God would give her the power to follow Him. She deliberately took up her pencil and wrote the answer to her first question. Slowly she finished the test.

Maria got a D– on the test. But she hadn't cheated. She promised herself that she would study next time. And she thanked God for giving her the power to stay firm to her commitment.

■ ■ ■ ■

But you will receive power when the Holy Spirit comes on you;
and you will be my witnesses in Jerusalem and in all Judea
and Samaria, and to the ends of the earth. Acts 1:8.

Riding in the Back Seat

I love to drive now. But when I was first learning, it terrified me. I was like a little old woman poking along at 10 miles an hour. A driving instructor had to be with me constantly in case I had any problems. Finally I got comfortable with driving, and then it was, Look out!

My Christian life was like that too. At first I wasn't sure what I believed, and I relied on God to tell me how to act and what to say in the same way I relied on my driving instructors to tell me when to shift from first to second gear or to guide me when I was parallel parking. But when I got some confidence, I took off on my own and left God standing on the corner!

It took me a long time to realize that I wasn't even supposed to be driving. I was supposed to be sitting in the back seat, letting God drive. That's the only way I'll end up where He wants me to go. If I go joyriding through life on my own, I could end up falling off some cliff. But when I let God drive, I know I will arrive safely, even when the road gets narrow.

■ ■ ■ ■

Before every man there lies a wide and pleasant road that seems right but ends in death. Proverbs 14:12, TLB.

Frogs in the Jacuzzi

*arning: Don't try this at home!*

Did you know that if you put a frog in a pot of hot water, it'll hop out? (So they say.) That's probably not surprising. Who'd want to hang out in boiling water?

But if you take the same frog, put it in a pot of cold water, and then heat that water slowly, the frog won't even try to get away. Heat it enough, and you'll cook the frog. Want to know why?

Because the frog won't notice the gradual change in temperature. By the time it realizes that it's in trouble, it will be too late. And face it, frogs aren't really intelligent in the first place—it may *never* realize it's in danger.

Satan tries to do the same thing with us. He doesn't tempt us with the big things, such as murder. He starts with the little things, such as murdering someone's reputation with gossip. One little thing leads to another, until our consciences get cooked.

The closer you stay to God, the easier it will be to tell when the temperature is starting to rise. Don't burn yourself. Hop out and stay cool for God.

Put on the full armor of God so that you can take your stand against the devil's schemes. Ephesians 6:11.

The Frogs and the Cream

I must be thinking about frogs a lot because it's springtime. My sister Aimeé sent me a poem attributed to T. C. Hamlet. It's about two frogs who fell into a can of cream. The first frog gave up and drowned. The second frog decided that the world didn't need another dead frog, so he swam for a few hours and was finally able to hop out of the can on the butter he had made.

Cute, huh? And a very valuable lesson. Imagine, learning something from frogs. The important question is: Which frog are you? You fall into a situation that looks hopeless, and everyone around you is muttering, "Oh, man! This is hopeless. We're never going to get out of here. Why should we even try?" What do you do?

Do you give up and drown like the first frog? Or do you start swimming, trusting that there's a way out of the situation even if it's not immediately obvious to you? I hope that you decide to try. Remember, no one ever lost anything by trying. And some, who shall remain nameless, lived "hoppily" ever after.

■ ■ ■ ■

Blessed is the man who perseveres under trial, because when he has stood the test, he will receive the crown of life that God has promised to those who love him. James 1:12.

Only Human After All

Have you ever wanted to give up? I mean really throw in the towel and *quit?* Elijah did. He had just experienced a great victory, and then Jezebel threatened his life. Elijah ran away and told God he'd had enough and he wanted to die.

Often when things are going great for us, we pull away from God, basking in our victory and patting ourselves on the back. We're like a toddler learning how to walk. "Look, Ma, no hands!" Then suddenly something knocks the pegs out from under us, and we take a nosedive onto the carpet. Ouch! How embarrassing! What went wrong?

Letting go and pulling away from God are big mistakes. Even when we're cruising along and everything is going our way we shouldn't pull away from God. That's a signal (a red flag, thumbs-up, blaring siren) that we should get even closer to God than we were before.

We need to lean on God at all times, but even more so during the good times. Then Satan won't be able to surprise us with a sneak attack that will leave us, like Elijah, discouraged and ready to quit. Instead we'll have one success after another.

■ ■ ■ ■

"I have had enough, Lord," he said. "Take my life; I am no better than my ancestors." 1 Kings 19:4.

Just Trust

Teon was only 3 when his father walked out on the family. Struggling to provide for five children, Teon's mom went to college during the day and worked as a nurse's aide in the evenings. When she got home late at night she was exhausted and short-tempered. Teon remembered vividly how she would yell and throw things around if she got mad.

Teon's grandmother watched them most of the time when his mother was gone. She was fond of telling the children how good-for-nothing they were. His grandfather strongly believed that sparing the rod would spoil the child, so he spanked the children for everything from spilling milk to forgetting to close the door.

When Teon heard about Jesus, he had a hard time believing that God could love him. Every other powerful figure in his life had abused or abandoned him. Then he learned that Jesus gave His life to God, His Father, because God could be trusted. And so did Teon. In God he found Someone who was really able to take care of his needs.

It is better to take refuge in the Lord
than to trust in man. Psalm 118:8.

Fake or Real?

endy was proud of her job as a bank teller. In all the years she had been working, she had come up short only one dollar, and she had been able to figure out what had happened. She had a great record, and she put 100 percent into her job.

One day in 1997, before the new bills came out, a man approached her window and handed her a $100 bill. "Can you give me change for that?" he asked.

Wendy took the bill and looked at it. "I'm sorry, sir, but this is not a genuine $100 bill."

"What do you mean?" the man yelled. "Of course it is."

"No, sir, it isn't. A real $100 bill has red and blue threads in it. The ink never completely dries. And the number in the seal matches the number place of the letter of the alphabet. This serial number begins with an A, but the number in the seal is five. A is the *first* letter of the alphabet, not the fifth."

The man tried to run off, but the police caught him only a few blocks away.

How did Wendy know that the bill was a phony? Because she had studied the real thing. When we study God and get to know Him, we'll be able to spot a fake. But if we don't know God, Satan will easily fool us.

■ ■ ■ ■

Test everything. Hold on to the good. 1 Thessalonians 5:21.

Good Gifts

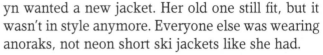

yn wanted a new jacket. Her old one still fit, but it wasn't in style anymore. Everyone else was wearing anoraks, not neon short ski jackets like she had.

"Please, God, give me a new jacket," she pleaded when she prayed.

Two months went by, and still there was no jacket.

"But I prayed," Lyn whined to her mom one day. "How come God didn't give me the jacket? It says in the Bible that He wants to give us good gifts. How can I trust God if He doesn't do what He says?"

"Actually, that verse you're talking about says that He wants to give us the Holy Spirit," Lyn's mom corrected.

"Whaaa . . ."

"It says that God is anxious to give us the Holy Spirit," Mom explained. "That is God's good gift to us. Maybe you should ask God for the gift He wants to give," Mom suggested.

There are a whole lot of things we want, that's for sure. But which of those things do we really *need?* God will always supply our needs. Sometimes before we even ask.

If you then, though you are evil, know how to give good gifts to your children, how much more will your Father in heaven give the Holy Spirit to those who ask him! Luke 11:13.

God Is on Our Side

J ob's head hung low as the afternoon sun shone brightly. His mouth was full of the taste of grit from the blowing sand mixed with the tears that coursed down his face, leaving muddy tracks in the ashes and grime. The scratchy and uncomfortable sackcloth on his body had rubbed his skin raw in spots. Painful boils covered his body.

It must have been hard for Job to think of even one positive thing in his life. His children were dead. His health was gone. His wife had turned against him. His best friends offered accusations instead of support. There wasn't a single bright spot in his universe.

Or was there?

Despite everything that had happened to him, Job was sure of one thing. He *knew* that God loved him and was with him. No matter what. And that was comforting. We can know that too. No matter how unfair life is, Jesus will come back and make all things right. God is on our side, even if we can't see Him right now.

Our Redeemer *lives!*

I know that my Redeemer lives, and that in the end he will stand upon the earth. Job 19:25.

The One About Seeds

armer Jones had to sow a lot of seed if he expected a good grain crop in the fall to feed his emus. They were hungry birds, all right. They'd be starving by winter if he didn't get the seeds planted.

He walked out into the field, and grabbing a handful of seeds he flung them over his head, aiming at a patch of bare ground. But oops! They fell on a big ol' rock in the field. Oh, well. They might grow there, but there wasn't enough soil. As soon as the sun came up, the plants would roast. Better try again.

He tossed the next handful a little too hard. Eeks! The seeds went into the briers. Some of them might grow, but those prickly bushes would choke them sure enough.

Farmer Jones took careful aim the next time, but lost his momentum at the last instant and dropped the whole handful on the path at his feet. The wild birds would come and eat the seeds. Those emus of his were surely going to starve.

He took one last handful and threw the seeds with all his might. They landed right in the good soil. And Farmer Jones had so much grain in the fall that his emus were positively fat.

Question: If the farmer represents Jesus, which ground are you?

■ ■ ■ ■

A farmer went out to sow his seed. Matthew 13:3.

That's Not Fair!

Have you ever watched two little kids playing with a toy? One kid has it. Then the other one grabs it. So the first one screams and tries to take it back. The second one holds it up so high the first one can't reach it. This, of course, is infuriating to the first kid, who bellows even louder.

Then Mom steps in and takes the toy. "If you can't share, then you can play with something else."

And what do the kids say? "That's not fair!"

God gave us a pretty strong sense of justice and fair play. We can spot unfairness at 40 paces. Imagine that you turned in a test and the teacher graded it. Out of 20 questions you and your friend each got five wrong. But you got a C and she got an A. What would you say?

"That's not fair!"

Lots of things in life aren't fair. Sometimes we can do something about it, and sometimes we can't. The important thing to remember is that even though *life* isn't always just and fair, *God* is. Remembering that (particularly when justice doesn't win the day) helps us to keep things in perspective. Especially when we get the short end of the stick.

How frail is man, how few his days,
how full of trouble! Job 14:1, TLB.

That's Dorcas

he boy shivered as he pulled the cloak tightly around his shoulders. He could hear his sick mother moaning in the other room, and his father was dead. Sometimes the boy went out on the street and begged for food, but he never got much. He was always hungry.

Suddenly there was a knock at the door. When the boy opened it, he saw two women standing there. One was his mother's sister, a widow who helped them as much as she could. The other woman had a kind smile. She cupped his cold face in her hands. And before he could speak she took off her own thick warm cloak and laid it across his shoulders. Then she took the steaming lentils and bread out of the basket she was carrying.

While the boy ate hungrily, the women took care of his mother. Before they left, the stranger promised to come again the next day.

"Who is she?" the boy asked his aunt in amazement.

"Why, that's Dorcas!"

Today, Dorcas means someone who helps others. Can you imagine being famous for doing good? What a great way to show people Jesus!

Your turn: What can you do today to be a "Dorcas" for someone else?

■ ■ ■ ■

In Joppa there was a disciple named Tabitha (which, when translated, is Dorcas), who was always doing good and helping the poor. Acts 9:36.

You're Awesome!

hat is your most valuable material possession?

If you asked me, I would have to say that my most valuable possession is my violin. Most everything else I have can be replaced, but not my violin. It's one of a kind. It has its own voice—no other violin has that same voice.

I'll tell you what God's most valuable possession is. It's *you!* That's right. God puts so much value in you that He gave His only Son to get you back. God, Jesus, and the Holy Spirit have been together since time began, whenever that was. They were never separated.

Then, to pay for our sins, Jesus came to earth. He was physically separated from God. That *had* to be hard. But then he was completely separated from God while He was on the cross (and later in the grave). And it hurt so much that it killed Him.

God considers us worth the cost of giving up the most precious thing He had (Jesus). So, what does that say about us? We are priceless to Him! Remember that the next time Satan puts you down. His love is so strong it raised Jesus from the grave. Where will it take you?

■ ■ ■ ■

I praise you because I am fearfully and wonderfully made; your works are wonderful, I know that full well. Psalm 139:14.

Want a Present?

Peter was loud, obnoxious, ornery, short-tempered, and impulsive. His friends would have voted him Most Likely to Stick His Foot in His Mouth. And he couldn't make up his mind to save himself. One minute he was telling Jesus that he'd die for Him, and the next he was cursing Him so that no one would guess they were friends.

But something changed all that. It wasn't the time he spent hanging out with Jesus, although that helped. He didn't suddenly see the light. No, it was a gift he received. Know what it was?

The Holy Spirit.

The Holy Spirit gave him the *power* to change. That's what the Holy Spirit is all about. He gives us power and wisdom to live the way God wants us to. Trying to be a Christian without the Holy Spirit is like trying to paddle a canoe upstream with our bare hands. We don't get very far.

But we can all have the gift of the Holy Spirit. All we have to do is ask for it. Go ahead. Your life will never be the same again. It'll be better than ever!

■ ■ ■ ■

Peter replied, "Repent and be baptized, every one of you, in the name of Jesus Christ for the forgiveness of your sins. And you will receive the gift of the Holy Spirit." Acts 2:38.

Free Will

hen I was in school we read a story called "The Lady, or the Tiger." In the story a man had to choose between two doors. Behind one was a beautiful lady. Behind the other was a very hungry tiger. One would love him. One would eat him. The choice was his.

In a way we all have a similar choice to make. Life or death. Love or *(gulp!)* being eaten by a ferocious beast (Satan). The only difference is that we can see behind the doors. We don't have to guess which one to open. We know that by choosing God we choose life and love. If we choose Satan, we're choosing death and destruction.

Why do we sometimes find it so hard to make the right choice? It's because Satan makes living for the moment sound more attractive than living for eternity. We settle for temporary things instead of permanent happiness. Not such a hot deal when you stop to think about it. The problem is that we don't often think about it.

Which door will you choose? We can put ourselves on God's side and choose to open His door. We can set our hearts in the direction of life.

See, I set before you today life and prosperity,
death and destruction. Deuteronomy 30:15.

It Is Written

Picture this: Joe Smith is walking down the street, minding his own business. He's whistling a happy tune, thinking about the great baseball game he just played. Suddenly out of a dark alley shoots a vicious dog! The dog snarls and leaps for Joe's leg. Light glints off his sharp teeth.

Joe says, "Hey there, pooch! What's the trouble? Lay off, will ya? Go back home and lie down by the fire."

Or he says, "Oh, please, don't hurt me. Nice doggie!"

Or he says, "Look, if you don't hurt me, I'll give you a nice bone. How about my sandwich? I have half left from lunch. Will you take a sandwich? Please?"

Would I be the only one who thought Joe was a little soft in the head? I mean, who would try to reason with a mad dog? Well, we do. When Satan attacks us we try to reason with him. But Jesus showed us the *only* way to fight Satan. "It is written . . ."

We shouldn't say, "It's only a *little* lie . . ." We should say, "Thou shalt not bear false witness" (Exodus 20:16, KJV).

We can't leave any room for Satan to argue. Unless we want to get our leg bitten off.

■ ■ ■ ■

Jesus answered, "It is written: 'Man does not live on bread alone, but on every word that comes from the mouth of God.'" Matthew 4:4.

You Are What You Think

ave you ever noticed how the world creeps in on you unless you're really careful? One day it's listening to the classic rock station on the radio. The next day it's watching a show that promotes questionable values or surfing to a vulgar site on the Internet. Then before you know it, you're stretching the truth and creatively manipulating your values to accommodate your new activities.

Satan is very clever in thinking up ways to compromise and destroy our values. He worms his way in here and there, and before you know it, God isn't in the picture at all. You're wondering where He went, but you don't realize that you pushed Him away yourself by letting in all the stuff He can't be a part of.

In Philippians Paul instructed the believers to guard carefully what went into their hearts. God won't stay where He isn't wanted. If you choose to put other things above God, His Spirit will leave you. When that happens, Satan can have a jolly old time.

What we watch, listen to, think, do, and look at *are* important. Don't settle for anything less than the very best. 'Cause you're worth it.

■ ■ ■ ■

Finally, brothers, whatever is true, whatever is noble, whatever is right, whatever is pure, whatever is lovely, whatever is admirable—if anything is excellent or praiseworthy— think about such things. Philippians 4:8.

Packing

Imagine with me that you're going on a trip. This is our imagination, so let's pick somewhere really fantastic. How about Alaska? Get your suitcase. We've got some serious packing to do. We don't want to go to Alaska unprepared. After all, the climate there isn't exactly forgiving.

Let's see, we'll need long underwear—the wool kind—and a hat, mittens, neck warmer, face mask. There—that should about do it. We're off. Isn't it breathtaking? Look at the view. Brrrr, pretty cold here, huh? Good thing we packed all that stuff. What? A coat? I'm sure it's in there. Look again. Didn't we pack a coat? No? Uh-oh . . .

Profound thought: You can't unpack what you didn't pack in the first place.

You're thinking I'm pointing out the obvious, aren't you? I'm not. How many times have you heard that the Holy Spirit will bring to mind Bible verses so we can answer for what we believe? How many have you learned?

Another profound thought: The Holy Spirit can't bring to mind something you never learned.

Learning memory verses isn't just something you did in kindergarten and primary. It's something we should be doing all the time. Challenge yourself. See how many you can learn. Pack the suitcase really full!

I have hidden your word in my heart that I might not sin against you. Psalm 119:11.

My Hiding Place

ave you ever been so beat up by life's punches that you needed a place to rest? to recover? to get a grip on yourself again? We have a place like that, and we can go to it any time we need to.

God is our hiding place. He will protect us against anything life dishes out. There are problems that we can't solve by ourselves. But the good news is that we don't have to. God is powerful enough to take on any of our problems and temptations. Let Him fight your battles. He always wins.

When we can't figure out a problem, we can be sure that God can. He knows our enemy (Satan) much better than we do. God knows his tricks and won't be fooled by appearances as we are. If we let Him, He will deliver us.

The weaker we are, the more we can see how strong God is. He loves us and wants us to come to Him with all our troubles. He never gets tired, and He's always ready to go into battle for us. He's on our side.

The Lord is a refuge for the oppressed, a stronghold in times of trouble. Those who know your name will trust in you, for you, Lord, have never forsaken those who seek you. Psalm 9:9, 10.

19 MARCH

For Such a Time as This

sther was nice and polite. She didn't talk with her mouth full. She took lots of baths, so she smelled really good. She was very pretty, too. *And* she was the queen, which was, in those days, a really big deal.

But Esther had a rather large, smelly problem. Haman, a really bad dude, managed to get Esther's husband, the king, to make a law that all the Jews were to be put to death. Esther might have been safe if she didn't tell anyone her secret—that she was a Jew.

Would you have risked *your* life to stop the law? Or would you have kept your mouth shut, hoping that no one found out you were a Jew? Esther could have kept quiet and laid low, but she didn't. She exposed evil Haman and saved her people. And for all we know, they lived happily ever after.

There are times when you have the opportunity to make a difference. Whether it is sticking up for a nerd at school or finding a home for a stray cat. Sticking up for what's right isn't always easy, but we can be pretty sure we were chosen "for such a time as this."

And who knows but that you have come to royal position for such a time as this? Esther 4:14.

Heavy Load

ook out! Oh, no! Now you've done it. You took the bag of bricks. Now you have to carry it. You can't put it down once you pick it up. Heavy, huh? What? You want to know how to get rid of it? There's only one way to get rid of it.

What's that? Oh, you want to know *how* to get rid of it? Well, you have to give it to Him. Who is He? Don't you recognize Him? It's Jesus. He's the only one who can carry those for you.

Why? Well, He paid for them. Why does He want a bag of worthless, incredibly heavy bricks? Because He wants to set you free. He knew that eventually the bricks would crush you, so He bought them.

Did He pay a lot? Oh, yes, a LOT. What? You're embarrassed? No need to be. He wants to help you. See? Look at Him. He's motioning you to come closer. That's right. Let Him take the bag. There, don't you feel a lot better now with that awful weight off you?

Remember: Sin is heavy. Confession is free. And forgiveness is as light as air.

Then I acknowledged my sin to you and did not cover up my iniquity. I said, "I will confess my transgressions to the Lord"—and you forgave the guilt of my sins. Psalm 32:5.

Get Lost!

I'm sure Peter thought he was being helpful. He didn't want Jesus to be discouraged. So when Jesus started talking about how He was going to die, Peter decided to put a stop to it. Immediately.

He pulled Jesus aside and said, "Now, listen here. We'll have no more talk of this. You're going to live to be 100." (Or something like that.)

Then he got the surprise of his life. Jesus said to him, "Get behind me, Satan!" Yikes! I can see the horror on Peter's face.

But peer pressure often comes across as "I'm only doing this or saying this for your own good. Come on, follow the crowd."

What if Jesus had said to Peter, "You're right, Peter. I know you only have My best interest in mind. We'll forget all about this dying stuff. Let's go fishing."

Horrors! If Jesus hadn't stood up for what was right, even though it was going to cost Him dearly, I wouldn't be writing this devotional right now, and you wouldn't be reading it. God's Word makes it plain what we should be doing. If anyone tells you differently, don't listen. Period.

Get behind me, Satan! You are a stumbling block to me;
you do not have in mind the things of God,
but the things of men. Matthew 16:23.

Redeemed

I f I needed money, I could take my violin (no, not my violin!) down to a pawn shop. They'd tell me what it was worth to them and lend me money. If I paid the money back (plus interest) by the deadline, they would return my violin. If not, they'd sell it. My loss.

Now suppose I didn't have the money to get my violin back, but my friend Michele wanted to "redeem" it for me? She would use her own money to buy *my* violin. Who would own it? Michele would. If she gave it back to me, who would own it then? I would! (Whew!)

But I didn't have to pay for it, did I? And that's exactly the way our salvation is. It cost a lot—death, in fact. We sure can't pay the price. Even if we could, it wouldn't be accepted, because we're not perfect. So Jesus paid it for us. He "redeemed" us from a pawn broker (Satan) who "owned" us.

And just as I could never pay Michele back for my violin and it would still be mine, we can never pay Jesus back for our salvation. We just have to accept it as His gift to us.

The Holy One of Israel is your Redeemer; he is called the God of all the earth. Isaiah 54:5.

Let Go and Let God

rs. Smith knew that some tough gang members wanted to harm her baby. She hid him for as long as she could. But when she could no longer hide him, she wrapped him up in warm blankets and many prayers, put him in a Macy's shopping bag, and left him in a taxi. And she sent his sister, Miriam, to ride along in the taxi and to see what happened to him.

Well, would you believe that the taxi stopped at the White House? The first lady took one look at the cute little bundle and decided to adopt him. His sister, Miriam, asked the first lady if she would like a nurse for the baby. Did she ever! So Mrs. Smith was hired as a nurse for her own baby.

Yes, you're right. This is a modern depiction of what happened to Moses. The actual story is recorded in Exodus. Just imagine how much Moses' mother trusted God to take care of him. We use the saying "Let go and let God," but that's not always easy to do. Next time you find yourself in a hopeless situation, why not try it?

■ ■ ■ ■

But when she could hide him no longer, she got a papyrus basket for him and coated it with tar and pitch. Then she placed the child in it and put it among the reeds along the bank of the Nile. Exodus 2:3.

She Made a Choice

ve was wandering around in the garden, minding her own business— Well, not really. Her business was obeying God, who wouldn't have wanted her wandering around alone. All of a sudden she spotted the tree of the knowledge of good and evil. And before you could say "Yum, yum" a snake popped out of the branches and started convincing her she should have a snack.

And then the snake picked a fruit and stuffed it into Eve's mouth before she could stop him. No, that's not how it goes. He pelted her with fruit, and some of it got in her mouth and she ate it. No, that's not it either.

Eve *took some and ate it.* Eve made a choice. She didn't *have* to eat the fruit. No one forced her to. Satan didn't twist her arm or cram it down her throat. She chose to disobey God. Why? Because the fruit looked good and she wanted some. She ignored the eternal consequences to have temporary fun.

We have the same choice to make each time Satan offers us something that catches our attention. How will *you* choose when he picks on you?

When the woman saw that the fruit of the tree was good
for food and pleasing to the eye, and also desirable
for gaining wisdom, she took some and ate it. Genesis 3:6.

Right Foot First

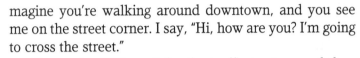magine you're walking around downtown, and you see me on the street corner. I say, "Hi, how are you? I'm going to cross the street."

You reply, "OK, wait for the traffic to stop, and then walk across. See you later."

Then you cross the street and go into a café on the other side of the intersection. You sit down and have a cup of hot chocolate.

But I'm still standing on the street corner. Other people stop and talk to me, and you see me point across the street. You figure I must be telling them that I'm going to cross the street, too.

You sit there for an entire half hour, but I never cross the street. You shrug and think that I probably wasn't too serious about crossing over if I'm still standing there.

Have you ever wondered if that's what God thinks when we tell everyone that we're Christians but we don't actually *do* anything Christlike? James tells us not just to listen to *how* to be a Christian, but also to actually *do it*. Spectator Christians don't make much of a difference in the world. We need full-contact players!

Ready? Hike!

■ ■ ■ ■

Do not merely listen to the word, and so deceive yourselves. Do what it says. James 1:22.

Unknown God

Ihave never seen God. I've never had dinner with Him. I've never been to His house. He's never been my pen pal. We never chat on the phone. And He doesn't send me e-mail.

So how can I know God if I've never seen Him, never corresponded with Him, and never talked to Him face-to-face?

God *wants* us to know Him, so He's given us some tools. The Holy Spirit is the most important one. He carries our thoughts to God and God's back to us. The Bible also tells us what God is like. And Jesus *showed* us what God is like.

Even though we've never seen God, we can know Him better than we know our best friends on earth. We can talk to Him constantly in prayer. Incredible, isn't it? God promises us that if we look for Him, we'll find Him. And not only that, but He'll help us look for Him, and He'll show us the best places to look to.

Seek and you will find. More than you ever thought possible.

I even found an altar with this inscription: To an Unknown God. Now what you worshiped as something unknown I am going to proclaim to you. Acts 17:23.

Gimme Oil

I have to admit that I always thought the five wise virgins Jesus talked about were just a tad on the selfish side. I mean, if they had enough oil, why not share? Why couldn't they have just said, "Sure, we'd be more than happy to help you out"? After all, we teach our children to share just as Jesus taught His disciples to share. But no, their reply was "Sorry, your loss."

Meanies.

But when I finally understood what the parable was talking about, it made sense. The five wise virgins couldn't share their oil because it wasn't actual oil. The oil represents the Holy Spirit, and we can't give *Him* to anyone! Each of us has to invite the Holy Spirit into our lives for ourselves. Other people can see His light in our lives. But we can't *give* the Holy Spirit to them. They have to go to God to receive the Holy Spirit.

Ask God to fill your heart with His Holy Spirit today, and you'll have plenty of oil to light your lamp.

Then all the virgins woke up and trimmed their lamps.
The foolish ones said to the wise, "Give us some of your oil;
our lamps are going out." "No," they replied, "there may
not be enough for both us and you. Instead, go to those
who sell oil and buy some for yourselves." Matthew 25:7-9.

The Walls Came Tumbling Down

Joshua was sweating. I mean, wouldn't you if you were out in the hot sun? And besides, there was this big wall he was supposed to be knocking down. He had ideas of jackhammers and chisels, but no, God said march. And march he did. Around and around the city until he was dizzy. I imagine he felt just a little foolish, too. ("Let me get this straight, Lord. We're going to knock the wall over by marching around it?")

The point is that Joshua, and the people, *did* march. No matter how foolish they might have felt. No matter how many tin cans or rotten tomatoes were rained down on their heads from the laughing crowds behind the safety of the wall, they marched. They took God at His word, even though it made no sense to them.

And the walls came tumblin' down.

That's what happens to all the walls in our lives when we ask God to knock them down. But we have to trust that He knows what He's talking about. Just as Joshua did.

■ ■ ■ ■

When the trumpets sounded, the people shouted, and at the sound of the trumpet, when the people gave a loud shout, the wall collapsed; so every man charged straight in, and they took the city. Joshua 6:20.

Under Cover

ammie O'Toole was a mild-mannered student by day, but at night she was transformed into Video Game Girl. Her schoolbooks and homework lay unopened on her desk as she sat for hours before a flickering screen evading enemy ships and vanquishing her electrical foes. Some days she even told her mom she was sick so that she could stay home from school just to play.

Sammie had a problem. She let part of her life control her. You and I have a similar problem when we try to follow God partway. It doesn't work. We can't keep part of ourselves hidden from God while we do things that God wouldn't approve of.

Some people think that we can make one decision for Christ, and that's it. But in reality we face lots of little decisions every day whether or not to follow Jesus. And the little decisions are every bit as important as the decision to become a Christian in the first place.

The devil will use anything he can to get in our hearts. He's like cockroaches. Once you have 'em, it's mighty hard to get rid of 'em. We need to get real with God and be willing to let go of the things that He doesn't approve of.

■ ■ ■ ■

Submit yourselves, then, to God. Resist the devil, and he will flee from you. Come near to God and he will come near to you. James 4:7, 8.

Wrong Way

omething was very wrong. Things weren't going the way he had expected. Jesus was being anything but cooperative. Why wasn't He rubbing shoulders with people in authority who could help Him become king instead of mingling with the dirty unwashed on the streets? What was wrong with Him?

Judas wasn't sure, but he wasn't going to stand for it. He'd fix it so that Jesus would be forced to show His power. The rest of the necessary events would follow right behind, just as thunder follows lightning.

But things didn't go as Judas had planned. They went from bad to worse! Not only did Jesus not free Himself, but He was going to be crucified! Oh, woe was Judas! He didn't even stick around to see how it all came out. He took his own life, and that was that.

It's easy to think, as Judas did, that we know better than God does. And as sinful human beings we naturally look after our own best interests first. But what we have to remember is that God is in charge. No matter what it looks like from where we stand.

■ ■ ■ ■

When Judas, who had betrayed him, saw that Jesus was condemned, he was seized with remorse and returned the thirty silver coins to the chief priests and the elders. "I have sinned," he said, "for I have betrayed innocent blood." Matthew 27:3, 4.

Something's Changed

aria sat with her best friend Julie in the cafeteria. As she began to eat, she noticed Julie looking at her funny. "What?" she asked. "Do I have something in my teeth?"

"No," Julie said slowly. "I was just wondering about something. I've noticed a big change in you. I know you cheat. I think everyone knows."

Maria felt her face burn with embarrassment. "So?"

Julie shrugged. "So I'm just saying, I haven't seen you cheat in weeks. What's up?"

Maria set her fork down. "Cheating isn't good," she said.

"Duh, no joke." Julie grinned.

"I mean it," Maria insisted. "Cheating is dishonest, and I got sick of being a poser. I want to earn the grades I get." She winced. "Even if they aren't as good as the ones I got before. I asked God to help me, and I've stopped cheating."

"You stopped cheating because of God?"

Maria nodded. "Yes. He helped me to stop." She stared hard at Julie. "He can help you too."

Julie shook her head hard. "I don't want help."

"Just the same," Maria said. "He *can* help you. All you have to do is ask."

Let us examine our ways and test them, and let us return to the Lord. Lamentations 3:40.

What's Love Got to Do With It?

My dog, Shadrach, is so old that he's deaf and blind. He's always underfoot because he can't hear you coming until you trip over him. And then he's too arthritic to get out of the way quickly enough to avoid you.

You probably wouldn't like Shadrach. He lives in his own little world of silence and darkness, so he's not much fun anymore. He mostly just sleeps and wanders around, getting in the way. He also does his "business" all over the house.

But I love Shadrach. When he was younger, if he heard me sniff and thought I was crying, he'd race to me from anywhere in the house. He'd climb onto my lap and lick my face. He was a great comfort to me.

No matter how bad he gets, I will always love him. If Shadrach wandered away, I would still love him. And I would look for him everywhere. It's the same with God. If we run away, He still loves us and comes looking for us. Remember that, if you ever find yourself lost in a strange place far from home where everything is dark and silent.

■ ■ ■ ■

The Lord, the Lord, the compassionate and gracious God, slow to anger, abounding in love and faithfulness, maintaining love to thousands, and forgiving wickedness, rebellion and sin. Exodus 34:6.

Insides and Outsides

She was soft-spoken and used her hands a lot when she was talking. I listened closely while she spoke. "I didn't like myself much," she said. "I looked around, and everyone seemed to be doing better than I was. But then I realized that I was comparing my insides to everyone else's outsides. Inside they're no better off than I am."

She was so right! We look at people and judge them by how great they look on the outside. As Samuel tried to do with Jesse's sons. He was looking for the best one—on the outside! But God can see what we look like inside, and to Him that's more important.

Our outsides are temporary. We will only have them while we're alive on earth. We may have accidents and lose our hearing or our sight or our legs. But our characters are what we'll take to heaven with us. That's why it's so important to make sure we let God clean up our insides.

But the Lord said to Samuel, "Do not consider his appearance or his height, for I have rejected him. The Lord does not look at the things man looks at. Man looks at the outward appearance, but the Lord looks at the heart." 1 Samuel 16:7.

Hide-and-seek

I'll admit, I get to play hide-and-seek pretty often. My kids are little, so I make them find hiding places inside or just outside the house so they'll be safe. Rachel can't stay hidden. She squeals and jumps out if you get anywhere near her. Josh is more savvy. He waits quietly and chooses some really good spots.

I sometimes play hide-and-seek with God, too, just as Adam and Eve did. I try to hide the parts of me I don't want Him to see. I stick them way inside and pretend they're not there so He won't talk to me about them. See, if I hide them well enough, I can keep them.

The problem is that in order for us to grow, we have to let God deal with the not-so-pleasant parts of our lives. That means we have to take them out of hiding. Remember, God loves us no matter *what* we have hidden away. And He'll always help us deal with it.

■ ■ ■ ■

Then the man and his wife heard the sound of the Lord God as he was walking in the garden in the cool of the day, and they hid from the Lord God among the trees of the garden. Genesis 3:8.

Bad Fruit

here's an old overgrown apple orchard in front of my house. Some farmer must have planted it a long time ago. Every spring the trees bloom with beautiful pink clusters of apple blossoms. But in the fall the only crop they bear is tiny, wormy apples.

Paul tells us we are like trees. The fruit we bear will reflect who we are. If we are being taken care of by the Holy Spirit, we will bear lots of delicious fruit—the things we do for God, such as being nice to others, controlling our temper, and being true to God. But if we're on our own like my apple trees, we'll have small, wormy fruit, such as being miserable to everyone around us, hurting others, and causing trouble.

An apple tree that has good fruit has to be pruned, and so do we. God will take all the bad branches out of our lives and leave just the good ones. Then we will have nice big apples that we can share with everyone!

But the fruit of the Spirit is love, joy, peace, patience, kindness, goodness, faithfulness, gentleness and self-control. Galatians 5:22.

Jump for Joy

I once listened to a tape on which the man talked about jumping for joy. Literally. No matter what happened. If he bumped his head on a doorway, he jumped for joy. If he burned his tongue on hot soup, he'd jump for joy.

The man felt like howling with frustration and anger. But he put himself on God's side by *doing* what the Bible said rather than relying on his emotions to tell him how to behave.

David did the same thing. Even when he was depressed and sad, he put his hope in God, and he *praised* Him. Why? Because God gave David salvation. How could problems compare to that? How bad could things be that he still couldn't be joyful about his salvation?

We forget what an awesome gift salvation is because we don't think about it as often as we should. Nothing, absolutely nothing—not the test you flunked, not the dog that ate your homework, not the brand-new skirt with the spaghetti stain on it—matters as much as the fact that you are saved! That's something to be joyful about *any* time.

Why are you downcast, O my soul? Why so disturbed within me? Put your hope in God, for I will yet praise him, my Savior and my God. Psalm 42:11.

Baggage

"O nce I thought I was wrong, but I was mistaken." Have you ever thought that way or wished you were always right?

I don't know anyone who likes being wrong. First of all, it's embarrassing. Second, when you're wrong, you often have to apologize. And third, it's so, well, humbling to admit that you aren't perfect.

But we all make mistakes, don't we? John says that if we *confess* our sins, God will forgive them. Confessing our sins means we have to own up to them. Then we have to give them to God. He will throw them out.

That's kind of like picking up my luggage at the baggage claim. When I see my hideous purple suitcase coming around, I have to claim it. Then I give it to God. Seeing God lugging my ugly purple suitcase to the dump makes me very sorry. He shouldn't have to deal with it.

God wants us to claim and hand over every suitcase in our lives. In exchange He'll give us brand-new luggage that we can be proud to carry around.

■ ■ ■ ■

If we confess our sins, he is faithful and just and will forgive us our sins and purify us from all unrighteousness. 1 John 1:9.

To Forgive
or Not to Forgive?

Saul and David didn't have the best relationship in history. Saul even tried to kill David a few times. David could have hated Saul, but he didn't. He had a chance to kill Saul, but he didn't. But even though David didn't hate Saul and he wasn't out to get revenge, David still kept his distance.

I assume that David forgave Saul. He sure didn't seem to hold any grudges against the guy. But they never made up. They were enemies all their lives because Saul wasn't willing to change. If David had showed up to try to be friends again, Saul would have killed him. It wasn't good for David's health to have a friend like Saul.

There are people in our lives who aren't good for us. And although we should forgive them as God forgives us, we don't have to hang out with them either. Forgiveness and reconciliation (making up) are two different things. If there is someone in your life who isn't good for you, do what David did. Maintain a healthy distance.

■ ■ ■ ■

When Saul realized that the Lord was with David and that his daughter Michal loved David, Saul became still more afraid of him, and he remained his enemy the rest of his days. 1 Samuel 18:28, 29.

8 APRIL

Uh, Excuse Me, Pardon Me

imon of Cyrene was probably a tourist in Jerusalem for the Passover. He is wandering around the city, looking at all the sights and minding his own business, when he bumps into a crowd. Eager to see something new, Simon politely squeezes his way to the front.

"Hey, guys, what's happening?"

He makes it there in time to see one of the most horrible sights he's ever witnessed. Three condemned men are being forced to carry the beams of their crosses down the narrow street. The beams easily weigh 30 or 40 pounds.

Simon watches one of the men struggling under the weight of the cross. Suddenly a soldier grabs Simon and hefts the struggling man's beam onto his back and tells him to move. Simon staggers ahead, proud to be chosen to help.

If the soldiers had grabbed you, would you have carried Jesus' beam? I like to think I would have. But Jesus doesn't ask us to do anything so spectacular or difficult. Maybe He's asking you to befriend a nerd or forgive a parent. Now, let me ask you again. Will you carry Jesus' beam?

"If anyone would come after me, he must deny himself and take up his cross and follow me." Matthew 16:24.

As they were going out, they met a man from Cyrene, named Simon, and they forced him to carry the cross. Matthew 27:32.

The Joy of the Lord

he joy of the Lord is your strength! I read that the other day. It was in a stack of promise texts that I had been memorizing. I thought, *Wow! The joy of the Lord is my strength!* And then I thought, *What on earth does that mean?*

It's great to memorize Bible texts such as this one. But to understand them better, it's good to find out why they were written in the first place. In this case the Jewish exiles who had been in Babylon were returning to Jerusalem. They had no clue about the laws of God, so the Levites read the Book of the Law of God to them. The people realized they had been sinning big-time and started crying.

We should be sad when we realize we have been sinning. But we have to remember that God doesn't leave us in our sins. He brings us out of sin and into the light. That is pure joy. Satan will try to keep us agonizing over our sins forever. But God wants us to put them behind us and walk with Him. His joy gives us the strength to go and sin no more.

"This day is sacred to our Lord. Do not grieve, for the joy of the Lord is your strength." Nehemiah 8:10.

What Is Man?

I t doesn't surprise us to see God's handiwork in the big, in-your-face places, such as the Grand Canyon, Niagara Falls, the starry nighttime sky, the endless oceans, or a sky-splitting rainbow. Looking at things so much bigger than ourselves makes us catch our breath and say as David did, "Wow, God is so amazingly mighty, it's awesome He even cares about our existence!"

But you know, God isn't in just the big stuff. He's there all the time, even when it's not as obvious. Such as when you're waiting in the rain for the bus and your friend's mom offers you a ride. Or when you're down and someone takes the time to make you smile. Those things aren't accidents.

God is there in the big things and the little things. He's there when you can see Him, and He's there when you can't. It's important to know that because when you're down it's easy to think He's abandoned you. Satan wants you to think that, but don't believe him.

God is with you every minute of every day. Look for Him. You might be surprised at some of the places you'll find Him.

What is man that you are mindful of him, the son of man that you care for him? Psalm 8:4.

Berry Juice

here's a patch of black raspberry canes at the end of my driveway. In the fall they're loaded with black raspberries. We pick them and make shortcake and berry cakes and put them in our cereal. But I never realized how much the juice stained until Josh started picking them with me.

I soon learned that berry juice is very stubborn. I tried everything to get the stains out of his clothes, but nothing worked. Then my friend Amy told me, "If you pour boiling water over berry juice, it will come out." I tried it, and do you know what? It worked. The stains melted away.

We try a lot of things to get our sin stains out. We try covering them up, ignoring them, or scrubbing them out ourselves. But until we let God take them out, they'll never be completely gone. He's the only one who knows the secret to removing our sins. You can trust Him with any stain. He'll make you white as snow.

■ ■ ■ ■

"Come now, let us reason together," says the Lord. "Though your sins are like scarlet, they shall be as white as snow; though they are red as crimson, they shall be like wool." Isaiah 1:18.

Life of Strife

urphy was smart. He's the one who wrote, "Anything that can go wrong will, and at the worst possible moment." This became known as Murphy's law because it happens so often. What Murphy didn't know is that the reason this law is so true is that Satan is more than happy to heap strife (bad stuff) on us.

Strife makes us sick because it wears out our bodies and minds. It makes us self-centered, because we're always trying to get what we want. And it makes it hard for us to pray when we're angry and upset all the time. Who wants a life of strife?

We have to face facts, though. Things will go wrong. And at the worst possible moment. That's life. But what's much more important is that God is in charge. He didn't leave us here defenseless against strife. He gave us a gift that fights strife. His peace. It is one of the most important gifts Jesus gave His disciples before He left.

If you want to know how important peace is, just ask the people of any country at war. It's crucial! Without peace there is no life, at least not a good one. "Seek peace and pursue it" (1 Peter 3:11).

■ ■ ■ ■

Better a dry crust with peace and quiet than a house full of feasting, with strife. Proverbs 17:1.

Getting Away With It

oes everything seem to turn out bad, even when you're doing all the right things? For example, studying hard for a test and failing anyway, or telling the truth and people hating you for it?

Your friend cheats on a test and gets an A+ and praise from the teacher. He lies, and people love him. It's sickening, isn't it? You wonder if it's really any use to do the right things when you could do them all wrong and be so much better off. Right?

Wrong. It may *seem* as though your friend who is cheating and lying is getting away with it and even getting *rewarded* for it. But no one gets away with doing wrong forever. In the end their cheating and lying will catch up with them. Maybe not now. Maybe it won't be until they are older. Maybe it won't *ever* catch up with them here on earth. But you can be sure that when the judgment comes, all the wrongs will be made right. When it really counts, good will be rewarded, not evil. And that reward will last forever.

Do not fret because of evil men or be envious of those who do wrong; for like the grass they will soon wither, like green plants they will soon die away. Psalm 37:1, 2.

She's So Blue-hoo-hoo

y kids love *Veggie Tales*. (OK, I like them too.) They're cute, and the songs are contagious. One of the characters, Madame Blueberry (she's a very blue berry), sings about being "blue-hoo-hoo." That's one of my favorites.

But being blue is really nothing to sing about. It stinks. People argue about whether or not God brings trouble to His people or if He just allows it. I don't think it matters much as long as you trust that He's in charge. Think of it this way. Say you had a big sliver. Would it matter to you if your dad removed it or if he let your mom remove it? Not really, as long as it was gone.

There are two important things to remember in the middle of being blue-hoo-hoo. First, it won't last forever, even though it may *seem* as though it will last for the rest of your life! The second thing to remember is to look for the blessing. There is always a blessing to be found. Sometimes it won't be easy to find, but look for it. It's there.

■ ■ ■ ■

Though he brings grief, he will show compassion, so great is his unfailing love. For he does not willingly bring affliction or grief to the children of men. Lamentations 3:32, 33.

Delight Yourself

y husband and I bought some paintings at yard sales and auctions. I don't know if anyone else would love them the way I do. When I look at them, a feeling of peace comes over me. I'm not kidding! Looking at beautiful things really makes me feel better.

That's one of the ways we can see God—in the everyday things. The butterfly dancing on the breeze. The sunshine in the morning. The puppy in the park. God finds millions of ways to reach out to us when we look for Him. We can *delight* in Him in the big things and in the small.

If we make God our delight, tell Him our concerns, praise His goodness, and do His work, He will fill up our hearts so that we will have everything we need. That doesn't mean He's like a genie. God knows exactly what you want and exactly what you need. He will give you "the desires of your heart."

■ ■ ■ ■

Delight yourself in the Lord and he will give you the desires of your heart. Psalm 37:4.

Good Advice

*ssst!* Hey you! Yeah, you. I've been keeping an eye on you. I know you really like that kid's watch, and I know a way you can get it. When he gets ready for gym, he leaves it in his locker. It's never locked, so all you have to do is take the watch. See? Simple."

Pop quiz: Is this good advice or bad advice?

If you said good advice, go back to the beginning of the book and start over. It's bad advice, way bad advice. The trouble is that sometimes the people we spend time with offer us bad advice. That's why it's important to have godly people around us whom we can rely on to give us good advice.

It's also a good idea to have more than one person we can rely on for advice. The more people we have to advise us, the better chance we'll have to make the right decision. One person can be wrong, but several people should agree. If they don't, that's a caution sign to take your time making a decision. Pray hard, and always let God have the last word.

For lack of guidance a nation falls, but many advisers make victory sure. Proverbs 11:14.

Narrow Escape, Part 1

arabbas sat in the cold, dark cell. He could see a flicker of dusty light coming in the high window overhead. It wasn't much, but he knew it was all he'd ever see. He was going to be put to death for committing murder during an insurrection.

A million thoughts collided around in his head. One minute he was defiant. Let them put him to death! The next he was terrified. He didn't want to die! He spent hours second-guessing himself. Maybe he should have tried to find a more peaceful solution. He realized that now. Now that it was too late.

He must have fallen asleep, because the next thing he knew, soldiers were yanking him to his feet and pulling him along the corridor. *This is it,* he thought. *The end.* He let his weight fall onto the soldiers, making them bear most of his weight as they dragged him along. *God save me,* he thought as they brought him out into the light.

■ ■ ■ ■

"Do you want me to release to you the king of the Jews?" asked Pilate, knowing it was out of envy that the chief priests had handed Jesus over to him. But the chief priests stirred up the crowd to have Pilate release Barabbas instead. Mark 15:9-11.

Narrow Escape, Part 2

arabbas heard the crowds and saw Him at the same time. Jesus was bloody and beaten. The mob that called for His death was dangerously murderous, and Barabbas could hardly believe his ears when they shouted for *him* to be set free. Jesus was going to die in his place.

The guards let him go, giving him a rough shove. He was free! Yet his feet hesitated. He wanted freedom, but could he let an innocent man take his place? Jesus had done nothing. Yet He was to be put to death for the crime Barabbas had committed. How could he just walk away and let someone else take his punishment? Everything that was going to happen to Jesus *should* happen to *him*. Instead he was walking away, which *should* have happened to Jesus.

We don't know what happened to Barabbas but, like him, each of us has committed crimes (sin) that we should have to pay for. Instead Jesus paid our debt for us. He took our place. What an awesome Saviour! Determine today to live your life in a way that will glorify Him, and thank Him for the sacrifice He made for you.

■ ■ ■ ■

But he was pierced for our transgressions, he was crushed for our iniquities; the punishment that brought us peace was upon him, and by his wounds we are healed. Isaiah 53:5.

The Secret of Being Content

I don't know about you, but I have a hard time being content. I'm impatient. In school my friends and I had a saying: I want what I want when I want it, and I want it now.

And then I remember Paul, and I can't help thinking that I must be missing something. I mean, here's a guy who spent a lot of his time hanging around prisons. Not doing prison ministry, though, I'm sure he did. But he wasn't allowed to leave at night and go home to his family. Still he was content.

How can that be? I think it was because he depended on God for everything. God created us, so He certainly knows how to give us contentment. But we have to let Him give it to us, which can be harder than it sounds. Being content means to stop striving for what we want. Not that we shouldn't want things, but we should want what God wants for us.

Our first question should be "What does God want?" Not "What do I want?"

I have learned the secret of being content in any and every situation, whether well fed or hungry, whether living in plenty or in want. Philippians 4:12.

The Real Deal

illy Sunday, one of the twentieth century's best known evangelists, once said, "Going to church doesn't make you a Christian any more than going to a garage makes you an automobile."

Being a real Christian means that you have a relationship with Jesus. You spend quality time with Him. You talk with Him, and you listen to what He says. You can share your problems with Him, and He helps you with them.

Being a Christian doesn't mean that you go to church so you can talk to your friends and get out of the house once a week. It doesn't mean that you carry a Bible around school to impress people without ever opening it.

You have to want to be a real Christian. You have to keep at it. But at the same time it will change your life. You'll have real power to live with. You'll have God's strength in you. What more could you ask for?

He humbled you, causing you to hunger and then feeding you with manna, which neither you nor your fathers had known, to teach you that man does not live on bread alone but on every word that comes from the mouth of the Lord. Deuteronomy 8:3.

The King and the Boulder

The story goes that a king put a boulder right in the middle of a road. Then he hid to see what would happen. Some of the most important people in the kingdom came along the road and just walked around the boulder, leaving it for the next person to deal with. Some of them complained loudly that the king didn't have the road cleared.

Finally a poor peasant came along with a load of vegetables. When he saw the boulder, he set his load down, and after a lot of pushing he rolled it out of the road. As he bent to pick up his vegetables, he saw a purse in the road where the boulder had been. Inside were gold coins and a note from the king stating that the money was for the person who moved the boulder.

Every obstacle is an opportunity to improve your position. You can go around it or complain about it, but what do you gain? Nothing. You can move it; what do you gain? Even if it's only the ability to walk along the road with no obstacles, it's worth the effort. Just ask the peasant. That's all he expected, but he got so much more.

As you know, we consider blessed those who have persevered. James 5:11.

Follow the Leader?

y daughter Rachel looks a lot like me. When people see us, they say it's easy to see she's my daughter. We have the same facial features and the same blond hair. She even *acts* a lot like me. She's quiet and shy, independent, and likes to do things by herself.

I think it's cute when Rachel acts like me. I can almost see what I was like when I was a little girl. The not-so-cute part is when she does something I don't like and I realize, "Hey, she's just like me!" I don't want to pass my bad traits on to her, just the good ones.

Unfortunately, that's impossible. We all get good *and* bad things from our parents. We don't have control over what we get. You can't choose your eye color, but you *can* choose how you act. It's no excuse to say, "Well, that's what my father did, and so I do it too." Instead do what your heavenly Father does. Then he'll smile and say, "Look, My child is just like Me!"

■ ■ ■ ■

Our kings, our leaders, our priests and our fathers did not follow your law; they did not pay attention to your commands or the warnings you gave them. Nehemiah 9:34.

Choice and Consequence

hoice, sin, consequence. It happens in that order. First you make a choice. Are you going to do what God wants you to do or are you going to sin? If you sin, you have to live with the consequences. For example, if you steal something, you'll feel guilty until you confess or are found out. And then you'll have to own up to what you did, pay for what you took or return it, and possibly face time in juvenile detention or jail, depending on the circumstances. None of these consequences are pleasant.

Some people, when they get caught, start making excuses. "It's not my fault because . . ." And *zip!* they skip right over learning anything at all. The lesson zooms over their head, and they'll probably end up right back where they started. Hopefully they'll learn the next time.

Other people, when they get caught, admit that, yes, they did something wrong. They take *responsibility* for what they did. They let the painful lesson of suffering for their sin turn them back to God. Instead of being destroyed by their suffering, they learn from it. And as they learn, they grow more and more like Jesus.

■ ■ ■ ■

*I am bowed down and brought very low; all day long
I go about mourning. Psalm 38:6.*

Your Sermons

onesty has a lot to do with what we say. We often lie with our lips. But that's not the only way we lie. We also lie by our actions. We say one thing and act another. That's a lie. Such as when we say we're Christians but try to see how far we can get on a date. You might as well scream, "I'm selfish, and I don't care about you at all." Is that a Christian message? No.

The biggest problem is that we don't really understand the damage we do when we act a lie. And you know what's scary about that? People will "listen" to what we do a lot harder than they'll listen to what we say. Because you can say anything you want to, it's how you act that will tell people what your heart's really like.

Can you remember what your pastor preached about last Sabbath? Maybe, maybe not. But you can be sure that people who were with you this last week will remember if you cut in the lunch line, cheated on a test, or passed on a nasty comment about someone. Your actions are like sermons, and your "sermons" will be remembered for a *long* time.

■ ■ ■ ■

Help, Lord, for the godly are no more; the faithful have vanished from among men. Everyone lies to his neighbor; their flattering lips speak with deception. Psalm 12:1, 2.

For a Change

I changed schools more often than some people change their socks. When you don't spend more than two years in the same school, you get used to making new friends and then saying goodbye. It wasn't easy for me. I make friends slowly, and when I say goodbye, it hurts a lot.

For a long time I resisted change. I rebelled against it. I pretended that it didn't bother me, but I never accepted it. I wouldn't let myself get close to people because I was afraid they would leave. Most of the time they did leave (or I did), so I did protect myself. But I also missed out on a lot of friendships because I was afraid to risk getting hurt.

Now that I'm older I can see that life is about change. Nothing ever stays the same. I can either accept that and enjoy what's here for the moment. Or I can protect myself by never really living so that I won't miss people or places if I leave or if they do. With everything we do, there's a risk of getting hurt. But we also know that Christians can be friends forever because this world isn't home forever.

There is a time for everything, and a season for every activity under heaven. Ecclesiastes 3:1.

26 APRIL

The Blame Game

ereza and Deb are putting some flowers in a vase. Deb has packed the vase so full it's hard to get more flowers in. Tereza jabs a stem in with more force than she intends. The vase teeters. It's so top-heavy that it topples off the table and shatters in a thousand pieces.

Tereza's father hears the noise and comes in the room. "Who broke the vase?" he asks.

Tereza points at Deb, and Deb points at Tereza. Who broke the vase?

Have you ever noticed that when you point a finger at someone there are always three fingers pointing back at you? In the case of Tereza and Deb, both were at fault. Deb for packing the flowers too tightly, and Tereza for trying to fit more flowers in. No one person was at fault.

Lots of factors contribute to the mistakes we make. They're rarely all anyone's fault. If you accept your part, you'll learn a valuable lesson, one that should prevent you from making the same mistake twice.

■ ■ ■ ■

And he said, "Who told you that you were naked? Have you eaten from the tree that I commanded you not to eat from?"
The man said, "The woman you put here with me—she gave me some fruit from the tree, and I ate it." Genesis 3:11, 12.

Pattern Pieces

I'm not much of a puzzle person. I can take them or leave them. But there is one thing I know about puzzles. If you don't put the pieces together the right way, you won't end up with a picture. You'll end up with a lot of scrambled pieces. Puzzle pieces fit together a certain way, and if you don't bother putting them together correctly, you might as well not bother at all.

This world is like a giant puzzle. Satan is trying to fit us all into his picture. It's not a pretty picture, either. His picture is full of drugs, divorce, scandal, betrayal, and every other bad thing you can name. But we don't have to be a part of it!

God wants us to let Him change our shape so we won't fit into Satan's puzzle. God knows that it isn't easy to stick out from the crowd. It isn't easy to be in the minority, but God's way is best. Stick with Him, and you'll always come out ahead.

■ ■ ■ ■

Do not conform any longer to the pattern of this world, but be transformed by the renewing of your mind. Then you will be able to test and approve what God's will is—his good, pleasing and perfect will. Romans 12:2.

Let the Light Shine In

ight is light, no matter what kind it is. At our house we have electric lights. We also have candles. When we go camping, we use propane lights and kerosene lanterns and flashlights. There is also firelight. Some of these kinds of light are bright. Some are soft. But the one thing they all have in common is that they light up the dark. If you wanted to keep a light from lighting up the dark, you'd have to cover it or douse it.

God put His light in our hearts for the same reason: to light up the darkness. First, He lights up the darkness in our hearts so that we can distinguish between right and wrong. And when the light is on in our hearts, it shines out of us and into the darkness of the world.

When you compare the darkness to the light, there's a big difference, isn't there? Satan and his demons scurry for cover. They don't want anyone to see what they're doing. So let your light shine, bright and strong.

■ ■ ■ ■

For God, who said, "Let light shine out of darkness," made his light shine in our hearts to give us the light of the knowledge of the glory of God in the face of Christ. 2 Corinthians 4:6.

Borrowing Trouble

he problem with borrowing trouble is that it's impossible to return it. Once you have it, you own it. It's like the sign in a store: "Lovely to look at, nice to hold. If you should break it, consider it sold." Trouble is like that. Once it's yours, it's yours to keep.

Have you ever tried to borrow trouble? Have you ever looked ahead to what's going to happen and started worrying? It's healthy to look ahead, but it's not healthy to worry ahead. Beyond making reasonable preparations for what's coming, there isn't anything you can do to change the future.

Do you know why Jesus told us not to worry about what was coming? Jesus knew that if we worried about everything, we wouldn't *do* anything. We'd get bogged down in the problems and not see the possibilities.

It doesn't do us any good to worry. Worrying won't change a thing, not the color of your bike or the grade on your test. So quit worrying, and give it all to God.

Therefore do not worry about tomorrow, for tomorrow will worry about itself. Each day has enough trouble of its own. Matthew 6:34.

Search Me

aria knelt by her bed to pray. While she was in the middle of asking God to bless the people in her life, she suddenly heard a quiet voice say, *Maria, what about your cheating?*

The voice wasn't out loud, but Maria "heard" it just as plainly as if it had spoken. She felt her face turn red. But she had really been doing better about not cheating. She hadn't cheated for weeks. In fact, she hadn't even thought about it in days. Why was God bringing it up now?

"What about my cheating?" she asked quietly.

How do you feel about your cheating?

Maria felt a flood of emotions: embarrassment, shame, guilt, horror, remorse, and regret. They all washed over her like a tidal wave, and she started to cry. "I'm so sorry about my cheating, Lord," she sobbed.

As soon as the words came out of her mouth she realized that she had never apologized to God for cheating. She had just told Him she was sick of cheating and she wanted to stop. Now she realized how very sorry she was for cheating.

"Please forgive me, Lord," Maria prayed. "Please forgive me. I want to be honest from now on. Thank You. Amen." A sense of peace filled her, and she smiled.

■ ■ ■ ■

Search me, O God, and know my heart; test me and know my anxious thoughts. Psalm 139:23.

Holy Spirit Power

I suppose from the Philistines' point of view the Israelites were a few fireworks short of a display. All week long they watched those crazy people march around their city to make the walls fall down.

I have a strong suspicion that the Israelites themselves weren't that enthusiastic about the plan. They didn't have the greatest record of following God's instructions in the first place, especially when those instructions didn't make sense to them. But here they were, being obedient, marching through the dust and around those massive walls, trusting that they would fall down.

You have to give them credit. It's not easy to do something just because God says so, especially when it doesn't make sense to you. Love your neighbor, even when they steal the dessert out of your sack lunch every day?

The thing is that we can't do it by ourselves. That's why we have the Holy Spirit. The Holy Spirit lives in us and gives us the power to do what God asks us to do. When we follow God, we can be sure that every wall blocking our path will fall down.

When you hear them sound a loud blast on the trumpet, have all the people give a loud shout; then the wall of the city will collapse and the people will go up, every man straight in. Joshua 6:5.

Go Ahead, Make My Day

et me guess. You were probably born at a hospital or at a birthing center or maybe even at home. When you were born, you were made in the image of your parents. Actually, you were made in the image of God since you're a descendant of Adam and Eve.

When you accepted Jesus as your Saviour, you were born *again*. Your *character,* all those things inside that make you special, was also made in the image of God. Since you were made in His image, people will be able to see God in you.

This can happen because God lives inside us. But He can do this only if (a) we want Him to, (b) we ask Him to, and (c) we keep wanting and asking Him to.

Having God live in you isn't something you can do just once. It's something you do every day. If you haven't asked Him to live in you today, take some time and do it now. It will make your day.

■ ■ ■ ■

Do not lie to each other, since you have taken off your old self with its practices and have put on the new self, which is being renewed in knowledge in the image of its Creator. Colossians 3:9, 10.

Please God

e know that Saul, or rather, Paul, had a massive heart transplant. One minute he was standing aside, holding cloaks for the men who were stoning the hated Christian Stephen. And the next he was being persecuted for preaching the very beliefs Stephen was stoned for.

Paul was a Pharisee of Pharisees. A big shot, we'd call him today. Men looked up to him. They wanted to be like him. If he lived today, they would probably make running shoes with his name on them. Saul liked all the attention.

But after the Damascus road meeting, the opinion of other people stopped being important to him. It didn't matter what people thought of him. His only concern was what Christ thought of him. Considering the account of his life, I expect Christ was well pleased.

There are many reasons for doing things. What we need to remember is that doing something for the good opinion of others is never a good idea. Instead, aim to please Jesus, and you'll never fall far from the mark.

Am I now trying to win the approval of men, or of God?
Or am I trying to please men? If I were still trying to
please men, I would not be a servant of Christ. Galatians 1:10.

Hope So

aron ran along the rough dirt path marked out for the race. He could see the backs of the long-distance runners from the opposing school.

Puffing and panting, Aaron looked into the crowd. Stretched along the sidelines were parents with cheering faces, shouting encouragement. In all those faces Aaron never caught a glimpse of his own father. This was his tenth meet of the season, and his father had yet to show up for even one. What a disappointment!

Sometimes we too become disappointed with the people in our lives when they let us down. It's hard to put hope in people. Friends can dump us. Parents can leave us. Teachers can betray us.

Jesus is the only one who will never let us down. He will never fail us. When we place our hope in Jesus, we are free to hope in others, too. If they let us down, He will keep us from falling.

■ ■ ■ ■

Jesus answered, "Everyone who drinks this water will be thirsty again, but whoever drinks the water I give him will never thirst. Indeed, the water I give him will become in him a spring of water welling up to eternal life." John 4:13, 14.

Fear Not

y horse, Cinder, was a beautiful gray quarter horse mare. She had quite a bit of Thoroughbred in her. You could tell by the way her hooves were shaped and by her sleek, racy lines. She loved to run, and she was so fast that I'd get tears in my eyes from the wind.

But there was one thing Cinder would not do: walk through water. She was scared of water. She would run away, jump over it (if it was narrow enough), even plunge through it if need be. But she would not walk calmly across it.

Fear is a powerful thing. And each person is afraid of different things. I'm afraid of speaking in front of crowds. You might be afraid of spiders. Not only is fear powerful, but it is destructive. It can keep us from doing the things we need to do.

God wants us to know that no matter what fears we have, we can always trust in Him. He will overcome our fear. Nothing is out of our reach when we trust in God. I can speak in front of huge crowds. And you can do whatever it is that frightens you—if you trust in God.

Do not let your hearts be troubled.
Trust in God; trust also in me. John 14:1.

6 MAY

Thy Will

o how do you show God you love Him? It's not as though you can get His slippers for Him after a hard day's work, do some chores for Him when He's had a bad day, make His bed when He's too busy, or help Him with His homework. These things may show your family members that you love them, but God?

John tells us that the way we can show God that we love Him is to obey His commands. Think about it. What if you do something your mom or dad asks you to do? It shows them that you love and respect them. It's the same with God. By obeying His commands, you are saying, "I love You, and I believe You have my best interests in mind."

God respects our choices. We can obey Him or disobey Him. He doesn't force us to do anything. That's why obedience is an act of love for God. We don't *have* to do it. But when we're obedient, all the forces of heaven are on our side and we can "overcome the world."

This is love for God: to obey his commands. And his commands are not burdensome, for everyone born of God overcomes the world. 1 John 5:3, 4.

Amazing Love

It isn't every day you see a cat on the news, but I remember one time in particular. A brave mother cat brought her kittens out of a burning building. She could carry only one at a time, so she had to keep going back in. Even after she'd been blinded by smoke and singed by fire, she kept going back into the building.

I'm not sure if she got all the kittens out, but she got quite a few. She was a hero, and all because she loved her kittens.

Imagine someone loving you enough to go into a burning building to get you out. Someone does! Jesus came to rescue us from this sin-filled earth. It's on fire with sin. The stench of it fills the universe. But just like the kittens, we will be saved if we let Jesus carry us out in His strong arms.

God is prepared to save us, one at a time, from this burning building we're in. Remember that the next time someone asks, "Who loves you?" Tell them God does. He loves you enough to go back in the building as many times as it takes to save you.

How can I give you up, Ephraim? How can
I hand you over, Israel? Hosea 11:8.

Bricks and Feathers

I want to show you something. You see those two bags over there. They look pretty much the same, don't they? Try picking them up. That one's light, isn't it? It has premium goose feathers in it. Now the other one. Careful. Don't hurt yourself. Why, as a matter of fact, I do have bricks in there. Are you OK? Good, then let me ask you a question.

If you had to carry one of those bags with you for the rest of your life, which one would you pick? Simple. I'd pick the one filled with feathers, wouldn't you?

But how often do we carry a bag of bricks around? Jesus says that His yoke is easy and His burden is light. Like the feathers. We can share our load with Jesus and go in His direction carrying feathers. Or we can carry a bag full of bricks by ourselves wherever we want to go.

Remember, if you get tired of carrying the load of bricks, Jesus is always ready to trade with you for a bag of feathers.

Take my yoke upon you and learn from me, for I am gentle and humble in heart, and you will find rest for your souls. For my yoke is easy and my burden is light. Matthew 11:29, 30.

Apples and Blossoms

We have a beautiful book about New England with photographs that show the countryside. There are pictures of fall leaves and pictures of the snow-covered mountains. There are covered bridges and maple trees being tapped for their sap. And there's a beautiful picture of a blossoming apple tree loaded with juicy red apples.

Hello. Did you catch that? The apple tree had blossoms *and* apples. Impossible! The trees bloom in the spring, and the apples are ripe in the fall. In order to get that picture the photographer had to tie apples onto the trees!

When we have a good relationship with Jesus, we bear fruit as naturally as an apple tree. But when we are doing "good" things just to please others or to impress God, our fruit is "tied on" like the apples in the picture. It's fake fruit. It's not coming from the tree. It's not living and growing.

When God is in you, your fruit will be real. And it'll keep on growing.

Remain in me, and I will remain in you. No branch can bear fruit by itself; it must remain in the vine. Neither can you bear fruit unless you remain in me. John 15:4.

10 MAY

Fw: Life

'm sure you've seen "forwards." They were invented with the birth of e-mail. If you sent a message to someone, they could instantly forward it to a hundred of their closest friends. Incredible! Most people forward inspirational stories, virus warnings (which are mostly jokes), actual jokes, and prayer requests. But you can forward anything you like, even bad things. This is why you need to be careful what you send.

The principal yells at a teacher. She goes home and yells at her son. Her son yells at his baby sister. And the baby sister turns around and kicks the cat. The cat didn't do anything, but he was at the end of a bad chain of events started by one person taking out his anger on another person.

It's easy to pass the bad stuff along. Sometimes it's easier than passing the good stuff. Remember, share only the good. Some cat will thank you for it.

■ ■ ■ ■

My dear brothers, take note of this: Everyone should be quick to listen, slow to speak and slow to become angry, for man's anger does not bring about the righteous life that God desires. Therefore, get rid of all moral filth and the evil that is so prevalent and humbly accept the word planted in you, which can save you. James 1:19-21.

Measuring Up

plumb bob is a cute little thing. It's shaped like a small pear with a pointy bottom. Because it's mostly brass, it's heavy. And when you hang one from a string (the plumb line), it will point downward. The plumb bob tells a carpenter if a wall is straight.

The Lord told Amos that He was putting a plumb line (a straight line) among His people. When He measured them against the straight line, He would know if the people were true to plumb (straight) or not. If they weren't straight, He wasn't going to spare them any longer.

We believe we're living in the last days of earth's history. Right now there is time to change if we aren't following God the way we should be. But very soon it will be too late, and those who aren't following God will not be spared.

Don't wait until the last minute. Get plumb today and follow God's straight line to heaven.

This is what he showed me: The Lord was standing by a wall that had been built true to plumb, with a plumb line in his hand. And the Lord asked me, "What do you see, Amos?" "A plumb line," I replied. Then the Lord said, "Look, I am setting a plumb line among my people Israel; I will spare them no longer." Amos 7:7, 8.

Hopping Mad

I t's a good thing we have traffic lights. Green means go. Red means stop. Yellow means slow down and get ready to stop. Signals are very helpful. Without them there would be a lot more accidents. We have some signals in us that we need to pay attention to as well. One of them is anger.

Sooner or later, you'll probably get angry. But doesn't the Bible tell us not to get angry? Actually, that was probably your mother. The Bible says not to sin in our anger. Anger becomes a sin if we don't deal with it properly.

Anger is a signal to us. Anger tells us that something is wrong. Someone has crossed our boundaries, and it gives us the energy to do something about it. When it is used this way, as a tool, anger is helpful. Where most people go wrong is in trying to deny that they are angry. Or they bury their anger. Then it turns into bitterness and resentment.

Anger becomes a sin only if we use it to hurt others or hang on to it. Use it to make your situation right again, and then let it go.

*"In your anger do not sin": Do not let the sun go down
while you are still angry, and do not give the devil
a foothold. Ephesians 4:26, 27.*

For Shame

ary hid her face and cringed, waiting, knowing that she deserved every rock the hostile crowd picked up. She hated herself so much for what she had done that she wanted to throw the stones herself. Even if by some miracle she came out of this alive, she couldn't live with herself. Her shame was too great.

When she looked up again, they were all gone. All except Jesus. Surely He would pick up all the dropped stones and hurl them at her. But He didn't. And then He said the one thing that took away her shame and gave her the courage to start over. "I don't condemn you either. Go and sin no more."

Shame is a tough emotion. Satan tries to clobber us with shame, hoping to make us believe that no one—most of all God—can ever love us after what we've done.

But the truth is that God forgives us no matter what we've done. He doesn't hold past wrongs against us. He gives us a fresh slate and expects us to go and sin no more. If anything, shame should motivate us to obey God because He loves us. It should never make us feel worthless.

If any one of you is without sin, let him be the first to throw a stone at her. John 8:7.

14 MAY

Doubt It?

If there had been an Olympics back then, I think Elijah would have won a gold medal in track and field for Israel. It's amazing how fast you can run when there's an angry queen on your tail. Elijah broke all land-speed records getting out of there. The interesting thing is that it happened immediately after he won a great victory for God.

Self-doubt happens to everyone. First you are flying high, sure you are doing what God wants you to do. And then *bam!* Something happens, and suddenly you're not so sure. Next thing you know, you're heading for the hills, giving Elijah a run for his money. Satan loves watching the race. If he can keep you running, there isn't a whole lot of work being done for God.

God gently helped Elijah through his self-doubt by reassuring him that he wasn't alone. And neither are we. By surrounding ourselves with people who love and care about us we can protect ourselves against self-doubt. They can help us remember the victories we have experienced and not focus only on the setbacks or obstacles.

After rest and reassurance we'll be ready to go back out there. We'll be so on fire for God that we'll be too hot for Satan to handle.

■ ■ ■ ■

Elijah was afraid and ran for his life. 1 Kings 19:3.

Saint Mittens

e have three black dogs, and lately a cat has been coming to visit. Guess what color he is. Black. We call him Mittens for the white on his paws.

I've never been much of a "cat person." The only cat I've ever really had is Scribbles, the cartoon one in my word processing program. Scribbles meows and purrs on my screen while I work.

Mittens isn't my ideal cat. If I chose a cat, I would pick a Burmese, Persian, Maine coon, or a tiger. I didn't really take to him right away. Then I saw him letting my kids carry him around like a sack of potatoes. It was amazing. If cats could be saints, Mittens would be one.

And I realized that it doesn't matter if he's not the "kind" of cat I would have chosen. What matters is the "kind" of cat he is—so sweet and loving. That's what matters, not because his fur isn't my first color choice or because he's not a breed I fancy. I love Mittens for *who* he is, just as God loves us for *who* we are. It doesn't matter *what* we look like. We're always God's type.

And God said, "Let the land produce living creatures according to their kinds: livestock, creatures that move along the ground, and wild animals, each according to its kind." Genesis 1:24.

Take It, It's Yours!

an you imagine how bad Paul must have felt? He was responsible for countless deaths among the Christians. They were terrified of him. I can imagine him staying awake nights agonizing over what he had done. In the end, though, he realized that God had forgiven him.

Some people have a hard time grasping forgiveness. They don't believe God can forgive them, because they can't forgive themselves. But what we have to realize is that forgiveness is ours. All we have to do is take it. God wants us to have it.

God sent Paul to tell people that there was forgiveness for sins. It was something they could have right away. They didn't have to wait. And there was nothing they could do to "pay" for it.

All we have to do is turn from the power of Satan to the power of God. If we confess our sins, we are forgiven. It's that simple. And that important.

■ ■ ■ ■

I am sending you to them to open their eyes and turn them from darkness to light, and from the power of Satan to God, so that they may receive forgiveness of sins and a place among those who are sanctified by faith in me. Acts 26:17, 18.

Kimberly, Jill, and Rebecca

eet Kimberly, Jill, and Rebecca.

"Hi! I'm Kimberly. I'm the greatest. You name it, and I can do it. Whatever you can do, I can do better. I'm more interesting than any 10 people you know."

"Oh, hi there. I'm Jill. I'm not bothering you, am I? Because if I'm bothering you, I'll go away. There's no reason you'd want to talk to me anyway. I'm nothing. I'm lower than nothing. I'm worthless. I should be going before I start bothering you."

"Hi, I'm Rebecca. Can I get anything for you? Have a seat. Let's get to know each other. Do you like books? What are some of your favorites? I'm a writer. I love books."

The most balanced person above is Rebecca. And Rebecca is the hardest person to be like. The media tells us we're great and we deserve everything we want. The Bible tells us to be humble and put others above ourselves. But real humility has dignity. It doesn't boast, but it doesn't make itself a doormat, either. When you find a balance, you'll have real humility.

For by the grace given me I say to every one of you: Do not think of yourself more highly than you ought, but rather think of yourself with sober judgment, in accordance with the measure of faith God has given you. Romans 12:3.

Gotcha Covered

alker" is my children's last name, but it isn't because they learned to walk more quickly than other babies. In fact, they were pretty slow about it. But do you know what? I love my children now, and I loved them before they could walk and before they could crawl. What they can do doesn't affect how much I love them.

God is the same way. He loves us all the time. He may not love what we do, but He loves us. And He always wants the best for us. When we fail, He cries with us. And when we succeed, He's our biggest cheerleader. He doesn't wait for us to be perfect, to have a perfect day, or to ace a big bad problem we've been struggling with, in order to love us. His love is right where we're at.

We don't deserve it. We mess up sometimes. That's what grace is all about. It's love and forgiveness given to us when we don't deserve it. Grace isn't something you can buy when you need it. It's God's character, God Himself, covering our shortcomings. We aren't even close to being perfect, but when God covers us we are perfect in Him.

And if by grace, then it is no longer by works; if it were, grace would no longer be grace. Romans 11:6.

Living Sacrifice

dmit it. The thought of being a sacrifice doesn't exactly make you feel comfortable, does it? *Sacrifice* is a painful word. Sacrifices were killed and then burned on altars. Gulp.

Isaac was a boy well acquainted with being a sacrifice since he came within a knife blade of becoming one. Lying there on that pile of wood, he was prepared to give up everything to be a sacrifice.

So what does Paul mean by being living sacrifices? Certainly he doesn't expect us to jump onto piles of wood and become actual sacrifices. No, that's not what he's talking about. The kind of sacrifice Paul is talking about is the kind that gives up its seat on the bus. It's the kind that gets up early to spend time with God before school. It's the kind that says, "Not my will, but Yours, Lord."

Every time we put others or God before ourselves we are a living sacrifice. We die to ourselves so we can be born to God. And in the same way that Jesus rose from the dead after becoming a sacrifice for us, we will rise with Him and receive our reward.

Therefore, I urge you, brothers, in view of God's mercy, to offer your bodies as living sacrifices, holy and pleasing to God—this is your spiritual act of worship. Romans 12:1.

Captain God

The ocean was so blue that it was hard to see where the water ended and the sky started. We plowed out toward the horizon in a boat that, if you thought about unpleasant sea creatures lurking beneath the waves, was uncomfortably small. When I looked back, I was shocked to find that land was no longer visible.

It was my first time out on the ocean with my house parents, the couple I was living with while I went to academy. David was steering the boat. His hand was going to guide us through the gigantic sea to an island we were going to explore. I had to trust that he knew where he was going. To my relief he did, and it wasn't long before we were exploring the island.

When we head out into life, sometimes forward and back look the same. We can't see where we're going or how we're going to get there. But if God is the captain of our boat, we can trust Him to get us to our destination safely.

■ ■ ■ ■

In your unfailing love you will lead the people you have redeemed. In your strength you will guide them to your holy dwelling. Exodus 15:13.

The Two on Either Side

here was a big difference between the thieves crucified on either side of Jesus. They had both done bad things, but the first one wasn't sorry for what he had done. He was sorry only that he'd been caught. He didn't like hanging on a cross, and he wanted out. He took his anger and frustration out on Jesus.

"Hey, you! Aren't you the Christ? Work a miracle, and get us down from here!"

The other man admitted he had done something wrong. He accepted his punishment as something he deserved, whether he liked it or not. He didn't try to make excuses or blame other people for what he had done. Instead, he took responsibility for his mistakes and realized that he needed forgiveness. He asked Jesus to remember him.

In order to be forgiven, we have to know we need it. We have to ask for it. And we have to accept it. The first thief denied that he had done anything wrong, and he lost out. The second thief admitted he had done wrong, and he gained Paradise.

We've all done something wrong. The question is Which side of the cross are you on?

We are punished justly, for we are getting what our deeds deserve. But this man has done nothing wrong. Luke 23:41.

New Every Morning

ittle Keturah peeked outside the tent. Even though it was hardly daybreak, she could see the glistening white carpet on the desert floor. The manna had arrived. She grabbed the basket she used every morning to collect the precious food and hurried out of the tent.

Soon she was crouched down on her knees, gathering manna into her basket. She must be sure not to gather too little or too much. Too little and they would go hungry. Too much and it would rot. The manna would not keep.

You may never have tasted manna in your life, but there is something God sends you every day that must be gathered just like the manna. It's God's compassion, His grace, His power. We have to ask for it (gather it) every morning, because it comes new every morning, just as the manna did.

You can't pray today for strength for tomorrow any more than you can expect to have strength today if you don't pray for it. It doesn't work that way. We have to ask God for His help day by day, moment by moment, problem by problem. In that way we'll have all the strength we need all day long.

Because of the Lord's great love we are not consumed, for his compassions never fail. They are new every morning; great is your faithfulness. Lamentations 3:22, 23.

Bringing in the Crops

omeo wanted to grow corn for his cows. But zucchini seeds were cheaper at the time and easier to plant. So in the spring he planted acres and acres of zucchini. Still, he was confident corn would grow despite that small detail.

When Romeo drove out to the field on his tractor, he didn't find a single stalk of corn. Instead, zucchini covered the field. Romeo stopped the big tractor and scratched his head. What had gone wrong?

Have you ever wondered where some of your behavior comes from? Maybe you yell or react violently when you're angry. You might not have to look farther than your television set or the books you read. What you put into your mind will come out. Just as Romeo couldn't plant zucchini and expect corn, you can't plant violence and expect patience. You can't plant immorality and expect virtue.

Be careful what you plant because whatever it is will grow in you. And like Romeo's zucchini it will be plain to everyone what kind of seeds you sowed.

Do not be deceived: God cannot be mocked. A man reaps what he sows. The one who sows to please his sinful nature, from that nature will reap destruction; the one who sows to please the Spirit, from the Spirit will reap eternal life. Galatians 6:7, 8.

Questions

I t's sometimes hard to admit when we need help. I remember having a difficult time in Algebra II. I just couldn't seem to get it right. I waited until everyone left class one day and slunk up to the teacher's desk.

"Umm, I need some help. Is there any way I could get some tutoring or something?"

"There's a study group after school," the teacher informed me. Did I imagine that she looked down her nose at me in disapproval?

I snuck into the study group later that day. Everyone there would now know that I needed help. How embarrassing. But you know what surprised me? Nobody thought I was stupid because I asked for help. Asking for help is a smart thing to do. The only people who stay in the dark are the ones who don't ask where the light switch is.

Earth can be a pretty dark place sometimes. God knows where all the light switches are in your life. If you ask Him, He will show you where to find them. He doesn't want His children stumbling around down here in the dark, alone and clueless. The only questions God won't answer are the ones you never ask.

I will instruct you and teach you in the way you should go;
I will counsel you and watch over you. Psalm 32:8.

The Book

here are a lot of expressions about "the book." By the book. Throw the book at him. The Good Book. Keeping the books. Buried in his books. And probably a lot more that I can't remember at the moment.

You probably lug around more books than you care to think about every day. There are millions of books in libraries all over the world. And sometimes I think I have half of them in my house, because my bookshelves are overflowing.

The most important book, however, is the book of life. And it's not even *on* earth. It's in heaven. That's the book that Jesus will write our names in if we are saved.

Admit that nothing you will ever do can make up for the fact that you were born a sinner. Understand that only Jesus was sinless, that only He can pay our sin debt with His perfect life. Accept Him as your Saviour. Then Jesus will take up His pen and carefully enter your name into the most important book—the book of life.

If anyone's name was not found written in the book of life, he was thrown into the lake of fire. Revelation 20:15.

God Loves Me, Even When I Don't Like Myself

ailure. It's a word that makes my palms sweat. Satan loves it, though. If he can convince me that I'm a failure every time I make a mistake, then he can keep me from trying again. Every time I fall he tries to convince me that I'm not good enough for God so I might as well quit trying to live the way God wants me to live.

But do you know what? No one can make God stop loving us. We might do things God hates, but God will never hate us. God loves us because He is God. He can do that.

Even if you take a nosedive at every step, He will still love you. And because God loves you, you can love yourself. And you can love others, no matter how many flaws they have. You can love them because God says you are full of worth. You are so valuable He gave His most precious possession to you. He gave you the gift of His Son.

No matter what you think of yourself, God loves you. Say it. GOD LOVES ME!

For God so loved _____ *(fill in the blank with your name) that he gave his one and only Son, that whoever believes in him shall not perish but have eternal life. John 3:16, my paraphrase.*

The Weeping Prophet

The book of Lamentations in the Bible was written by the prophet Jeremiah. It records his sadness over the people of Israel, who refused to listen to God and were taken captive by a heathen nation. No wonder Jeremiah was known as the weeping prophet. He had a lot to cry about as Israel lived with the shame she had brought upon herself.

Maybe you've never done anything you were ashamed of. I have. And Satan often reminds me of the things I've done. But I don't have to listen to his accusations.

God says, "You have sinned, but I have forgiven you. My compassion never ends. My mercy has kept you from complete destruction. I am forever faithful, and every morning when you seek Me, you will find My love for you is just as fresh as it was before you sinned."

No matter how hard Satan tries to destroy us and no matter how many times he knocks us down, God will help us back up. And as long as we keep walking toward Him, we will be going in the right direction. One step at a time.

■ ■ ■ ■

The Lord is good to those whose hope is in him, to the one who seeks him; it is good to wait quietly for the salvation of the Lord. Lamentations 3:25, 26.

28 MAY

Washing the Dishes

I like washing dishes by hand. I like making dirty dishes clean again. I like rinsing the suds off in hot water. Using hot water makes the dishes dry faster. I wash, and God dries. That's how it's always been.

My dishes wouldn't get very clean, though, if I cleaned only the outside, would they? The inside is the dirtiest part. All the food goes on the inside. So it wouldn't do me much good to give the outside a good wipe and put it in the dish drainer.

It's the same with us. We have to let God clean us up. The Pharisees were famous for hiding parts of themselves inside. Jesus told them that they'd never get clean if they kept washing only the outside. They had to wash the inside, too.

When we confess our sins, we let God clean our insides. The soap might sting, and the hot water might be uncomfortable, but when He is through we will be clean all over. In this case God does both the washing *and* the drying.

You clean the outside of the cup and dish, but inside they are full of greed and self-indulgence. Blind Pharisee! First clean the inside of the cup and dish, and then the outside also will be clean. Matthew 23:25, 26.

Fooled Ya

ave you ever seen anyone you thought was just perfect? I have news for you. They're not. We like to take ordinary people (movie stars, sports figures, singers, and—horrors!—even writers) and make them into role models. But these people struggle with their problems just as everyone else does. They might fight with their friends, disappoint their loved ones, or even battle horrible problems we know nothing about.

Olympic skater Oksana Baiul is one example. Many factors in her life made it easy for her to have a problem with alcohol, and for a while her life was really messed up. Now she is starting over, admitting her problems, and trying to do what's right. Anyone who thought of her as a role model was probably disappointed in her, but they shouldn't be. She's back on track and working at staying there.

Everyone sins. The only sinless person is Jesus. He is the only role model who's perfect. We can place *all* our trust in Him because He will always live up to it. Cut people slack. Everyone messes up. Take what good you can from people, but place your trust in Jesus.

■ ■ ■ ■

If we claim to be without sin, we deceive ourselves
and the truth is not in us. 1 John 1:8.

Blind Trust

bram really trusted God. I mean he *really* trusted God. When his herdsmen and Lot's were fighting and causing problems, Abram suggested they split up. He and Lot stood on a hilltop and looked out over the land God had given to *Abram*.

Did Abram say, "Well, this is my land, after all. I want the best part of it"? No, he let Lot choose where he wanted to go.

Lot took the best of the land for himself, and look what happened to him. He lived near Sodom, which got fried to a crisp, and his wife turned into a pillar of salt. Bad decision, Lot.

Abram, on the other hand, let God lead him. He selflessly gave Lot the best part of the land, and look what happened to him. God blessed him and gave him a son and made him the father of a nation. We can always trust God, even when it looks to us as though we're getting the short end of the stick.

So Abram said to Lot, "Let's not have any quarreling between you and me, or between your herdsmen and mine, for we are brothers. Is not the whole land before you? Let's part company. If you go to the left, I'll go to the right; if you go to the right, I'll go to the left." Genesis 13:8, 9.

Coming Clean

aria was studying when her mom looked in on her after supper. It was getting late, but Maria had one more science chapter to read before she could turn in.

"You've been spending a lot more time studying lately, Maria. Is something wrong? Have you been doing poorly in school?"

Maria felt her face flush with embarrassment as she laid down her pencil. She had been thinking it was time to tell her parents about her cheating, and now was as good a time as any. "Yes, Mom, my grades have been worse than before. But they're honest grades. I—" Maria could hardly bring herself to say it, "I used to cheat. But I've asked God to forgive me, and I've stopped."

Maria watched her mother's face, but it didn't change. "Maria, I am very proud of you. It took a lot of courage for you to admit that. I think it's important that we tell your dad and your teachers too."

Maria nodded. Now that she had told her mom, she felt much better, almost light with relief. It gave her the courage to tell the others.

"Thank You, God, for taking away my sins," she prayed.

■ ■ ■ ■

Therefore confess your sins to each other and pray for each other so that you may be healed. James 5:16.

Vacation

ummer vacation used to seem endless. It seemed to stretch on forever. Until the first week of school came. And then it seemed much too short.

As the school year ends, you're probably ready to start summer vacation. Maybe you're already finished with school (lucky you!) and are enjoying days that start slow and linger dreamily, full of sunshine and fluffy clouds and lemonade. OK, maybe I *am* starting to sound like a commercial, but I *miss* summer vacation.

Jesus must have enjoyed vacations, too. He worked hard, but He also rested. In the book of Mark particularly we read about Jesus taking a lot of time off. No joke! He often went off by Himself.

During the time He spent alone He talked to God, and that's where He got the strength to keep going. It's sometimes easy to overlook. We can get pretty busy. But it's important for all of us to slow down often and take time-outs with God. Not just in the summer, but all year long. This summer vacation, be sure to spend time with God.

■ ■ ■ ■

So they went away by themselves in a boat
to a solitary place. Mark 6:32.

Mean Old Mister Strife

I picture the Demon of Strife as a really ugly dude. Tall, scowling, messy complexion, stringy hair, bad breath. You can tell Mr. Strife is around when your insides start to feel like a rubber band being stretched further than it can handle. The good news is that we don't have to let Mr. Strife hang around. In fact, we don't have to let him in at all!

Mr. Strife uses three doors to get into our lives: the door of our lips, the door of pride, and the door of debate. The Bible tells us to keep our tongues from evil. That will keep the door of our lips shut. Jesus taught us to think of others first. That will keep the door of pride shut. We also need to remember that it is our job to present the truth, and it's the Holy Spirit's job to convict people of truth. The door of debate will remain shut.

If you follow these tips, Mr. Strife will be stuck outside in the cold. That's where he belongs!

■ ■ ■ ■

Since the children have flesh and blood, he too shared their humanity so that by his death he might destroy him who holds the power of death—that is the devil—and free those who all their lives were held in slavery by their fear of death. Hebrews 2:14, 15.

3 JUNE

Left Behind

braham and Sarah weren't at home when Sarah died. They were visiting a foreign land. Can you see Abraham, tears running into his beard, sitting beside the road? Then can you see him slapping his knees and saying, "Well, I'll miss her, but there's no time to bury her. I'll just leave her beside the road and get moving"?

Horrors! No way! He bought a field and a cave to bury Sarah in. And he mourned for Sarah before he moved on.

When we lose something, a person or something else very dear to us, we can't expect just to forget that it happened. When my dog died, it took me a long time to get over it. But the only way we'll ever really be able to move on is if we let ourselves feel the sadness that comes with loss.

The good news is that no matter what we are sad about it won't last forever. God promises, "I will turn their mourning into gladness; I will give them comfort and joy instead of sorrow" (Jeremiah 31:13). I can't wait for that day. How about you?

Sarah lived to be a hundred and twenty-seven years old. She died at Kiriath Arba (that is, Hebron) in the land of Canaan, and Abraham went to mourn for Sarah and to weep over her. Genesis 23:1, 2.

Warning Signs

I f you're driving along and all of a sudden you see a "Bridge Out" (or "Road Closed" or "Caution—Steep Hill") sign, and you ignore the sign, what would happen? Well, I shudder to think. Let's just say I hope I'm not in the car with you at the time. You could very well end up seriously hurt or, worse, dead.

That also happens when we ignore the signs God gives us in our lives. Whenever we sin, God starts flashing signs in our conscience. "Danger!" If we ignore the signs, we could drive right over a cliff.

Our job is to read the signs (the Bible) and see where we should be driving in the first place. If a bridge is out, the signs will tell us. If a road is dangerous, they will tell us that, too. But just as real drivers can go on the Internet for up-to-the-minute travel advice, we can pray anytime, and God will give us directions.

So don't ignore the signs God gives you. He has promised to be our travel agent and make sure we reach our final destination: heaven. The ultimate joy ride.

Whether you turn to the right or to the left, your ears
will hear a voice behind you, saying,
"This is the way; walk in it." Isaiah 30:21.

On the Battlefield

ook, hence in yonder castle turret! Cast your gaze across the battlefield and upward. Tell me, do you see a maiden of fair complexion, with skin like rose petals, and hair of spun gold, held captive in the tower prison?

Yeah? Well, her name is Jenny, and she's got a temper that can be measured on the Richter scale. She's also not above lying when it suits her purpose. She talks about people behind their backs, and she does some highly questionable surfing on the Internet. But she has just decided to be free from all that. She's asked her King to save her.

Now, do you see the Rider over there? The One coming across the battlefield? He's going to free her from the tower.

"Rejoice greatly, O my people! Shout with joy! For look—your King is coming! He is the Righteous One, the Victor!" (Zechariah 9:9, TLB).

Our lives are battlefields. And sometimes it can seem like we're stuck in the prison tower for good. But we're not. Jesus will rescue us if we want Him to. We don't have to be perfect. We don't have to be model citizens. We just have to be willing.

■ ■ ■ ■

Together they will be like mighty men trampling the muddy streets in battle. Because the Lord is with them, they will fight and overthrow the horsemen. Zechariah 10:5.

The Flowers

I heard a story about a little girl who loved flowers. She took some of her allowance money and bought some fake flowers and a vase. She loved them and kept them on her bureau, even though they didn't have any smell at all.

A few weeks later her dad was tucking her in, and he asked her if she loved him. She said, "Yes, Daddy."

Her father replied, "Then give me your flowers."

The little girl was sad because she just couldn't bring herself to do it. She loved her flowers too much.

This went on for a month. Finally the little girl handed over the flowers, and do you know what happened? Her daddy gave her a bouquet of red roses. He'd been waiting all that time for her to give up the cheap stuff so he could give her the real thing.

Are you holding on to any cheap stuff in your life? Give it to God, and He'll give you the real deal. You won't be sorry you did.

■ ■ ■ ■

Now Joshua was dressed in filthy clothes as he stood before the angel. The angel said to those who were standing before him, "Take off his filthy clothes." Then he said to Joshua, "See, I have taken away your sin, and I will put rich garments on you." Zechariah 3:3, 4.

7 JUNE

A Broken Heart

I can remember being about 12 and feeling smug because I was a pretty good kid. I was a Catholic at the time, and in confession I was supposed to tell the priest my sins. My biggest sin was probably that I made things up so that I'd have something to say!

Young David was like that too. He once said, "Don't treat me as a common sinner. . . . No, I am not like that, O Lord; I try to walk a straight and narrow path of doing what is right; therefore in mercy save me" (Psalm 26:9-11, TLB). And then came his relationship with Bathsheba and his murder of her husband, Uriah. It took a fall for David to realize that everyone needs a Saviour. Big sins, little sins, it's all the same.

I've taken plenty of nosedives in my life by now. I'm not so smug anymore. But like David, I understand that when we are truly sorry for our mistakes, God will forgive us and comfort us and heal us. The size of the mistake doesn't matter. Just the sincerity of your heart.

■ ■ ■ ■

You do not delight in sacrifice, or I would bring it; you do not take pleasure in burnt offerings. The sacrifices of God are a broken spirit; a broken and contrite heart, O God, you will not despise. Psalm 51:16, 17.

Chicken Feed

y neighbor has a chicken, a little reddish hen;

She often jumps the fence to escape the confinement of her pen.

Little does this chickie know what awaits in the nearby field,

Where a wily fox is likely to think she'd make a great free meal.

OK, so I'm not a poet, but the story is true. One of my neighbor's chickens is a Houdini chicken, and she thinks she's found freedom. What she doesn't realize is that there's a fox living around here in the meadows. He has had many free chicken lunches over the years, and she's likely to be next on his menu.

Sometimes the commands in the Bible and the rules our parents give us look like fences meant to keep us in. They are actually fences put up to protect us. Like my neighbor's chicken, we struggle to find a way out, only to meet danger waiting on the other side ready to gobble us up. If we stay inside the fence, we need never fear what's on the outside.

For I command you today to love the Lord your God, to walk in his ways, and to keep his commands, decrees and laws; then you will live and increase, and the Lord your God will bless you in the land you are entering to possess. Deuteronomy 30:16.

The "Good" Life

here are a lot of shortcuts in life. You can cheat. You can lie. You can gamble. You can cut in line. But none of these shortcuts will get you any closer to a good life. A good life isn't about shortcuts at all. It's about taking the road less traveled. You get to the good life on the high and narrow road, not the easy, wide road.

The devil likes to tempt us with shortcuts because we humans tend to like doing things the easy way. He even tried to tempt Jesus to take a shortcut. Jesus came to earth to save human beings the hard way, through His life, death, and resurrection. But Satan offered to "give" Him all of humanity if He would bow down and worship him.

Jesus told Satan to get lost. And when Satan offers us a shortcut, we should tell him the same thing. A shortcut through life may be easier. But when you reach your final destination, you'll find yourself in a far different place than where you wanted to be.

Again, the devil took him to a very high mountain and showed him all the kingdoms of the world and their splendor. "All this I will give you," he said, "if you will bow down and worship me." Matthew 4:8, 9.

Brand Spanking New

**H**ave you ever taken something that was absolutely filthy and cleaned it up? The sweatshirt you wear to play tag football? The dress you wore to the banquet and spilled grape juice on? The bike you mud-dog on? Your room?

It's especially amazing when you don't think the grime will ever come out. You resign yourself to having something with a stain on it forever. But then, almost miraculously, the stain is gone!

It's like that with our hearts, too. From the time we're born they are dingy. The more we sin, the dirtier they get. But when we give our hearts to Jesus, He cleans them, and they're even better than new!

We might sometimes go around acting as though they're just the same old dirty hearts, when really they're as clean as snow. That's how Jesus sees us. And that's how we should see ourselves. We're not second-class citizens on a foreign planet, biding our time until Jesus comes back. We're children of the heavenly King.

Jesus has placed infinite value on our worth and given us every treasure heaven has to offer. We're new creatures. We don't look the same or act the same. We're "new and improved"!

■ ■ ■ ■

Therefore, if anyone is in Christ, he is a new creation;
the old has gone, the new has come! 2 Corinthians 5:17.

11 JUNE

Body Parts

I have pretty eyes. No joke. People tell me that all the time. And while I appreciate my eyes very much, I hate my feet. I think they're ugly. Of course, if I had to choose between having my ugly feet and having no feet, I'd keep them. They don't *have* to be attractive. They just have to be functional.

I think we overlook that too often. We give a lot of attention to some people or jobs in the church body. Everyone admires the kid who can get up and play a fantastic piano solo for special music, and it's great that he's using his talent to glorify God. But who admires the kid who makes money by assembling bikes and donates it to build churches in developing countries? His contribution is just as important. Just ask a little Bolivian girl who attends a church built with those funds.

Not everything that God asks us to do is exciting or popular. But whatever He asks us to do is *ours*—our particular job. We can do the most humble job with pride when God asks us to do it.

After all, no one ever hated his own body, but he feeds and cares for it, just as Christ does the church—for we are members of his body. Ephesians 5:29, 30.

Heavenly Gatorade

here's nothing I like so much after a long run or bike ride as a couple gallons of water or Gatorade. I wouldn't dream of drinking piping hot herbal tea after exercising. That would just make me hotter, and it wouldn't quench my thirst at all.

All of us have the same kind of thirst in our lives. We can try to satisfy it with stuff such as video games, wrong relationships, exciting books, TV, movies, music, and more, but that would be similar to drinking something hot after you exercise. It would only make you want more, but it would never satisfy you.

God promises to give us heavenly Gatorade when we come to Him for a drink. When He fills us, we won't want or need anything else. The world will leave us wanting more. God will completely satisfy. Ask Him to fill you today.

■ ■ ■ ■

Say there! Is anyone thirsty? Come and drink—even if you have no money! Come, take your choice of wine and milk—it's all free! Why spend your money on food that doesn't give you strength? Why pay for groceries that don't do you any good? Listen and I'll tell you where to get good food that fattens up the soul! Come to me with your ears wide open. Listen, for the life of your soul is at stake. Isaiah 55:1-3, TLB.

Sparrows and Chimney Swifts

hen we were in Tennessee visiting some relatives, we heard an odd scratching behind the chimney. My husband, Rob, looked behind the fireplace and pulled out a little grayish brown bird that had gotten trapped in the fireplace. It was a chimney swift, and it looked almost dead.

Rob gently put the bird on the porch. The poor little thing tipped forward onto its face, stunned. But before we could even blink, it righted itself, jumped into the sky, and flew away. Just like that.

Does it amaze you that God knew where that chimney swift was before we found it? That He knew that it was going to be OK even before we did? He knows everything about the smallest, most trivial forms of life on earth. And He knows all about you, even the things you don't tell anyone else.

Nothing you could ever do would make Him stop loving you. He's there for you when you want to share something exciting or a problem that breaks your heart. Whatever it is, He's interested. He knows where the sparrows are, and He knows where you are, too.

Are not two sparrows sold for a penny? Yet not one of them will fall to the ground apart from the will of your Father. Matthew 10:29.

Passing the Baton

I t was our track and field meet. I was the only girl on our relay team. The pressure was on. The boys on my team didn't have any confidence in me. I was new, and I was a girl.

Guy went first and passed the baton to Scott, who passed the baton to me. I tore down the track, passing two boys. When I passed the baton to Brian, it wouldn't be my responsibility anymore. My part would be done. Brian grabbed the baton, and he was gone, legs churning. He passed everyone ahead of him, and we won the first-place ribbon.

I try to remember my relay-racing days when I get hurt, because I tend to carry my hurts around with me. I circle the track, refusing to pass my baton of hurt to God, even though I know He's the only one who can win the race. The thing is, I can run around the track until I keel over. But until I forgive and pass the hurt to God, I'll never get over it and finish the race.

When someone hurts you, don't hold on to the baton. Forgive the person, and pass the hurt to God.

Forgive us our debts, as we also
have forgiven our debtors. Matthew 6:12.

He Was Here

ould you like to visit the Holy Land? My dad and grandmother once went there. I have a bottle of water from the Jordan and some sand from the Dead Sea that my dad brought back with him. The thing that draws people to the Holy Land is that it's possible to actually *walk where Jesus walked.* You can see things He saw. The sunrises, the sunsets, the lakes, the mountains, and the landscape might be different, but *He was there.*

"God has no idea what I'm going through," we say when we're having trouble. And you know, it couldn't be further from the truth. God knows *exactly* what we're going through. Jesus was HERE. He walked in your shoes when you're lonely, when you're frightened, when you're tempted. Whatever you go through, He went through. He can identify. God isn't just looking down on us; He walked with us too.

That's why you can approach Him with any problem that you have. Maybe it's not exactly the same thing, but problems are timeless. They don't change. Rejection is rejection, no matter in which century or in what part of the world you experience it. Jesus understands. Share your burdens with Him, for He *cares for you.*

■ ■ ■ ■

Because he himself suffered when he was tempted, he is able to help those who are being tempted. Hebrews 2:18.

War

ou're a jerk," Tanya spat. "I don't know why I ever liked you."

Nicole bit her lip. It was on the tip of her tongue to lash back at Tanya. Instead she said a quick prayer for control and asked God to forgive Tanya for her nasty words.

Let's see that again the way heaven sees it:

"You're a jerk," Tanya spat. Evil angels crowded around her, egging her on.

"She's not good enough to be your friend," one of them taunted.

God's angels clustered around Nicole, ready to defend her. When she prayed, even more angels came to her side. They pushed the darkness back.

Tanya, feeling their influence, suddenly saw how wrongly she had behaved. She flushed with shame. "I'm sorry, Nicole. I was angry. Please forgive me?"

Prayer is the mightiest weapon we have on earth to fight Satan. His evil angels are always looking for ways to hurt us, but we can overcome them by claiming God's power.

■ ■ ■ ■

The weapons we fight with are not the weapons of the world. On the contrary, they have divine power to demolish strongholds. We demolish arguments and every pretension that sets itself up against the knowledge of God, and we take captive every thought to make it obedient to Christ. 2 Corinthians 10:4, 5.

Whale of a Tale

J onah was in a huff about the people of Nineveh—their repenting had upset him. He stomped off to a hill nearby to see what would happen. While he was there God sent a vine to grow and give him some shade. Jonah had been hot and uncomfortable, and the vine gave him some relief. The vine grew, and Jonah got real attached to it.

When God sent a worm to eat the vine and kill it, Jonah was, well, extremely angry! He was so angry and frustrated that he just wanted to die. Why? Jonah hadn't planted, fertilized, or watered the vine. He had done nothing to make it grow. God had given him a gift, and when it was gone, he grumbled about it.

Don't we do the same thing? Even about small matters, such as sunshine? When it rains, we get disagreeable. But why? We didn't have anything to do with the sun shining. God controls all that. We need to learn to accept everything He allows, trusting that He will always help us through the tough times.

■ ■ ■ ■

But God said to Jonah, "Do you have a right to be angry about the vine?" "I do," he said, "I am angry enough to die." Jonah 4:9.

Walking With God

I like to walk four miles a day. It's a hard four miles: up, up, up a hill and then down, down, down that hill. And the hills are steep. This is Vermont, after all. They don't call it the Green *Mountain* State for nothing.

One day my 6-year-old son, Joshua, decided to come with me on my walk. He was sure he could do it. I wasn't so sure, because I walk pretty fast.

He did it, though. His little legs moved quickly, and his face got red. He invented a run/walk combo kind of thing to keep up. By the end of the four miles he was pretty exhausted. Walking with Mommy wasn't as easy as he'd thought it would be.

I'm glad that walking with God isn't that challenging. We assume that because God is, well, God, He will be impossible to keep up with, but that's not the case at all. There is nothing God would rather do than walk with us. He matches His steps to ours. He even takes time to stop and smell the roses along the way.

■ ■ ■ ■

I will walk among you and be your God,
and you will be my people. Leviticus 26:12.

Great Faith

he woman crept up to Jesus. She knew she had a lot of nerve approaching Him in the first place. She could see annoyance on the faces of His followers, but the kindness in Jesus' eyes gave her courage. Her daughter was ill, tormented constantly by a demon, and the woman was ready to do whatever she had to in order to get help.

Jesus' answer to this woman's request always surprised me. He seemed almost rude to her. First He ignored her. And then He told her, "I was sent to help the Jews, not the Gentiles."

But that didn't stop her. And Jesus *knew it wouldn't*. He knew her faith was strong, and He wanted to impress the disciples with it. He was saying, "Look, you guys! This woman isn't even a Jew, but she knows who I am and that I can help her!"

The Samaritan woman received her miracle because she trusted Jesus to give it to her. She braved the disapproval of the disciples, worked up her courage, and asked for it. She was persistent. She believed. Think of her story the next time *you* need a miracle.

Then Jesus answered, "Woman, you have great faith!
Your request is granted." And her daughter was
healed from that very hour. Matthew 15:28.

Camping Out

aiting beside the Pool of Bethesda must have been frustrating for the invalid. He had been disabled for 38 years! He went as far as he could go, but even though he could see the finish line he couldn't make it on his own.

Even though I'm not like the man at the pool, I have a lot of other disabilities. I sometimes wonder how God can love and accept me with all my problems. But we don't have to be perfect before God accepts us. He makes up for what we lack.

Jesus healed the man at the pool. The man became as good as new. Maybe even better. We might not be perfect people here on earth, but with Jesus in our lives we'll be able to join the pool guy, leaping and shouting for joy throughout eternity.

■ ■ ■ ■

"Sir," the invalid replied, "I have no one to help me into the pool when the water is stirred. While I am trying to get in someone else goes down ahead of me." Then Jesus said to him, "Get up! Pick up your mat and walk." At once the man was cured; he picked up his mat and walked. John 5:7-9.

21 JUNE

Did Not, Did Too

id not."

"Did *too!*"

Arguments are dangerous creatures. Even friendly ones can end up in disaster with two angry people stomping off to neutral corners. God doesn't expect us to agree with everyone. There are principles and positions we should defend. But we have to choose our battles.

Most arguments aren't about anything important. Avoid them like bad hair days. Pride forces us to prove that we are indeed, as always, right again. When this has been established, we can stand on the head of our victor and listen to the cheering. But think about the position of the guy who loses. No one likes being wrong. We don't show our love for others by being right but by being kind.

The arguments that matter are the ones you have to handle carefully. Pretend your words are dynamite. You don't need a lot of dynamite to make a big hole. Listen and pray before you say anything. Ask God to give you words that won't stir up anger but will show truth instead.

When you walk away from an argument having respect for the other person, you will know that you did it the right way.

Will too!

Don't have anything to do with foolish and stupid arguments,
because you know they produce quarrels. 2 Timothy 2:23.

Love in Action

Jill is shy. She volunteers after school tutoring younger students. She helps her folks make sunshine baskets for the homeless, and she gives Bible studies by e-mail. But every time she tries to pray out loud, she trips up or clams up. She just can't do it.

Billy is on the football team. Everyone knows he's a Christian. They can see him praying before every game. When the team wins, Billy gives all the glory to God. He doesn't attend many outreach activities because of practice, and he has time to be friendly only to his friends.

Quiz: Of the two kids above, which one is following Jesus' command to "love one another" better? Does it always matter that people hear us declare that we are Christians? What if our actions don't match our words?

Satan wants us to think that love is a feeling that comes and goes, but that's not true. Love is an action. You love someone by choosing to do what is best for them no matter what happens and no matter what you feel like. Loving actions are really love *in* action.

A new command I give you: Love one another. As I have loved you, so you must love one another. By this all men will know that you are my disciples, if you love one another. John 13:34, 35.

Oh, Joy! (Part 1)

o you think of God as a joyful being? Because He is. He's the most joyful being in the universe. Can you imagine what His creation might have looked like if He wasn't joyful?

Day one: God created something, but it was boring, so He stuck it in His homework folder and forgot about it until day two. On that day He made water and sky, but just barely. On day three he made some grass and vegetables and stuff, but He got sick of it after a while and didn't finish.

Day four He was in a hurry, so He made only a couple stars—two, in fact—and the sun and moon. Day five He created a goat and a horse and decided that would be good enough. Day six He made people, and on day seven He took a nap, glad that it was all done.

Aren't you glad God is joyful? He loved what He created. He had fun. He made lots of interesting things. He didn't *have* to. He could have made everything the same.

If you're ever tempted to think that God drags around heaven with a long face, remember the platypus or the giraffe. No joyless fuddy-duddy could have dreamed *them* up!

■ ■ ■ ■

*I have told you this so that my joy may be in you
and that your joy may be complete. John 15:11.*

Oh, Joy! (Part 2)

od wants us to be joyful—joy filled. Today, not tomorrow. Not next week after we've passed an exam. Not this summer during vacation. Now! Immediately.

David says, *"This* is the day." Not tomorrow. Today.

C. S. Lewis, a great writer, said, "Joy is the serious business of heaven."

Joy is important stuff. Do you know why? Sin looks a lot less tempting to us when we are happy. It can help us follow God. That's why Jesus wanted *His* joy to be complete in us, to give us strength.

But joy doesn't just happen. We have to practice it. We have to determine that we will be joyful today no matter what the circumstances.

One way to do that is to remember that today is minor in the scheme of things. Even if everything goes wrong today, so what? It's only one day out of your life. In the end you will still have all of eternity for everything to go right. Every moment of every day, forever and ever and ever, to be absolutely stuffed full of joy.

This is the day the Lord has made; let us rejoice and be glad in it. Psalm 118:24.

Don't Judge a Book by Its Cover

I noticed the black horse immediately. He was galloping at top speed around the field. When he got close to the other horses, they laid back their ears and threatened to bite. They hopped a little to show him that if he got closer he could expect to get kicked.

This horse was a handful. I could just imagine what he'd be like to ride (and fall off of, I'm sure).

A few days later I walked by the herd of horses again. They were closer to the fence. The black took one look at me and began to walk toward me. I could hardly believe it. He stuck his neck over the fence, asking me to pet him. He might very well be a spunky ride, but what he really wanted was attention.

There are people in life who give others a hard time. They can be annoying and even mean. If you assume that they are just bad apples, you could be missing a whole other side of them. The side that just needs a little attention. Don't be quick to judge. Ask God to show you how you can reach them.

■ ■ ■ ■

Stop judging by mere appearances,
and make a right judgment. John 7:24.

Cracked Pots

I have a really pretty jar that my husband picked up for me at a yard sale. It's orange, but not a hideous orange. Rather, a nice burnt orange like sunflowers. The color is so cheerful and warm that just looking at it reminds me of warm sand, summer sun, and blue sky. I keep cough drops in it in my kitchen.

During one spell of colds I moved the jar so that my children couldn't get into it by themselves. As I tipped it to put it farther back on the countertop, the lid slid off and fell into a glass jar, breaking in two! My husband came running when he heard me scream. He offered to fix it with glue. Now my cover is in one piece, but it will never be "new" again.

Our hearts are damaged, but God wants to fix them for us. He won't just glue the pieces together so that the cracks will be a constant reminder that the heart's been broken. He gives us a completely new heart. It's not like the old one. It's His heart. He puts it in us so that we can act and think and love as He does.

Those who belong to Christ Jesus have crucified the sinful nature with its passions and desires. Galatians 5:24.

Bail Out

I decided to take my horse, Cinder, out for a ride. We cut across the schoolyard and rode on the trails in the back. As we walked calmly through the playground, minding our own business, without any warning we were attacked by a vicious, horse-eating string!

Cinder saw a string, which was caught on her shoe, slipping through the grass like a 10-foot-long snake. Her legs went stiff, and she shot into the air. I tried to pull her in, but her eyes were rolling wildly, and I knew that whatever I did was not going to stop her. So I jumped off.

That's right. I jumped off.

Sometimes you have to do that in life. There are situations that will get worse no matter what you do to stop them. Then the best thing to do is get out. Remove yourself from the danger. Bailing out may seem cowardly, but it's not. It takes a lot of courage to admit that something is more powerful than you are, and then get away from it. But sometimes it is the wisest choice you can make. (As for Cinder, she circled the school twice before I caught her.)

Flee the evil desires of youth, and pursue righteousness, faith, love and peace, along with those who call on the Lord out of a pure heart. 2 Timothy 2:22.

Clay Pots

Ialways thought that pottery looked like a lot of fun. And easy. It looked so easy to sit there with a lump of clay turning on a wheel. You'd put your hands on it, and the wheel would turn. Presto! A cup or a bowl or a jug or a vase would miraculously appear.

It seemed like a no-brainer, so I decided to give it a try. It was fun but not at all easy. You have to put a lot of pressure on the clay in order to shape it. What looked so effortless was really a combination of skill and downright muscle power. But not *too* much power. Too much, and it would collapse into a pile of mud again. Too little, and it wouldn't make anything except a pile of mud.

In today's verse God is our potter. He shapes us carefully, not pressing too hard so that we collapse, but not so lightly that we stay shapeless lumps on the wheel. The pressure may not always feel good to us, but sometimes it's necessary in order to shape us into beautiful vessels that hold the Potter's love.

■ ■ ■ ■

Yet, O Lord, you are our Father. We are the clay, you are the potter; we are all the work of your hand. Isaiah 64:8.

Our Help

If you don't plug a lamp in, will it shine? (This is not a trick question.)

You and I are a lot like lamps. *God has to fill us with the Holy Spirit, and we need to stay "plugged in" to Him.* Sometimes I get on a goodness kick, and I determine to be good from now on. But pretty soon I fall on my face. Why? Because I can't be good on my own. Only God can show me what He wants and help me to obey Him. Then my light will shine. I can't do it on my own, just as your lamp can't shine if it's not plugged in.

The Bible tells us that God even has to help us to *want* to obey Him. We'd rather follow the desires of our hearts (which are "deceitful above all things and beyond cure" [Jeremiah 17:9]). But when we invite the Holy Spirit into our hearts, God will help us not only to obey Him, but to want to obey Him. So plug in to His power, and shine your light today!

■ ■ ■ ■

***For God is at work within you, helping you want to obey him,
and then helping you do what he wants. Philippians 2:13, TLB.***

A Clean Slate

aria had another test. She had done her homework, paid attention in class, and studied for a week. But she still wasn't sure she knew the material well enough to get a good grade. She was pretty sure she'd pass, but what she really wanted was to get a good grade again. Lately C+ and B– were the best grades she'd been able to pull off.

As she sat down to take the test, a thought flew through her mind. *If you cheat, you'll definitely get a good grade.* Immediately she said no in her mind. She actually screamed the word in her head. She was not going to cheat.

Maria suddenly realized that not only did she not want to cheat now, but she didn't want to cheat ever again. Quickly she bowed her head and silently prayed, *Lord, thank You for helping me to stop cheating. Please take away my desire for cheating, and help me to know that getting a good grade isn't the most important thing. Being honest is more important. Please help me with my test. Thank You. Amen.*

■ ■ ■ ■

We were therefore buried with him through baptism into death in order that, just as Christ was raised from the dead through the glory of the Father, we too may live a new life. Romans 6:4.

Innies and Outies

aybe you've noticed, but there are two groups in every school. The "in" group and the "not-so-in" group (or, as I like to call them, the "outies"). I was one of the "outies" in school, so I know what it feels like. But you might be surprised how many great, popular, fun adults were very shy, clumsy, unpopular kids in school. Jack Hanna, of wild animal fame, once laughed himself silly when I asked him if he had been popular in school.

Whether you are popular in school or not doesn't really matter. Being unpopular won't doom you to a life of being a nobody. And being popular won't guarantee that you'll be rich and famous when you grow up. What's a lot more important are the kinds of friends you have, popular or not. The Bible warns us that bad friends can have a bad effect on us.

It's OK to have friends who are not Christians. Jesus demonstrated this for us by accepting people who weren't at all religious. But His closest friends were His disciples. We should make sure that our closest friends, the ones who influence us, are Christians who put Christ first. They will help us to be strong during tough times and rejoice with us in the good times.

Do not be misled: "Bad company
corrupts good character." 1 Corinthians 15:33.

Face Plant

I think one of the funniest and saddest stories in the Bible is the story about the Philistines capturing the ark of God. I can imagine the celebration as they carried their prize to Ashdod. Then the Philistines took the ark into the temple of Dagon and set it right beside the heathen image. The next day, *wham!* Dagon was on his face in front of the ark of God. The people scratched their heads and stood him back up again.

The next day it was even worse! Dagon had done another face plant, but this time his arms and head had broken off. Soon after that, the Philistines were afflicted with tumors. They knew immediately that it was because of the ark of God. But instead of worshiping God rather than Dagon, they sent the ark away.

We do that when we try to put things into our lives that are wrong. When God tells us they're wrong, we send Him away if we don't get rid of them. We need to remember that there is only one true God, and we should worship Him.

■ ■ ■ ■

Then they carried the ark into Dagon's temple and set it beside Dagon. When the people of Ashdod rose early the next day, there was Dagon, fallen on his face on the ground before the ark of the Lord! 1 Samuel 5:2, 3.

Baby Steps

hen my son, Joshua, was a toddler he decided to learn how to walk. That's a good thing too, because I couldn't imagine carrying him around for the rest of his life! He pulled himself up and took one step before falling down. I watched proudly until the minute he fell. Then I ran over, paddled his bottom, and said, "You horrible baby! Get on your feet this instant! You can do better than that!"

You gasped with horror, didn't you? Well, gotcha! I said no such thing. I helped him get up and try again.

See, you couldn't believe *I* would be disgusted with my baby for not being able to walk, but don't we often think God is disgusted with us when we fail? One of the biggest lies of all time is that God can never love us because we aren't perfect.

The truth is that God loves us. Period. And He will help us to walk the way any parent helps a child to walk—one step at a time, helping and encouraging all the way.

I have seen his ways, but I will heal him; I will guide him and restore comfort to him, creating praise on the lips of the mourners in Israel. Isaiah 57:18, 19.

Spread Your Arms

Jesus loves me! this I know . . ."

We all know this, right? Still, when I do something wrong I get the picture of Him being very upset. Mad even. And then if something goes wrong or I have a bad day, it's like He's out to get me, maybe paying me back for something I did wrong. Have you ever felt that way?

It's so untrue. We know it is, in our heads. But our hearts have to realize it too. We have no idea how much God loves us. We really don't. I want you to do something: spread out your arms really wide.

Now say, "How much does God love me? He loves me this much."

He loves you so much that He stretched out His arms and died for you. Think about that. Let it sink in. He put Himself between you and forever death. Even though the Romans meant the cross to be a terrible thing, look at Jesus hanging there. His arms are outstretched, welcoming you. When you remember that, it's hard to believe Satan's lie that God doesn't love us, isn't it?

But God demonstrates his own love for us in this:
While we were still sinners, Christ died for us. Romans 5:8.

The Attack of the Weeds

eeds are vicious little creatures. They sneak up on your garden like a well-trained army. One day you look around, and they have invaded your territory. Sin is like that too. It pounces on us for a surprise attack, and before we know it, our life is full of it.

In a garden the best way to manage weeds is one at a time as they come up. If you let a few slip by, your whole garden will soon be choked with them. Sin is the same. We let a few smaller ones sneak up on us, and then soon we've forgotten all about God and doing what's right.

Paul tells us to keep the harvest in mind so we won't get discouraged. A gardener looking at a bare field that has just been planted imagines the vegetables that will be ready for eating in a few months. But if he gets discouraged waiting, there won't *be* any vegetables.

Don't get discouraged if it doesn't look like you are growing. Just keep doing what you know you should, and trust that God will help your garden grow.

■ ■ ■ ■

Let us not become weary in doing good, for at the proper time we will reap a harvest if we do not give up. Galatians 6:9.

Measuring Up

here's a story about a girl named Kathy, who thought she had it pretty bad. She complained to God about her problems one day. "You said my burden would be light," she pointed out, "but it isn't. I want to trade burdens with someone else."

"Help yourself." God pointed to a row of bundles with names on them. One bundle belonged to Diane, the most popular girl in school, who was beautiful, tall, slim, and smart.

"I'll take that one," Kathy exclaimed, but when she tried to pick it up, she could hardly carry it. "What's in here?" she wondered. Opening the bundle, she found a stepmother who couldn't be pleased and a father who was always traveling. And she found that a baby brother had died with Diane's mom in a car accident.

"I'll keep mine," Kathy decided quickly.

Comparing ourselves with others is never a good idea. We can easily be fooled by appearances. Even so, we will always find some who appear better than us and some who appear worse. We should carry our own loads as well as we can. God will help us if we ask Him to.

■ ■ ■ ■

Each one should test his own actions. Then he can take pride in himself, without comparing himself to somebody else, for each one should carry his own load. Galatians 6:4, 5.

Choosing Sides

icture life as two teams. God and Satan are the team captains, and they're choosing sides. But instead of them picking the players, they're letting the players choose the team. So you don't have to worry about being picked last. You just have to decide which team you want to play on.

There are some people who say they're on God's team, but they keep scoring goals for Satan. And there are some people who keep switching sides. Other players are sitting on the bench because they can't figure out which side they want to be on in the first place.

Deciding which team to be on is the most important decision we'll ever make. After we choose a team we will make decisions every day about how we play for our team. Our decisions won't affect whether or not the team wins. God's team has already won. How we play will determine whether or not we stay on the team.

I want to be there on the winner's platform when they play the anthem of heaven and God passes out the gold medals. Don't you?

Elijah went before the people and said, "How long will you waver between two opinions? If the Lord is God, follow him; but if Baal is God, follow him." But the people said nothing. 1 Kings 18:21.

Heaven, Here I Come

I can remember hearing about Jesus coming back to take us all to heaven and praying that He'd wait just a little while longer. There were so many things I had to do. Go on a date. Graduate from high school. Get married. Have kids. Live, basically.

Of course, my idea of heaven at that time was being dressed in white and floating around on clouds playing a harp from morning until night. It didn't seem very exciting to me.

But I changed my mind over the years as I learned a little more about heaven. It's going to be a wonderful place, so much better than the sinful world we live in today! I won't have to worry about getting shot in a grocery store. Punks won't push drugs on little kids to support their habit. Hurricanes won't destroy people's homes. And there will be no more death.

Heaven is going to be better than anything we can even dream about here. The Bible promises us that. So live every day as though Jesus is coming, because one day He will.

■ ■ ■ ■

You ought to live holy and godly lives as you look forward to the day of God and speed its coming. That day will bring about the destruction of the heavens by fire, and the elements will melt in the heat. But in keeping with his promise we are looking forward to a new heaven and a new earth, the home of righteousness. 2 Peter 3:11-13.

Baron's Master

aron was a great dog, except that he had some problems. He killed chickens. And he chased bicycles. And he mauled cats. And he bit people. Pretty soon he ended up at the pound.

At the end of the day Baron's master picked the dog up from the pound and brought him home. He fed him the best dog food, even after all Baron had done. Miserable dog though he was, he was home with the master because he was loved.

Have you ever felt like Baron? Paul did. He tried to be good, but he ended up doing bad things. No matter how hard he tried, eventually he messed up. It was frustrating. But he was never defeated, because he realized that no matter how badly he did, Jesus had paid the penalty for his sins. He wasn't going to stay in the pound forever. At the end of the day he was going home with the master.

■ ■ ■ ■

So you see how it is: my new life tells me to do right, but the old nature that is still inside me loves to sin. Oh, what a terrible predicament I'm in! Who will free me from my slavery to this deadly lower nature? Thank God! It has been done by Jesus Christ our Lord. He has set me free! Romans 7:23-25, TLB.

Bullies

iz hated me, but I never found out why. For some reason she singled me out for particular nastiness, tormenting me in any way she could imagine. And Liz had quite an imagination.

She was bigger and older than I was. I didn't fight back. I didn't invent any wisecracks when she picked on me. I did nothing. I just stared at her in paralyzed fear when she started up. If it got real bad, I stared at the floor.

Even after all these years I don't know what I should have done. I try to imagine what would have happened if I had said something, such as "You know, it hurts my feelings when you say that." Chances are that's what she was trying to do!

I did learn one thing, though. Because I didn't participate in her attacks, they stopped after a while. I was no fun to pick on, because I never reacted.

My horse, Cinder, used to freak out just to watch me leap around in panic. Once I got used to her, I stopped leaping, and she stopped freaking out. I wasn't fun to watch anymore. That's what bullies want—a show. When we don't give it to them, they'll stop. Solomon must have known that when he suggested being gentle with our answers.

A gentle answer turns away wrath, but a harsh word stirs up anger. Proverbs 15:1.

Mirror, Mirror

K; trick question: Why do you look in a mirror?

To see yourself, of course. (I told you it was a trick question.)

But did you realize that you also look at other people to see yourself too? When your best friend tells you that you look horrid in glasses, or your granny tells you that your voice is not as nice as your brother's, or your teacher tells you that your handwriting is atrocious, you take that message in and believe it about yourself. *You see yourself the way other people see you.*

The problem is that other people see you because of the way they see themselves, and the way *other people* saw them, and on and on. This is dangerous. The only true picture of yourself you will ever get is the one you see when you look at Jesus. His reflection of you is the *real* you, the *true* you. It's the only picture that matters. He sees all your flaws, but He also sees your perfection because He is in you making up for whatever you lack.

You + Jesus = your perfect reflection.

■ ■ ■ ■

Now we see but a poor reflection as in a mirror; then we shall see face to face. Now I know in part; then I shall know fully, even as I am fully known. 1 Corinthians 13:12.

Fall From Grace

They say it's a true story. It might be. It was supposedly found in an old family heirloom Bible. It's about the painting *The Last Supper,* by Leonardo da Vinci. Da Vinci used real people models for his paintings, and he saw hundreds of young men to find a face full of innocence and beauty to model Jesus. Finally he found the right young man and began the portrait.

Seven years went by as he found, one after the other, models for each of the disciples. Last to be painted was Judas, but Da Vinci could not find someone he thought looked bad enough to be Judas. Searching for the right face, he went to a dungeon in Rome, where he found the perfect man. A special order from the king allowed the man to be released long enough to be painted.

When Da Vinci finished and the man was being led away, he cried, "Da Vinci, look at me! Do you not know who I am? I am the man you painted seven years ago as Christ! O God, have I fallen so low?"

No matter how far we fall, Jesus can bring us back up again. That's why He came and died for our sins.

■ ■ ■ ■

For the Son of Man came to seek
and to save what was lost. Luke 19:10.

Walk Softly

our ego is the part of you that wants to be noticed. It's the part that does something nice for someone or aces a test and then screams, "Hey, look what I did! Did you see that? I'm awesome! Let me tell you all about it."

There's nothing wrong with ego, particularly. Everyone wants to be appreciated and noticed for the things that they do. Or do they?

Can you find one instance in the Bible where Jesus pointed the finger at Himself and said, "Did you see that? Did you see what I did? Am I great or what?" No, Jesus went about quietly doing good, trying *not* to attract attention.

We don't mind doing good (as long as someone notices it), but try doing good and not getting caught at it. Man, you could just burst to tell *someone,* couldn't you? Just one person. Let me impress just one person. But that's not how Jesus did things.

Try this: Every day this week, do one good thing. But don't get caught at it. And don't tell anyone. See if it's easy or hard. Let Jesus feed your ego. He's the only one who can keep it well fed and satisfied.

Do nothing out of selfish ambition or vain conceit, but in humility consider others better than yourselves. Philippians 2:3.

When the Going Gets Tough

eisha hated playing the violin. She wasn't any good at it. So late one night she crept outside and buried her violin in a hole. The next day her violin teacher wanted her to play the new piece they were working on so he could see her progress.

Leisha said, "Sir, I knew you were a cruel master and wanted more than I could give, so I buried my violin in the ground. I refuse to play."

The violin teacher's mouth dropped open. "Wicked student!" he said. "The least you could have done was practice your scales. At least then you'd have something to play. But now we're going to have to sit here for an hour twiddling our thumbs until your mother comes to pick you up."

When the going gets tough, giving up can seem like the easiest thing. But God gave each of us unique gifts, and He wants us to use them. Even the slightest improvement, the tiniest good deed, is better than doing nothing at all.

■ ■ ■ ■

Then the man who had received the one talent came.
"Master," he said, "I knew that you are a hard man,
harvesting where you have not sown and gathering
where you have not scattered seed. So I was afraid and
went out and hid your talent in the ground." Matthew 25:24, 25.

Great Value

Jeff rode up to the front of the school on his new Fuji bicycle. He stopped with a flourish, his tires spitting a cloud of dirt at the kids standing nearby. He put his bike in the rack and walked past a group of boys known to be thieves and troublemakers. Six hours later he came out to find his bike gone. "Aw, man, why did this happen?" he wailed.

How many times have you put something even more precious than a bike in front of the wrong people and had it trampled all over? Some people think that being a Christian means you have to be a doormat, not caring about your own feelings or rights. That's not true.

If someone makes you uncomfortable or hurts you, you don't have to take it. Tell an adult. Get someone to help you. It's your right. You are valuable to Jesus. He wants you to take care of yourself the way He would.

■ ■ ■ ■

Do not give dogs what is sacred; do not throw your pearls to pigs. If you do, they may trample them under their feet, and then turn and tear you to pieces. Matthew 7:6.

No Fear

y dog Indy and I went hiking on Vermont's biggest mountain. Alone. It was just me, Indy, and . . . the bears! Let me tell you, I was pretty scared. I went hiking by myself to conquer my fear of being alone and ended up with a new fear of bears. I don't like to think of myself as a fraidy cat, but there are a few things I'm scared of: airplanes (actually, crashing), anything with more than four legs (such as spiders), and stuff like that.

Some fear is good for you. For instance, I will never again go into the woods without protection. (A snoring dog does not count.) That's a good thing. It might save my life. Being scared of crashing in an airplane, on the other hand, is pointless. God knows when I'm going to die. There's no sense in my worrying about it. And my fear of flying could keep me from some great experiences.

Bill Cosby once advised, "Decide that you want it more than you are afraid of it."

I think that's good advice. Realize that God is protecting you no matter what. Use fear to help you stay safe or else let it go.

The Lord is my light and my salvation—
whom shall I fear? The Lord is the stronghold
of my life—of whom shall I be afraid? Psalm 27:1.

17 JULY

But I'm So Humble Already

It never fails. Whenever I'm feeling full of myself, such as when I have a new outfit or my hair looks great or I say something I think is particularly brilliant, *something happens.* I spill ketchup on my skirt, it rains and my hair loses all sense of style, or I end up putting my foot in my mouth. All of Murphy's laws are about this sort of thing. His basic law was that if something could go wrong, it would and at the worst possible moment.

Some people call it tempting fate or jinxing yourself. But that's not it at all. Proverbs 16:18 warns us that "pride goes before destruction, a haughty spirit before a fall."

We should never depend on ourselves. Even when we think we're strong or great or intelligent, we're not nearly as strong, great, or intelligent as we could be if we let God call all the shots.

Humbling ourselves doesn't mean letting other people walk all over us. It means we let God lead us. When we take ourselves out of the center of our universe and put God there instead, we can treat other people the way God would treat them—with dignity and understanding.

■ ■ ■ ■

For everyone who exalts himself will be humbled, and he who humbles himself will be exalted. Luke 18:14.

Attitude of Gratitude

ave you ever felt that things could not possibly be worse? They can be a lot worse. Want to know how? Try this: hold your breath. . . . Go ahead. I'll wait. Hold it until you can't hold it anymore.

There now, aren't you glad you can take a breath?

Breathing is important, because if you are breathing, it means you are still alive. Be thankful for your breath. It means that no matter how badly you've messed up, you can try again. It means that you can start over. It means that all is not lost.

I read a story about a man who had cancer. He had chemotherapy to get rid of it, and when he was tested at the end of his treatment, they found the cancer was not only still there, but even worse than before. It was his death sentence.

Then they discovered that they had made a mistake. They had read the wrong results! He was actually cured. He would live. Everything in life was wonderful to him.

Be grateful for the gifts God has given you today. Praise Him in your prayers and in your conversations with friends. And live today like there is no tomorrow.

Let the word of Christ dwell in you richly as you teach and admonish one another with all wisdom, and as you sing psalms, hymns and spiritual songs with gratitude in your hearts to God. Colossians 3:16.

Forgive Them?

I have to admit that I have trouble with today's verse. I read it and think that God has to be kidding. I mean, love my enemies? I don't feel like doing that. I feel like plotting a very complicated, painful revenge. That's how I feel.

But read the verse again. Nowhere does it say to love my enemies only when I feel like it. This isn't a request or even a suggestion. It's a command. Such as when I tell my son to put away the dishes. He may not *feel* like it. He may really hate the idea of putting the dishes away, but he obeys *regardless of how he feels.*

The command Jesus gave us doesn't hinge on our feelings. We can feel downright hostile toward our enemies, but we are still commanded to pray for them and do good to them.

There are two reasons it's good to love our enemies. First, praying for them might help them realize how they're hurting us. And second, praying for them makes us vulnerable to God. You might start praying for someone you don't like. But in the end you will realize that you care about that person, because your prayer will have changed *you.*

But I tell you who hear me: Love your enemies,
do good to those who hate you, bless those who
curse you, pray for those who mistreat you. Luke 6:27, 28.

Be All You Can Be

y friend Robin was a great inspiration to me. She was shy, studious, and very talented, and she didn't care what other people thought of her. She wanted to be in our school plays, so she joined the drama club. Her bravery inspired me to join too.

Neither one of us ever took the lead in anything besides our own daydreams, but we stretched and tried something new. We had fun and learned new things (how to project our voices without spitting on our fellow actors, how to change clothes very fast, and important stuff like that).

The thing is, there are new experiences everywhere for you to try. But they aren't going to just happen to you. You have to make an effort to find them. Sure, there will be obstacles. But don't see them as stumbling blocks. See them as stepping-stones, helping you to reach higher than you can reach without them.

Believe that you have the potential to be everything God wants you to be, and then take that confidence with you into all you do. You have a world inside you waiting to happen. Go and build it with one incredible experience after another.

■ ■ ■ ■

Be very careful, then, how you live—not as unwise but as wise, making the most of every opportunity, because the days are evil. Ephesians 5:15, 16.

Wait-a-Bit Bush

I magine you're walking down a road in Jamaica. You see a shrub growing by the side of the road. You think, *H'mm, what an interesting shrub. I think I'll check it out.* So you go closer to examine it.

But when you try to pull away, yikes, it's caught you! Tiny thorns with little barbs have snagged your clothes and skin. The harder you struggle to get away, the more hopelessly you are caught. Finally you give up and wait for someone else to come and help you. What you've run into is what the islanders call the "wait-a-bit" bush.

There are a lot of "wait-a-bit" bushes in life. Satan uses them to attract our attention and then hook us. Sometimes the "wait-a-bit" bushes are easy to spot, like alcohol, smoking, or premarital sex. Other times you don't really notice them until you're already caught.

But you don't have to be fooled by one of Satan's "wait-a-bit" bushes. You have a Master Guide who will walk with you and point them all out. In the journey of life you don't ever have to "wait a bit."

■ ■ ■ ■

All a man's ways seem right to him, but the Lord weighs the heart. To do what is right and just is more acceptable to the Lord than sacrifice. Proverbs 21:2, 3.

Service With a Smile

heri Peters has led a remarkable life. I met her at the Discover the Power Pathfinder Camporee in Oshkosh, Wisconsin (was that awesome or what?).

Talking to Cheri, I would never have guessed that she ended up on the streets at the age of 12. Heroin addicts taught her how to take care of herself. When she went home 10 years later, she found out that nobody had missed her!

Cheri decided to kill herself. It wasn't her first suicide attempt, but it was her last. She moved in with a friend's sister, who told her about Jesus. Cheri felt the presence of God and decided to become a Christian.

Cheri believes that serving others is the way to find God. She should know. She works constantly with teens, helping them to escape the kind of life she once had. "The only way to find God," says Cheri, "is through service. Any other way is like trying to take swimming classes through a correspondence course."

■ ■ ■ ■

It is absolutely clear that God has called you to a free life.
Just make sure that you don't use this freedom as an excuse
to do whatever you want and destroy your freedom. Rather,
use your freedom to serve one another in love; that's
how freedom grows. Galatians 5:13, Message.

Dis-Appointment

hen God created Adam and Eve, He had great things in mind for them. They would have an eternity to experience all the good stuff. Of course, we know the rest of the story.

Adam and Eve ended up on the wrong side of the garden, and until they died they lived in dis-appointment. They missed the appointment they had with God. He created a beautiful, perfect life for them, but they missed the boat. They took the wrong train. They got off on the wrong foot.

Centuries later we're still living *in* dis-appointment and *with* dis-appointment. Why? Because we are missing the life God has appointed for us. In that life He is the center of our universe, the axle on which our whole life turns.

If life were a skateboard ramp and we were skateboarders, God would be our center of gravity. Instead He's stuck cheering us on while we try to do McTwists on our own and skin our knees. He *wants* us to succeed, but He knows that as long as we insist on running the show we'll keep falling. Life here will never be perfect, but with the right Center we can do perfect Ollies every time.

■ ■ ■ ■

For all have sinned and fall short of the glory of God, and are justified freely by his grace through the redemption that came by Christ Jesus. Romans 3:23, 24.

The Third Wheel

odie was my friend. When my family moved away, I missed her a lot. Sometimes I called her or wrote her letters, but it wasn't the same as being together. And then the most wonderful thing happened. My parents said I could invite Jodie over for Christmas weekend.

It was great seeing her again. I decided to take her caroling and invited Macy along, a friend I'd met in my new town. Before our noses even had time to freeze, Jodie and Macy were the best of friends. Suddenly I was the one out in the cold.

It was hard losing my friends. Neither one of them really cared about me after they found each other. Eventually I moved on and made some other friends, but I was afraid that the same thing would happen again.

The only friend you can really trust with all of yourself is Jesus. He is the only one who will never desert you, never betray you, never choose someone else over you. No friend in the world can take His place, and you shouldn't depend on any other friend to love you as much as He does.

A man of many companions may come to ruin, but there is a friend who sticks closer than a brother. Proverbs 18:24.

Just a Little Bit

ave you ever seen a mustard seed? When I was little I had a glass locket with a real mustard seed in it. At the time I thought it was one of the only mustard seeds on the planet, sort of like a relic or something. It wasn't, but my thinking so added to its mystery. I would stare at it and think about what Jesus said about faith. Surely the apostles weren't trying hard if they didn't have even that much faith.

It would be nice if you could check your faith to see how much you have before you need it. But you can't. Faith is kind of like a muscle. It has to be exercised constantly so that it's strong when you do need to use it. If you don't use a muscle, it gets smaller. So does faith.

There are lots of ways we can exercise our faith. Believing in Jesus takes faith. Trusting that He is going to help us through any problem we have takes faith. Relying on Jesus every day will keep your faith strong enough to move mountains and mulberry bushes.

■ ■ ■ ■

The apostles said to the Lord, "Increase our faith!" He replied,
"If you have faith as small as a mustard seed, you can
say to this mulberry tree, 'Be uprooted and planted
in the sea,' and it will obey you." Luke 17:5, 6.

JULY **26**

He's Been There

olchester, Vermont, doesn't mean anything to most people. It's just a little town in a little state. But if the news were suddenly flooded with reports that a bomb had been dropped on it, I would be heartbroken. Why? Because I grew up there.

Colchester was my home for 10 years. I rode my bike with my friends up and down the streets. I remember the ice-cream stand, the little green store around the corner where we bought candy, and the school I attended.

Most people hearing about the bomb would shake their heads, but it wouldn't mean anything to them. The difference is that I've been there. They haven't. And when you've been there, it makes all the difference.

There is no part of life or living that God has not experienced. No matter what we go through He can say, "I have been there. I know what it's like." The best Person to talk to is someone who has been there, done that. Jesus was here. He walked the walk and talked the talk. Jesus was here. He understands, better than anyone else can, exactly what you're going through.

■ ■ ■ ■

For you, Bethlehem Ephrathah, though you are small among the clans of Judah, out of you will come for me one who will be ruler over Israel. Micah 5:2.

Now Serving

Jones was a servant. A butler, to be precise. He shined shoes, made sure the sheets were aired, served refreshments, and generally made himself as useful as possible. If you needed a letter mailed immediately, Jones was the person to send to the post office. If you wanted to go out to eat, Jones made the reservations.

So? Big deal, right? What's so great about that?

Well, what if I told you that Jones was also a king? That's right. Charles James Douglas Richard Jones, otherwise known as King Charles. A king serving like a butler would make a big difference, wouldn't it?

King Charles, the butler, lives only in my imagination. But when King Jesus lived here on earth, He served the people every day as though He were a butler. He didn't do it because He had to or in order to get a paycheck. He did it because He wanted to.

If King Charles were real, do you suppose he'd choose to be a butler over being a king? Jesus did. Would you?

■ ■ ■ ■

Your attitude should be the same as that of Christ Jesus: Who, being in very nature God, did not consider equality with God something to be grasped, but made himself nothing, taking the very nature of a servant, being made in human likeness. Philippians 2:5-7.

The Good Word

op quiz: Quick. Tell me where your Bible is right now.

Give yourself 10 points if you knew immediately where it was. Give yourself five points if you went looking for it and found it in the bottom of your backpack. Give yourself a stern talking-to if you had no idea where it was and when found it was covered with dust.

The Bible is God's Word and contains guidelines to live by. There is only one way for Bible verses to be fixed on our hearts and minds. We have to read them. They won't seep into your head if you put your Bible under your pillow at night. They won't march off the pages and plaster themselves to your forehead. You have to read them.

Not only that, but memorizing Scripture is a great way to "fix" it in your head. Scripture is a powerful weapon against Satan. Remember when Satan confronted Jesus in the wilderness? Jesus used Scripture to send him packing. You can too.

Make it your goal to memorize one of the verses in the devotional each week for the rest of the year.

Fix these words of mine in your
hearts and minds. Deuteronomy 11:18.

Combat Optional

always thought that if I was nice to people, everyone would like me and I would avoid conflict. Of course, the older I became, the less this seemed to be the case. Conflict happens to everyone. It doesn't really matter how nice you are. Even if you were nice every minute of your life from the second you were born (like *that's* possible), someone somewhere isn't going to like you. Not only that, they are going to be downright mean to you.

Even though we can't avoid conflict, we *can* avoid combat. God gave us creative minds to work things out. The most important words you can say to avoid combat are "I'm sorry." These words stop a lot of fights before they start.

If a problem still exists, talk it out. Don't blame. Don't say things like "You always . . ." or "You never . . ." Stick with the facts. And don't go back in history to bring up a list of wrongs that are over and done with. With love you can turn an enemy into a friend.

■ ■ ■ ■

But love your enemies, do good to them, and lend to them without expecting anything back. Then your reward will be great, and you will be sons of the Most High, because he is kind to the ungrateful and wicked. Luke 6:35.

The Hot Seat

I'm sure you never liked to be spanked when you were a little kid. And you probably aren't too fond of the discipline your parents dream up for you now: grounding, loss of privileges, or fines. Maybe you're tempted to think, *They hate me!*

But you know what? Your parents don't hate you. If they hated you, they would let you grow up to be a hoodlum, and then they wouldn't visit you in jail, where you would likely spend the rest of your life.

We hate discipline, but it's for our good. I'll let you in on a little secret. It's no picnic for the person who has to discipline either. It's hard to enforce a punishment on someone you love. But when you know that it will help them grow up to be a better person, you do it because you love them.

God's discipline helps us to grow as mature Christians. Is it painful? Oh, yeah! Is it difficult? Oh, yeah! Does He do it because He loves us? Oh, yeah! Just like your earthly parents, God wants what is best for you.

Our fathers disciplined us for a little while as they thought best; but God disciplines us for our good, that we may share in his holiness. Hebrews 12:10.

Eyes of Love

aria, honey, what's wrong?"

Maria looked up quickly as her mom walked into the kitchen, her arms full of grocery bags. Maria tried to wipe the tears off her face, but it was too late. Mom set the bags down on the counter and put her arm around Maria. "Is there anything I can do?"

"Oh, Mom," wailed Maria, "I feel so bad about cheating on my tests at school. I asked God to forgive me, but how do I know that He did? If He forgave me, wouldn't I feel better about this?"

"No, you shouldn't rely on your feelings," Mom told her. "Satan will try to make you feel guilty even though you've been forgiven. When he tries to do that, repeat a Bible verse about God's love and absolute forgiveness. Satan will also try to tempt you in other areas, hoping to make you fall. That's why you should ask God every day to keep you strong."

Maria smiled weakly. "I will, Mom. Thanks."

This is the confidence we have in approaching God: that if we ask anything according to his will, he hears us. And if we know that he hears us—whatever we ask—we know that we have what we asked of him. 1 John 5:14, 15.

Payback Time

evenge is hot. Many action films and video games center on revenge. Somebody does somebody wrong, and that person's going to pay up! You can probably think of several instances when someone hurt you. Maybe you even imagined how you would pay them back. Most of us have done that.

However, God doesn't want us to pay people back when they wrong us. He wants to be our superhero. He wants to swoop down and rescue us. He doesn't always do it the way we want Him to, so we take it into our own hands and mess things up. Only when God is leading will all things end up right.

If someone stole your lunch because he hadn't eaten in a week, would you be mad? See, we don't know everything that's going on. We don't know why people do the things they do. If we looked only at the stolen lunch and not the starving person, we would get a completely different picture. (Not, of course, that stealing is OK.) Fortunately, God sees every picture. That's why we should leave revenge to the expert Judge. He doesn't make mistakes.

■ ■ ■ ■

Do not say, "I'll pay you back for this wrong!"
Wait for the Lord, and he will deliver you. Proverbs 20:22.

The Borrowers

I have a deep, dark confession to make. I have shelves and shelves of books, books, and more books, and I don't like to lend them to people. *Gasp!* The reason is that I have lent books out and found them squashed between the sofa cushions at my friend-who-shall-remain-nameless's house. Worse, some books have walked away and left me for good, never to return.

Maybe it has something to do with the fact that I'm a writer, but books are like friends. We should treat them with respect. We shouldn't crack their bindings, rip their pages, leave them on the floor, or abuse them in any way. So here's my dilemma. Do I lend books? Or do I keep them for myself?

The answer might surprise you. I lend them. After all, our possessions belong to whom? (God.) Would God lend me a book? (Yes.) Would He expect me to take care of it? (Also yes.) Respect for others and for their possessions is very important. Their property ultimately belongs to God, just as yours does. If God lent you something, how would you take care of it?

■ ■ ■ ■

The wicked borrow and do not repay,
but the righteous give generously. Psalm 37:21.

The Light in the Woods

It was dark, and the loons were calling across the lake. The forest around me felt close and confining just beyond the rim of the flickering light cast by the campfire. Someone suggested flashlight tag. Immediately players grabbed flashlights and scurried for the woods. I'd never played before, but I decided there was a time for everything and now was the time to play flashlight tag.

I stumbled into the woods and crouched behind a log. Tree branches poked me with their bony fingers. I looked for the ideal time to make my move to safety. How could I get from my log, through the downed limbs and gullies of the forest floor, to the "safe" tree? There was only one way. I had to turn on my light. If I didn't, I'd be stuck in the forest, surrounded by obstacles I couldn't see.

Jesus called Himself the light of the world. Only by following Him can we make it through life, with all its hidden obstacles and pits. If we don't let Him shine in front of us, there's no way we'll make it out of the woods.

■ ■ ■ ■

When Jesus spoke again to the people, he said, "I am the light of the world. Whoever follows me will never walk in darkness, but will have the light of life." John 8:12.

I've Got That Joy, Joy, Joy, Joy

ave you ever read the text for today and wondered what the joy was that was set before Jesus? I mean, there couldn't be any joy in the Crucifixion, could there? Not only did Jesus face the physical pain of Calvary and the pain of having our sins heaped on Him, He faced the worst pain of all: separation from His Father. They had never been separated before. So that couldn't have been the joy before Him.

No; His joy was having us in heaven with Him for eternity. Imagine! Jesus endured Calvary and separation from His Father so that you could be in heaven with Him for eternity. And He didn't think of it as some kind of chore or distasteful duty to get through. He considered it a joy!

Think of that today when you face something you don't really feel like doing. Remember Jesus and all He did for you and consider whatever task you have to perform as if you were doing it for Jesus. It will become a pure joy!

Let us fix our eyes on Jesus, the author and perfecter of our faith,
who for the joy set before him endured the cross, scorning its
shame, and sat down at the right hand of the throne of God.
Consider him who endured such opposition from sinful men,
so that you will not grow weary and lose heart. Hebrews 12:2, 3.

Don't Sweat the Small Stuff

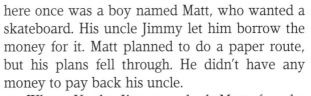

Theme once was a boy named Matt, who wanted a skateboard. His uncle Jimmy let him borrow the money for it. Matt planned to do a paper route, but his plans fell through. He didn't have any money to pay back his uncle.

When Uncle Jimmy asked Matt for the money, Matt pulled his pockets inside out and said, "I'm sorry, Uncle Jimmy. I don't have the money. But I will get it." Uncle Jimmy told him to forget about it.

Matt, however, hunted his friend Brian down, grabbed him by the throat, and shook him. "Give me back the lunch money you owe me!" he demanded.

Matt seems—what is the word?—ungrateful? Uncle Jimmy gave him a wad of cash for his skateboard and Matt's bent out of shape over a couple bucks. What gives?

We could ask ourselves the same question. It's hard for us to forgive people who hurt us. But all we have to remember is the great amount that God forgave us. He's forgiven us everything we've done to deserve death. Surely we can forgive the small stuff others do to us. And trust me, compared to what we've been forgiven, it's *all* small stuff.

■ ■ ■ ■

Forgive, and you will be forgiven. Luke 6:37.

Up, Up, and Away

he other day my little friend Camille handed me a toy airplane from United Airlines. I usually fly United, and I thought they did a pretty good job of making it look realistic. I noticed a button on top and pushed it. Immediately the scream of a plane engine began, revving up as though the plane were hurtling down the runway. I broke out into a sweat.

You see, I have this thing about planes. I don't like them. It's not the planes themselves, although I'm probably about as crazy for airline food as you are for cafeteria food. (I think they get it from the same place.) No, my problem with planes has more to do with the thought of them crashing.

You might be afraid of growing up, dating, getting a job, going to college, getting married, and having children. There is a time for everything in life, and it will happen whether we are afraid or not. Worrying about it won't help. But as Christians we don't have to worry. God is in control of our whole life. We can confidently leave the future in His hands and enjoy the present.

There is a time for everything, and a season for every activity under heaven: a time to be born and a time to die. Ecclesiastes 3:1, 2.

Oops

ave you ever done something wrong without knowing it? You didn't feel bad about it then. After all, you didn't *know*. This happened just before Christmas with my son, Josh. He was teasing his friend Taylor about the frogs in her fish tank. She thought he was serious, and she got upset.

Josh didn't know that he had hurt her feelings until later. *Then* he apologized. He couldn't have apologized *before* he knew that he had hurt her feelings. So he apologized *after*, even though it was weeks later when he found out.

In the Bible the Israelites had a special offering for when they committed a sin without knowing it, which tells us that unintentional sins are just as wrong as intentional ones. God forgives all of our sins, but we need to acknowledge and correct our unintentional sins as soon as we discover them. We shouldn't feel that just because they are in the past, they aren't important.

Joshua could have said, "Well, I didn't know I hurt Taylor's feelings. It's too late now." If he had done that, he and Taylor might not be friends now. But they are. Because he was willing to correct his mistake, he saved a friendship.

■ ■ ■ ■

But if just one person sins unintentionally, he must bring a year-old female goat for a sin offering. Numbers 15:27.

The Great Adventure

inger Steven Curtis Chapman describes life as "the great adventure." He pictures Christians saddling up their horses and galloping into the world to take it by storm, shaking the strongholds of Satan, and spreading the good news that Jesus has come and is soon returning. The way he sings about it, I can smell the saddle leather and feel the horse straining beneath me as we tear across the terrain.

Is your life a great adventure? Do you wake up in the morning excited about what God might do in your life and through you during the day? You're one of His riders! Jump out of bed, grab the saddle, scream "Yee-haw!" at the top of your lungs, and ask Him what adventure you're going to tackle today. Roping demons, saving souls, avoiding stampedes—it's all in a day's work for God's riders.

So ask God for an adventure with Him. Saddle up, follow Him, grab the horn (that's the little handley thingy sticking up in the front of your saddle), and hang on because you're in for the ride of your life!

■ ■ ■ ■

I press on toward the goal to win the prize for which God has called me heavenward in Christ Jesus. Philippians 3:14.

Mystery Words

y horse could fly like the wind and buck like a seasoned bronco when she felt like it. I rode her a lot, but I did *not* want to fall off. No way! I was determined not to fall, even if I ended up hanging from her neck. And I did *not* fall off that horse. Ever.

There are two words in the English language that cling to the back of our throats. They seem determined not to escape our lips, not to fall out, just as I was determined not to fall off the horse. The two words are so hard to choke out that some people hardly ever say them. Can you guess what they are?

"I'm sorry." They're two short little words, but it takes a brave person to say them. When we say "I'm sorry," we admit to making a mistake, and no one likes to do that. But you know what? No one is perfect except God, and the closest we can come to perfection is admitting we have none. Admitting that helps to push "I'm sorry" out of our mouths when we need it.

■ ■ ■ ■

Therefore, if you are offering your gift at the altar and there remember that your brother has something against you, leave your gift there in front of the altar. First go and be reconciled to your brother; then come and offer your gift. Matthew 5:23, 24.

Lying for Dummies

his class is called Lying for Dummies. Nothing gets you out of a jam faster than an old-fashioned lie. It gets you right out of one jam and into another bigger one, and then another one after that. Soon you wish you had told the truth the first time around.

Lies are hard to keep up with. They grow like crazy snowballs, getting bigger the longer they live, the farther they roll, and the more people they crush.

For example, let's look at a history case. Here we have an angel with one of the highest positions in heaven. Is he happy? No, he wants more out of life. Go figure. So what does he do? Lies. And he goes from Paradise to hell in no time. Now tell me, does that sound like an intelligent thing to do? I don't think so.

The angel (you know him better as Satan) isn't any happier about life now than when he was in heaven (surprise, surprise). It just keeps getting worse and worse. But he won't tell you that. Because he's good only at lying, which is, as we learned, for dummies.

When he lies, he speaks his native language,
for he is a liar and the father of lies. John 8:44.

Whatever the Cost

he way I see it, Isaac had two choices when he saw his father preparing to (gulp!) sacrifice him on the altar. He could let his father do it, or he could run for it. Young and strong, he could easily outdistance his old father. Die or run for his life?

Isaac decided to do what God had in mind for him. Even though it wasn't what he had in mind for himself. Even though it seriously messed up his plans for the rest of his life. Even though it was likely to be very painful. No matter what the cost.

Can you say that about your life? Are you willing to follow God's plan for you no matter what it is or what it costs you? Are you willing to lay down your life for God and to trust Him to take care of you the way He cared for Isaac?

As far as Isaac was concerned he was a dead man. But did he die? Not then. He lived to be an old man. He trusted God regardless of the cost. Do you?

■ ■ ■ ■

When they reached the place God had told him about, Abraham built an altar there and arranged the wood on it. He bound his son Isaac and laid him on the altar, on top of the wood. Genesis 22:9.

Simply Salvation

hen we mess up, we often bargain with God. "I promise, I'll never do that again." Or "Next time I'll try harder." What we're really saying is "I can be a better person. Let me show You."

But that's not the point. Yes, the guilt we feel should prompt us into a deeper relationship with God and a new determination to follow Him, but it can't buy us deeper forgiveness. It can't make up for what we did. It can't add to our salvation. God's forgiveness is complete. Jesus' salvation is perfect.

It's important to take the time to experience forgiveness for our sins and to realize our total need for salvation. Kneel down, and confess your sin. Then thank God for forgiving you.

Experience the forgiveness, and be thankful for Christ's salvation. Let the Holy Spirit convict you of your need for a Saviour. Realize how much you need to depend on Jesus, and listen to what He says. Then go and sin no more.

You will go on before the Lord to prepare the way
for him, to give his people the knowledge of salvation
through the forgiveness of their sins. Luke 1:76, 77.

Friends

Pretend that you are going to place two ads in the newspaper. The first ad reads "Wanted: A Friend." The second ad reads "For Sale: A Friend."

List on one side of a piece of paper all the things you would want in a friend if you could advertise for one. On the opposite side of the paper, list all the things you could offer as a friend. Then compare both sides of the paper. Are you asking for more than you are offering? Are you offering more than you are asking for from a friend?

To be lasting, a friendship should be balanced. I don't mean that you should be just like your friend. Life would be pretty boring if the only people we were friends with were just like us. But friendships should be give and take.

Sometimes we find good, lasting friendships. Other times we might become hurt. But the risk is worth it when we find the treasure of a true friend. Think about how you can be a true friend to someone. And remember, Jesus wants to be your best friend. He is a "friend who sticks closer than a brother" (Proverbs 18:24).

A friend loves at all times. Proverbs 17:17.

Love: The Real Deal

ave you ever felt as though you were too bad for Jesus to love? I sometimes feel that way.

I was sitting on the edge of my bed one night, thinking about that, when I felt a strong sense of peace come over me. It was as though Jesus had wrapped His arms around me and said, "I love you. I *love* you."

There is no question about it. He loves me before I mess up, He loves me when I mess up, He loves me after I mess up, and He'll love me even if I mess up again. That doesn't mean He loves my messing up. But He loves *me,* and that doesn't ever change.

Satan wants us to think that Jesus can't stand us when we do something wrong, but that's not true. The kind of love Jesus has for us is the real deal. It never changes. It never gets smaller. It never goes away. If we could realize how much God loves us, it would fill us with a desire to love Him back and a desire *not* to hurt Him by sinning.

■ ■ ■ ■

But from everlasting to everlasting the Lord's love is with those who fear him, and his righteousness with their children's children—with those who keep his covenant and remember to obey his precepts. Psalm 103:17, 18.

Practice, Practice, and More Practice

hen my friend Kirsten plays the piano her fingers fly over the keys. She makes it look so easy! I used to be able to play just the way she does but not anymore. I haven't played the piano seriously for years. Now my fingers sound more like sick elephants staggering on top of the keyboard.

So I practice. And practice. And practice some more. I enjoy practicing most of the time. I know that while I practice I am building strong playing skills that will help me to shine when I perform. That's when all the practicing will pay off.

Having a relationship with Jesus is sometimes like learning to play the piano (or anything else we don't know how to do). We have to put in "practice" time—read the Bible, pray, and have devotions. But when we "practice," it isn't hard to live a Christian life. We will make it look easy.

Other people will look at us and say, "Wow, where can I learn to live like that?"

And you can say, "Practice, practice, and more practice."

■ ■ ■ ■

Everyone who competes in the games goes into strict training. They do it to get a crown that will not last; but we do it to get a crown that will last forever. 1 Corinthians 9:25.

The Third Strand

They say there is strength in numbers. Or is it safety? They definitely say the more the merrier. That's because it's awfully hard to hang out with a bunch of people and be droopy for very long. Pretty soon someone will make you laugh, and then someone else will tell you an interesting story, and before you know it you'll be feeling better, even if you started off feeling pretty rotten.

Friends are wonderful people. They can help us back up when we feel down. They can pray with us when we are having a hard time. They can bring us down a peg when we're feeling too full of our own importance. The list is practically endless.

Make a list of all your friends. Then put a star next to your very, very close friends, the ones you would call if you had a really bad day.

Jesus chose 12 friends to be with Him all the time. They were the people closest to Him. He relied on them for support. And He knew that when He left, they would be able to lean on each other when things got discouraging. Why? Because that's what friends are for. Which is another thing they say.

Though one may be overpowered, two can defend themselves. A cord of three strands is not quickly broken. Ecclesiastes 4:12.

Falling Forward

I've been cross-country skiing since I was 3 years old. I used to ski in Stowe at the Trapp Family Lodge owned by Maria von Trapp of *Sound of Music* fame. Once when I was a little girl I met Maria on the trail, and she stopped to talk to me for a few minutes. I didn't find out until later who she was. (Hey, I was young. I expected her to look like Julie Andrews.)

Because I have skied for so long I'm pretty good at it, which means I don't fall much. My husband, on the other hand, is a frequent faller. He tries to tell me he's looking for something in the snow, but I don't swallow it. Most people would rather not fall if they can help it. They'll do whatever they have to do in order to avoid it, whether it's falling on skis, skates, or falling by failing in a test. Falling is failure.

But we can use failure to our advantage. By falling forward, learning from our fall, and using what we learned to move us forward, falling isn't a failure at all. It's a learning experience.

■ ■ ■ ■

Examine yourselves to see whether you are in the faith; test yourselves. Do you not realize that Christ Jesus is in you—unless, of course, you fail the test? 2 Corinthians 13:5.

Running and Leaping!

Imagine that every day on your way to school you pass a man who can't walk. He sits with a sign around his neck that says "Can you spare any change? I'm hungry." Every day you give him some of your lunch money. But one day you forget your lunch money, so you decide to pray for him instead. When you stop praying, he *gets up and walks.*

Or imagine that there's a blind girl in your class named Ellen. You decide to pray for her too. Instantly she can see! Everyone is so thankful that they sing and shout and dance.

Why do you suppose it is that we don't ever feel that thankful, as a general rule? Walking and seeing are things that will be gone only temporarily, while we are on earth. But Jesus healed us from something much worse than lameness or blindness. He healed us from *sin.* Are you grateful for that? Are you as grateful as if He solved one of your daily problems for you?

Praise God today for healing you not just from the things that keep you from enjoying life on earth, but from the sin that keeps you from enjoying eternity.

■ ■ ■ ■

The people were amazed when they saw the mute speaking, the crippled made well, the lame walking and the blind seeing. And they praised the God of Israel. Matthew 15:31.

Thank-you Note

t my house a lot of conversations go like this:

Josh: "Hand me the book."

Me: "Hand me the book what?"

Josh, after thinking for a minute: "Hand me the book, *please.*"

Or like this:

Me: "Rachel, here are your crackers."

Rachel: (Nothing.)

Me: "You're welcome."

Rachel: "Oh . . . *thank you.*"

I want my kids to be polite when they grow up, and the best way for them to learn to be polite is if *I'm* polite and if my husband is polite. We try to be. Sometimes it's natural, and sometimes we just plain forget.

When Jesus healed 10 lepers, apparently nine of them forgot to say thank you! When we complain about our life instead of praising God for giving us everything we have, we are like the ungrateful lepers. Instead we should praise and thank God for each new day He gives us.

Jesus asked, "Were not all ten cleansed? Where are the other nine? Was no one found to return and give praise to God except this foreigner?" Luke 17:17, 18.

Lost and Found

Simon Peter lost something that was very important to him—his faith. He thought he knew right where he had put it. He thought he could pull it out whenever he wanted and even show it off if he felt like it.

But when he really needed faith, Simon Peter reached inside himself to pull it out, and it was missing. At least, it seemed to be missing, and that's when he went AWOL (absent without leave). He cursed Jesus and denied ever knowing Him.

But Simon Peter went on to write Bible books, lead the disciples, and live a spectacular life of faith. In other words, he found his faith again, and it was even stronger than before he had lost it. His faith stayed strong because he didn't let go of it. Even when he couldn't be sure he had it anymore, he didn't let go. Jesus rewarded him by giving him even more faith.

Be sure to hang on to your faith. And trust God no matter what happens.

"Simon, Simon, Satan has asked to sift you as wheat. But I have prayed for you, Simon, that your faith may not fail. And when you have turned back, strengthen your brothers." Luke 22:31, 32.

Bloom, Baby, Bloom

I n August when you read this, the gladiolas will be blooming up a storm. But right now, as I write, there is snow outside the window, and gladiolas are a whole summer away. The first flowers won't even think about coming up above the soil for another two months.

That's a long time to wait for flowers, so I bought some at the store to cheer me up. They remind me that there is more to life than snow, ice, and mud. They remind me that winter won't last forever. They make me think of spring and hope and new life. And do you know what? They do all that even though they're *dead.*

Cut flowers are dead flowers. But even in death they can remind me of life. And that's kind of like our job here on earth. In a world of death and sorrow we are to remind others that there is more to life than dying. There is life in heaven. There is a "to be continued" after this world is over.

■ ■ ■ ■

Therefore, as we have opportunity, let us do good to all people, especially to those who belong to the family of believers. Galatians 6:10.

Make Up Your Mind

Peter seemed to have trouble making up his mind. One minute he was swearing eternal devotion to Jesus, and the next he was cursing His name and claiming he never knew Him. How could he be so wishy-washy?

Sometimes pressures and fear can get in our way and affect our thinking. We do or say things that make others wonder just how much *we* really love Jesus. We might wonder ourselves if we really love Jesus. If we do, how could we hurt Him?

Peter wasn't the only one of God's followers who deserted Him in a moment of weakness. Jonah ran away. So did Moses. And Elijah. And Jacob. They made wrong decisions. But God wasn't finished with them. Ultimately they came back and allowed God to lead them.

Satan tries to get us to make wrong decisions and to lead us away from God. One wrong decision after another will lead us in Satan's direction. But we can change directions at any time. When we make a wrong decision, it's important to get back on our feet and run straight back to God.

■ ■ ■ ■

When they had finished eating, Jesus said to Simon Peter, "Simon son of John, do you truly love me more than these?" "Yes, Lord," he said, "you know that I love you." John 21:15.

Heart Man

ave you ever been afraid and wondered if the whole world knew it? You think people must be able to hear your heart pounding like a kettledrum. Sometimes they can.

When my pastor was in college, he was asked to have prayer before a huge audience. When he bowed his head to pray, he laid the microphone against his chest. The audience heard not only his prayer but also the *thumpity, thumpity, thumpity* of his heart, racing a mile a minute because he was nervous! This earned him the nickname "Heart Man."

Society views fear as something very undesirable, even cowardly. One antiperspirant company's logo is "Never let them see you sweat." But while we try to convince ourselves and everyone else that we can do anything, we sometimes ignore the very greatest source of power in our lives.

You don't have to be weak, unsure of where to go or what to do. Let God step in, flex His fingers, and say, "Watch this." He'll do incredible things in your life that you would have missed completely if you had muscled on ahead without Him. When you feel weak, stand back and watch what He can do.

■ ■ ■ ■

But he said to me, "My grace is sufficient for you, for my power is made perfect in weakness." 2 Corinthians 12:9.

What Friends Are For

I was in a crank not too long ago. Satan was busy trying to keep me thinking about the negative things in my life, and there sure seemed to be a lot of them. The more I thought about those negative things, the worse they seemed! And the worse they seemed, the more I complained.

My friends got sick of hearing me complaining. I know this because one day I received a book in the mail. It was about strife, and there was a note from my friend Michele, saying, "I love you enough to say you need this." I learned that strife is something you let into your life *by the things you do.* I was miserable because I was letting Satan cover my life with strife.

Close friends, like the Bible talks about, are the ones who love you enough to point out your faults. They don't beat you over the head with them, but they help you overcome them.

That's why you can trust the "wounds from a friend." They have your best interests in mind. They won't "poor baby" you and throw you a pity party. They'll get right in there and help you with the dirty work of gaining victory over Satan's schemes. And *that's* what friends are for.

Wounds from a friend can be trusted,
but an enemy multiplies kisses. Proverbs 27:6.

Separation Anxiety

Joshua cried this morning because I'm leaving on a trip tomorrow. I'll be gone only over the weekend, from Friday to Sunday, but to him that's a long time, and he doesn't want me to leave.

There was a time when Jesus felt even worse than Josh. He had to be separated from His Father over the weekend, from Friday to Sunday, for the first time ever. And He didn't want to go. Calvary wasn't only about physical pain. What hurt Jesus even more, what He dreaded enough to sweat drops of blood over, was being apart from His Father.

The sad part is that my little boy misses me when I'm gone more than I miss God when I don't spend time with Him. Jesus died so that we can be "with" God any time we want. The Holy Spirit can live *in* us.

Ask God to help you miss Him when you don't spend enough time with Him. Pray for a little separation anxiety. Absence might make the heart grow fonder, but nothing beats being there.

Going a little farther, he fell to the ground and prayed that if possible the hour might pass from him. "Abba, Father," he said, "everything is possible for you. Take this cup from me. Yet not what I will, but what you will." Mark 14:35, 36.

Awesome Power

o you believe in God?" he asked, holding a gun to her head.

She could have lied. It might have saved her life. Instead the 17-year-old Christian said, "Yes, I believe in God."

"Why?" he asked. But before she could say anything he shot her.

Cassie Bernall didn't expect to go to school one day and get shot to death. But what makes her and other kids like her different is that in death they shone as stars in the universe. Many people heard their stories and marveled at their faith and love for Jesus.

We don't have to be missionaries in some far-off land to be martyred for our faith. We don't even have to die. Every day Satan tries to show Jesus up by picking on His followers. Every time we act like Jesus we show the world His awesome power and offer them the kind of life we have. The kind of life in which an ordinary kid can become an extraordinary light.

Do everything without complaining or arguing, so that you may become blameless and pure, children of God without fault in a crooked and depraved generation, in which you shine like stars in the universe as you hold out the word of life—in order that I may boast on the day of Christ that I did not run or labor for nothing. Philippians 2:14-16.

246 / MORE POWER TO YA

Pray for Each Other

One of the most awesome responsibilities God gives us is praying for each other. How many times has someone said to you, "Would you pray about . . . ?" And you say, "Oh, yeah, sure, definitely."

The next week they thank you for your prayers, and you suddenly realize that *you forgot to pray!* Embarrassing, isn't it? I know. It's happened to me.

But do you know what? We don't ever need to forget to pray again. God is "open" 24 hours a day. We can pray at any time, anywhere.

Try this: Take a small notebook, the kind you write your assignments in, and put it with your Bible. The next time someone asks you to pray, write the person's name and request in your notebook, and pray about it immediately. You can also use the notebook to record the answers to prayer. Don't forget to record your own requests and God's answers so that you can see God working in your life.

Finally, "pray without ceasing" (1 Thessalonians 5:17, KJV), because our need for prayer never ends.

With this in mind, we constantly pray for you, that our God may count you worthy of his calling, and that by his power he may fulfill every good purpose of yours and every act prompted by your faith. 2 Thessalonians 1:11.

Planting Good Seeds

I know when I plant my garden that if I put beans here and cabbages there and carrots down the middle, the beans will come up here, the cabbages will come up there, and the carrots will grow right down the middle. The seeds I plant determine the crops I grow. I can count on that, and so can you.

The seeds we plant in our lives will determine what we grow. For example, if we plant seeds of honesty, we will grow the reputation of an honest person, and we will be rewarded with trust and responsibility. If we plant seeds of dishonesty, we will reap distrust and suspicion.

We will reap whatever we plant, so we should be very careful to plant good things. Bad things might still happen to us, but we won't be the cause of the them, and we won't cause bad things in other people's lives, either. God will harvest the good seeds we've planted when He's ready. We will reap what we have sown.

■ ■ ■ ■

Sow for yourselves righteousness, reap the fruit of unfailing love, and break up your unplowed ground; for it is time to seek the Lord, until he comes and showers righteousness on you. Hosea 10:12.

Scripture Arrows

Jesus was tired. He was tired and hungry. He was tired, hungry, and thirsty. And hot, too. He'd been in the barren wastelands of Judea for 40 days and nights. There was sand in His clothes. There was sand in His hair and beard. His eyes were gritty, and whenever He licked His lips He could feel sand grate between His teeth. He wasn't exactly in the best condition to meet His mortal enemy.

But then, *it wasn't up to Him.* Sure, He was God, but when He was tempted He didn't rely on Himself. He relied on God the Father, just as He relied on the Father for everything else in His life. When Satan taunted Him with promises of bread, a kingdom He didn't have to die for, and a dramatic rescue, Jesus didn't try to explain to Satan why He didn't want those things. Jesus rebuked Satan with Scripture. He told Satan what God said.

This is an important lesson for us. Scripture is a powerful tool against Satan. Make a commitment to learn your memory verse every week, then the next time you need an arrow to fight Satan, you'll have a whole quiver full of them.

■ ■ ■ ■

My son, keep my words and store up my commands within you. . . . Bind them on your fingers; write them on the tablet of your heart. Proverbs 7:1-3.

Better Than

an you imagine what would happen if you were required to win a beauty contest and have a high IQ in order to enter heaven? Maybe an angel would be at the entrance, scoring you on your looks and passing out IQ tests before letting you into heaven. He'd say, "I'm sorry, but I'll have to take off points because you don't know the capitals of all the countries in the world. Oh, and that blemish will cost you, too." Crazy, huh?

Looks are important to us. We all want to look our best, and we want to hang around with people who look their best. Looks make us important because *people* judge us by the way we look.

But have you ever met someone you thought looked great until you got to know the person? Maybe he or she had a real sour disposition or was loud and obnoxious. Suddenly the person didn't seem so attractive, huh?

Our inner beauty (or lack of it), the part that God looks at, shines through no matter what our physical looks are. We might be able to hide our inner self from other people for a while, but sooner or later it's pretty obvious that looks aren't everything. Character is.

Charm is deceptive, and beauty is fleeting; but a woman who fears the Lord is to be praised. Proverbs 31:30.

The List

aria sat at a table in the library with her notebook open in front of her. She picked up a pen and looked at the blank page. She had decided to make a list of all the people she had hurt by cheating on her tests. Then she intended to go to each one and tell them how sorry she was.

Julie plunked down at the table next to her just as Maria wrote her name at the top of the list. "Whatcha doin'? Writing me a letter? You don't need to do that. I'm right here."

"I'm not writing you a letter," Maria said quietly. "I'm making a list of all the people I hurt by cheating."

Julie looked at her blankly. "So why is my name on there? You didn't hurt me."

"Yes, I did," Maria said. "I hurt you by encouraging you to cheat too. At first it seemed like a game and a great way to be sure of good grades. And if we didn't have to study, we had more time for fun. But I was wrong. Will you forgive me?"

Julie was silent for a moment. Then she nodded. "Yes. Now will you tell me more about why you think it's wrong to cheat?"

Forgive us our sins, for we also forgive
everyone who sins against us. Luke 11:4.

Grace Flight

I'm sorry, but I can't let you on that plane," the woman at the United Airlines desk said. "There's a 15-minute cutoff. You missed it by five minutes."

Secretly I didn't want to fly on that tiny plane anyway. I had flown to Pennsylvania on it, and we had been thrown around in the sky. I had been green by the time we had arrived. But that plane was my only ride home.

I was going to be stuck in Pennsylvania for two more days. I started crying. I was tired. I wanted to get home. I missed my family.

In desperation I took my ticket to the Delta counter and asked if they would take it and put me on one of their planes. And behold, they did. I later realized on the plane that if I had known how it would all end, I wouldn't have been so heartbroken in the first place. Not only did God get me home the same day, but He put me on a much bigger plane, and I didn't get airsick.

Faith is believing that God is in control no matter what things look like. And grace is God giving you far more than you ever expected.

■ ■ ■ ■

Wait for the Lord; be strong and take heart
and wait for the Lord. Psalm 27:14.

Curveballs

J onah was seriously upset about the way things were going. He'd come all the way to Nineveh to tell the wicked people that God was about to toast them for their wickedness, and what did they do? Repented! Now he was sitting around angry because God had decided not to destroy them.

Jonah had come. He had proclaimed. They had repented and thrown him a curveball. No doubt about it. Life throws us curveballs. For Jonah it was a city. For me it was a plane (see September 1). What is it for you?

When we are headed in a particular direction and our course suddenly changes, it's important to stay in close contact with God. We can make all the "travel" plans we want in our life, but God is the only one who can see our final destinations. The closer we stick to Him, the less off-balance we'll be when life throws us a curve.

But Jonah was greatly displeased and became angry.
He prayed to the Lord, "O Lord, is this not what I said when
I was still at home? That is why I was so quick to flee to
Tarshish. I knew that you are a gracious and compassionate
God, slow to anger and abounding in love, a God
who relents from sending calamity." Jonah 4:1, 2.

Fear Not

Her name was Christy, and we were best friends. And then one day we fought about something. I don't even remember what it was about. But it was a bad fight, and we didn't speak to each other for the rest of the year.

In seventh grade we attended the local high school and didn't have any classes together. I wonder what junior high would have been like if Christy and I had still been friends. I had some friends, but none like Christy.

I saw her years later after we had both graduated from high school. It was uncomfortable at first, but neither one of us could remember what we had squabbled about.

Silly, isn't it, the things that keep us apart. Jacob and Esau were separated most of their lives over a bowl of soup!

Some of you may be growing up with a mother or father or grandparent or friend who cut you out of his or her life. Ever since Lucifer plotted against God, relationships have been cracking up. Not all relationships will be fixed here on earth, but God is the only one who can put them back together.

■ ■ ■ ■

Save me, I pray, from the hand of my brother Esau,
for I am afraid he will come and attack me, and also
the mothers with their children. Genesis 32:11.

Superstars

e call them heroes or superstars or role models. They are the people who determine what brand of shoes we wear or the way we dress or the kind of cereal we eat for breakfast. We look up to them—until they make a mistake and fall down.

Hard times reveal a person's character, the place inside that God sees. A strong person will rely on God, get back up, and try to learn from his or her mistakes. A weak person will give up.

We learn more from people when they make a face-plant in life than when everything is going their way. When you see someone getting up and going on after messing up, be their cheering section. The next person who falls could be you. Wouldn't you rather have people cheering for you than shaking their heads at what a disappointment you are?

It takes guts to get up, admit you were wrong, and go on. And only God can fill you up with that kind of guts. He is always your biggest cheering section.

Then they prayed, "Lord, you know everyone's heart. Show us which of these two you have chosen to take over this apostolic ministry, which Judas left to go where he belongs." Acts 1:24, 25.

Up in Flames

The story goes that the only person to survive a great shipwreck washed up on the shore of a deserted island. He prayed for God to rescue him, but no one came. Reluctantly he built a small hut to live in while he waited. Then one day while he was out hunting for food his little hut burned to the ground. He came back to find smoke billowing up into the sky, his only shelter destroyed.

"How could You do this to me, God?" he screamed, overcome with grief and anger.

But the next day he woke up to the sound of a ship coming to the island. He was rescued! He asked his rescuers how they had found him.

"We saw your smoke signal," they said.

It can be so easy to think that God has deserted us when things aren't going our way. But God is always working in our lives, even when things seem utterly hopeless. Even when our hut burns to the ground we can be sure that God is watching over us. He will work things out in a way that will bless us if we'll just look for the blessing instead of zooming in on the bad stuff that's happening.

■ ■ ■ ■

Though he slay me, yet will I hope in him;
I will surely defend my ways to his face. Job 13:15.

No, No, Not One

I watched an interview of a man who was with "friends" who dragged a Black man to death behind their truck. There was a moment, he said, when he could have done something that might have prevented the whole tragedy. But he didn't do it. Why? Because he was scared.

When we watch other people mess up, it's tempting to think that we would never, ever, not in a million years do what they did. As I listened to the interview I thought, *If it had been me, I would have taken the chance.*

The problem with my reasoning is that:

A. It's hindsight. We can always see the choices we had *afterward,* but they may not be so obvious to us at the time.
B. I wasn't in his shoes. I couldn't feel his fear. Maybe if I had, I would have done exactly what he did.

The Bible tells us that there are all kinds of sins. And there are all kinds of people. The only thing that keeps any one of us from committing the very worst sins is the grace of God. Which is just one more reason we should ask for God's grace every minute of every day.

There is no one righteous, not even one; there is no one who understands, no one who seeks God. Romans 3:10, 11.

MPTY-9

The Struggle for Life

here's a story about a man who happened to be watching a cocoon when he saw a tiny hole appear. As he watched, a butterfly began to struggle through the hole. The man watched the struggle for hours. Finally he couldn't take it anymore, and he took some scissors and made the hole bigger so the butterfly could get out.

The butterfly came out, but its body was swollen, and its wings were shriveled. The man watched the butterfly closely, expecting to see it spread its wings and fly away. Instead it spent the rest of its brief life crawling around on the ground. It never flew.

What the man didn't understand was that the butterfly needed the small opening and the struggle toward life in order to survive. The struggle would force fluids from its body into its wings so that it would be ready to fly when it was finally free.

Sometimes we also need struggles to gain strength for our lives. If we didn't have them, we would be like the butterfly, never reaching our potential to fly high.

I consider that our present sufferings are not worth comparing with the glory that will be revealed in us. The creation waits in eager expectation for the sons of God to be revealed. Romans 8:18, 19.

For Trade: One Soul

magine if an angel suddenly appeared to you and said, "Here are 1,000 sparkling widgets. This is what your soul is made up of. Now you can either trade your widgets for something here on earth, or you can save them and turn them in to get into heaven. Remember, the admission price for heaven is 1,000 widgets. Any less, and you can't get in."

Wow, 1,000 sparkling widgets. What would you do with them? Would you put them in a safe-deposit box at the bank so that they could never be lost? Or would you trade them for things that catch your eye here on earth?

The sad fact is that every day we trade in some of our sparkling widgets for things that we want. The things we buy often have nothing to do with heaven, and we enjoy them for only a little while.

The good news is that when we realize what a mistake we've made and want our widgets back, Jesus will go and collect them for us. Isn't He wonderful?

Self-help is no help at all. Self-sacrifice is the way, my way, to finding yourself, your true self. What kind of deal is it to get everything you want but lose yourself? What could you ever trade your soul for? Matthew 16:25, 26, Message.

The Potter's Wheel

y first attempts at throwing clay on the wheel went well. So when I tried again later on and everything I touched turned to mud, I was frustrated. I was *trying* to make a teacup like the one my sister Aimeé had sent me from Korea.

"Why don't you touch up the top and let me fire it in the kiln?" suggested Helvi, who was helping me make something presentable. "You can always use it as a pencil holder."

A pencil holder. A rather humble destination for what was supposed to be a Korean teacup. It was serviceable, however. And after it had been fired I saw new possibilities for it. Sure, it wasn't perfect, but what is?

The pencil holder actually reminds me of myself. There are things about me that make me a far from perfect vessel to contain God's work. Still, when it comes right down to it, I'd rather be God's pencil holder than the most exquisite teacup in someone else's hands. What would you like to be?

So I went down to the potter's house, and I saw him working at the wheel. But the pot he was shaping from the clay was marred in his hands; so the potter formed it into another pot, shaping it as seemed best to him. Jeremiah 18:3, 4.

Un Cadeau

I am trying to learn French, *savez-vous* (you know)? And at times it is *très difficile* (very difficult). I've always wanted to speak French fluently, but now I have an even more important reason. I'm planning a trip to France. And I'd really like to speak the language when I get there. Of course, I'll never speak French like a native because I'm not a native.

But what if someone handed me *un cadeau* (a gift), and when I opened it—*voilà!*—I could speak French fluently? *Magnifique!* No work. No conjugating verbs. No memorization. Would I have earned it? No way. Would it be mine? You betcha!

Salvation is kind of like that. We can work at it. We can be pretty good on our own. But we'll never be truly good from the inside out. We need the *cadeau* (gift) of salvation because we can never work hard enough to earn it ourselves. Salvation is a one-size-fits-all *fantastique* kind of gift. *N'est pas* (isn't it)?

When we receive a gift, what do we say? *Merci!* (See? You're learning too!)

Now when a man works, his wages are not credited to him as a gift, but as an obligation. However, to the man who does not work but trusts God who justifies the wicked, his faith is credited as righteousness. Romans 4:4, 5.

Boomerang

ou know that kid in your class, the one they call lamebrain? You know, the one who wears his pants as though he's expecting a flood and scratches his armpits when he thinks no one is looking? Exxon could drill for oil in his hair, and he's liable to be voted most likely to embarrass his class.

Well, imagine now that you've graduated from college, and you're going for your first job interview. You look sharp. You are ready. You are . . . sitting in front of lamebrain. Only now the lamebrain is the president of Yeehaw Software Company and making a bazillion dollars a year, and you're asking *him* for a job.

Quick! How did you treat him in school? Did you pick on him like the other kids did? Did you ever sit with him at lunch when he was sitting all alone? Did you ever choose him to be on your team? If you treated him badly, you might as well leave now.

What we give out to people always comes back to us in one way or another. That's one reason it's important to treat everyone we meet with kindness and respect. The most important reason, however, is because Jesus asked us to follow His example.

■ ■ ■ ■

So in everything, do to others what you would have them do to you, for this sums up the Law and the Prophets. Matthew 7:12.

Promises, Promises

avid made a promise to Jonathan, his very best friend, to treat Saul's family well. Years later, after Saul and Jonathan were dead and when David was finally king, he remembered his promise. And whaddya know, Jonathan had a son Mephibosheth still living. David made a place for Mephibosheth at his table, as though he were one of his own sons. Mephibosheth even moved to the palace to live.

It's easy to make a promise. But it's much harder to keep it. Sometimes it's impossible, no matter how hard we try. When that happens, we break a trust that was between us and the person we made the promise to. That's why it's important to be careful about making promises. Don't promise things you can't deliver.

David didn't have to honor his promise to Jonathan. He could have said, "Aw, Johnny's dead. No one will ever know." Instead he honored his promise, and by doing that he made Mephibosheth's life better. Promises may not be easy to keep, but if it was worth making a promise about in the first place, it's important enough to honor it.

■ ■ ■ ■

David asked, "Is there anyone still left of the house of Saul to whom I can show kindness for Jonathan's sake?" 2 Samuel 9:1.

Fill Your Well

ere's a bucket. Please go to the well, and draw up some water."

You scamper down to the well, toss your bucket over, and in a few seconds hear it clunk at the bottom of the well. Clunk? Not splash? You look over and find the well is as dry as the dust in the apostles' sandals. You tell me that the well is dry and that you can't give me what you don't have. None of us can.

When we have to make a decision, we base it on what we believe about ourselves. We can't do more than what we believe we can do. That's why it's important to fill the well of our self-esteem so that we have plenty to draw from.

Having healthy self-esteem doesn't mean thinking you're better than other people or believing you're the greatest. It means believing that you have the ability to reach your potential and that if God calls on you to do more, He'll fill your well to overflowing. Believe that, and your well will never run dry, because God never fails.

■ ■ ■ ■

Again, the kingdom of heaven is like a merchant looking for fine pearls. When he found one of great value, he went away and sold everything he had and bought it. Matthew 13:45, 46.

Watching and Waiting

o you know that it's possible to have a talent and not even know it? Amazing but true. Take me, for instance. If you asked me what my gifts were, I would list writing but never speaking. Speaking in public terrifies me.

Here's the deal, though. When I let God use me, He can do great things with my speaking. But I have to be humble enough to let Him use me, rather than being hung up on how I'm going to do, look, sound, or perform. That's not important. The important thing is what God wants to say through me.

You might have gifts you're not even aware of. Maybe you aren't outgoing, and suddenly you are asked to help out during a crisis. You discover that God has given you the gift of comforting people, and you never knew you had it!

God can use the gifts we know about and the ones we don't know about if we are willing to give them all to Him. He can do wonderful things through us if we are willing to be used.

Be dressed ready for service and keep your lamps burning, like men waiting for their master to return from a wedding banquet, so that when he comes and knocks they can immediately open the door for him. Luke 12:35, 36.

Generosity

ot too long ago, I gave each of my kids a bag containing five Hershey kisses. I told them that for that day they were angel kisses. After they did a good deed for someone, they were to leave an "angel" kiss to show that they had been there. The good deeds had to be done in secret. It was great fun. They had a ball thinking up good deeds and not getting caught doing them.

Somebody came up with a similar idea and called it committing "random acts of kindness and senseless acts of beauty." The basic idea is to go around doing nice things for other people (without getting caught). Just because. Just because you can. Just because God has filled you so full of His grace that you can't help yourself, and you abound in every good work.

Why not commit some random acts of kindness yourself this week? Take a tip from my kids and leave "angel" kisses wherever you go. There are only two rules: you can't eat the kisses yourself, and your good deeds have to be a secret. Oh, and one more rule: Have fun!

■ ■ ■ ■

And God is able to make all grace abound to you, so that in all things at all times, having all that you need, you will abound in every good work. 2 Corinthians 9:8.

What's in a Name?

y name was almost Chantal. I wish it had been. A few years ago I discovered that my name should have an accent mark! Now my name is written Céleste, which I like better. It means "heavenly."

Do you know what your name means? You can probably find out in a baby name book.

Names used to have much more meaning. Parents chose them to describe what they hoped for their children or told of the circumstances of their birth. Some friends of mine take Hebrew names to describe their new lives in God. If I had a Hebrew name, I'd like Keturah, which means something like "to turn into fragrance by fire, as an act of worship," sort of like the fragrance of incense.

God's different names describe aspects of His character. Each tells us something about Him. See how many of God's names you can find. What do they say about Him? Which ones do you like best? Praise Him by all His names!

Moses said to God, "Suppose I go to the Israelites and say to them, 'The God of your fathers has sent me to you,' and they ask me, 'What is his name?' Then what shall I tell them?" God said to Moses, "I AM WHO I AM. This is what you are to say to the Israelites: 'I AM has sent me to you.'" Exodus 3:13, 14.

Speeding Through Life

he story goes that a man was speeding on his way home. You guessed it. He heard a siren behind him and pulled over. Imagine how embarrassed he was when he looked in the rearview mirror and saw that the policeman was someone he knew from church!

He fully expected a ticket, but he tried to talk his way out of it the whole time the officer was scribbling away in his notebook. The policeman didn't say anything. He just ripped the ticket out and handed it to him. But when he looked at the ticket, it wasn't a ticket at all. It was a note telling how the policeman's little girl had been killed by a speeding car and asking him to drive safely.

Have you ever pictured God as "the big policeman in the sky"? You do something wrong, you hear the siren, and you pull over to try to talk your way out of a ticket. But God doesn't give you a ticket, does He? He asks you to be careful because His Son was killed by a speeder like you.

Live safely. And when the time comes, drive safely.

If a righteous man turns from his righteousness and does evil, he will die for it. And if a wicked man turns away from his wickedness and does what is just and right, he will live by doing so. Ezekiel 33:18, 19.

There, But for the Grace of God

I f you don't know who Winston Churchill was, ask your parents or your history teacher. (He was the British prime minister who said, "Never in the field of human conflict was so much owed by so many to so few.")

Anyway, the story goes that Churchill had a political opponent named Cripps. Nobody liked Cripps, because he was smug and self-righteous and thought he was better than anyone else. One day as he passed by, Churchill quipped, "There, but for the grace of God, goes God."

To some degree there's a little of Cripps in all of us. Ever since Eve fell for Satan's line about being like God if she ate from that tree, we've all secretly wished to be "like God." But when we put ourselves in the place of God and believe we are all-powerful, we'll find there is nothing else to lean on for help. Only by kneeling at the throne will we find the strength we need to live every moment by the grace of God.

■ ■ ■ ■

"You will not surely die," the serpent said to the woman. "For God knows that when you eat of it your eyes will be opened, and you will be like God, knowing good and evil." Genesis 3:4, 5.

The Great Race

here were two athletes competing at the race. Neither won the blue ribbon. They tied for third place.

After the games a man approached them. "I've been watching you two," he said. When he gave his name, the two athletes recognized him as one of the best coaches in the country. "Even though you didn't win, I am impressed with both of you, and I'd like to train you," he told them.

The first athlete was delighted. "Sir, I accept," he said. The second athlete shook his head. "Nah, I'm going to win next time; I don't need your help."

A year later the two athletes met again at a competition. The one who had been coached came in first place. And the one who refused? He carried water and towels out to the other athletes. Without the proper coaching he pushed himself too hard and pulled a muscle so he couldn't compete.

We have the same choice as the athletes did. We can accept God's offer to coach us so that we can win in the race of life. Or we can refuse and take our chances. What will you do today?

■ ■ ■ ■

As a father has compassion on his children, so the Lord has compassion on those who fear him; for he knows how we are formed, he remembers that we are dust. Psalm 103:13, 14.

Time-out

Joshua and Rachel hate time-out. They have to sit in a chair and be quiet, and do you know what? They hate it. But sitting in time-out can be a blessing, as well as a punishment. When we sit outside the situation for a little while, we can see things so much clearer.

Jesus also had a lot to do. But He made sure to take time out just to be with His Father. And He made His disciples take time-out too. When the crowds got too big, He made them get away by themselves. Jesus knew that when we're outside a situation a little, we can understand better what's going on. We can regroup, rethink, and recharge. Try it the next time you are confused or overwhelmed. Get away from the situation for a while. Pray about it and ask God to show you what to do about it. (Coming out of a time-out, we'll be ready to hit the road again with Jesus.)

■ ■ ■ ■

Immediately Jesus made his disciples get into the boat and go on ahead of him to Bethsaida, while he dismissed the crowd. After leaving them, he went up on a mountainside to pray. Mark 6:45, 46.

Tongue-lashing

I heard a story about a kid who kept losing his temper and saying mean things to people. He asked his dad how he could stop doing it. His father gave him a hammer and a bucket of nails. "Here, son," he said. "Every time you lose your temper, instead of saying something mean, go pound one of these nails into the fence."

A week later the kid went back to his father and said, "Dad, I don't lose my temper anymore."

"That's great, son," the father replied. "Now go and pull out one nail for each day that you keep holding your temper."

The son did that, and when the nails were all gone, he went back to his father. They walked over to the fence together. "You've done a good job, son, but do you see all these holes? The fence won't ever be the same. Every time you hurt someone in anger you leave a scar, just like the holes in the fence. And they can't ever be completely fixed. Remember that the next time you're tempted to say something in anger."

The tongue is a pretty deadly weapon, isn't it? Dedicate it to God instead of running around leaving holes in other people's fences.

■ ■ ■ ■

But no man can tame the tongue. It is a restless evil, full of deadly poison. James 3:8.

Power-tripping

**W**hen Josh was about 3 years old, I jokingly told him one day that I got to make the rules because I was the big kahuna. A week or so later I gave him a chore to do and kidded him, "Because I'm the what?"

He thought for a few seconds and then declared, "Because you're the big tuna!"

Aw well, kahuna, tuna, whatever. It's a real power trip to be important and well-known. As a sorta famous Adventist writer, I've had my share of rocket trips to the moon when people recognize me ("Can I have your autograph?") and more than my share of humbling experiences ("I'm sorry, who did you say you were again?").

One of the biggest obstacles on the road to heaven is our pride. I'll admit that my head inflates at an embarrassingly fast rate. But I try to remember that it doesn't matter who I am, but who He is and whether I know Him. That's what's important. The next time you're tempted to take off on a power trip, remember what's *really* important.

Work happily together. Don't try to act big. Don't try to get into the good graces of important people, but enjoy the company of ordinary folks. And don't think you know it all! Romans 12:16, TLB.

Give It Up!

ave you ever fasted? I have. The last time I fasted was for World Vision, the 30-hour famine, to see what it's like to go hungry the way many people do every day.

There are lots of reasons to fast. And there are many ways to fast. Fasting is usually associated with not eating, but we can also give up things we like so that we can concentrate on what's most important.

What can you give up? Video games, TV, shopping? What do you spend a lot of time doing? (Homework doesn't count!). Fast from it. Set apart a week or a couple days, and use the time you would have spent on that to get to know God better. If you have friends who are willing to fast with you, make it a joint effort. Fasting with friends helps us keep going when we hit the wall and feel like quitting.

No matter what you give up, you will get much more. God tells us that when we seek Him, we will find Him. Go, fast, and seek.

■ ■ ■ ■

While they were worshiping the Lord and fasting,
the Holy Spirit said, "Set apart for me Barnabas and
Saul for the work to which I have called them." Acts 13:2.

Whisper a Prayer

I was having a rough time, and my friend Michele said, "I'll pray for you." We all like people to pray for us. But she didn't just pray for me. She sent me the prayer that she prayed in e-mail!

I read her prayer, and I was so impressed by it that I printed it out and hung it on my wall so that I would have it the next time I needed it. Her prayer comforted me when I saw it even more than if I had just known that she had prayed.

The next time someone asks you to pray for them, be sure to do so. But you can also let them hear your prayer. If you're too shy to pray out loud with someone, write your prayer down in a card, a letter, or an e-mail and send it to them. These whispered prayers mean so much to the person who is being prayed for. They can be carried around and re-read over and over.

David's prayers were written out as psalms, and they can be very comforting. When you can't think of your own prayer, you can always pray a psalm.

As for me, far be it from me that I should sin against the Lord by failing to pray for you. 1 Samuel 12:23.

Going to Extremes

acchaeus was a horrid little man. At least, that's how people saw him. But guess what? When Zacchaeus became a follower of Jesus, he didn't just pay back what he owed people. He didn't just give them back the things he had taken from them.

"Uh, let's see . . . I owe you one stereo set and a camcorder. And you, I owe you an Oriental rug and a pair of candlesticks."

Zacchaeus could have done that. That's all that was really required of him. Instead he gave back *four times* what he had taken. He gave back four stereo sets, four camcorders, four Oriental rugs, and four pairs of candlesticks (in a manner of speaking). Zacchaeus went beyond payback. He filled people's needs.

What really amazes me is how people's worst attributes become their greatest assets when they follow Jesus. Zacchaeus was greedy; everyone agreed about that, even Zacchaeus. But following Jesus, he became *generous* in the extreme.

Give yourself to God, and watch Him go to extremes.

■ ■ ■ ■

But Zacchaeus stood up and said to the Lord, "Look, Lord! Here and now I give half of my possessions to the poor, and if I have cheated anybody out of anything, I will pay back four times the amount." Luke 19:8.

Because I Said So

I hate to admit this, but when I was a teen I liked a truly awful song that was popular at the time. Don't ask me why. I have no idea. Every time it came on the radio I turned it up loud and sang along. The only reason I remember it so well is because my mother *hated* it. When I asked her why, she said, "Just because."

Now that I'm all grown up I know exactly why she didn't like it. The lyrics are horrible. I sometimes wonder if I would have liked the song so much if my mother had explained to me what was wrong with it.

Parents (and I know, I'm one of them) have a standard phrase: "Because I said so." This is meant to explain everything from mealtime to curfews. It isn't that they don't want to explain their reasons, but this blanket phrase is just easier to use at times.

If you don't understand your parents' reasons for something, ask them. They'll probably be happy to tell you if they know you really want to listen.

But in your hearts set apart Christ as Lord. Always be prepared to give an answer to everyone who asks you to give the reason for the hope that you have. 1 Peter 3:15.

27 SEPTEMBER

Prepare a Room

There once was a town that was in the middle of a drought. There hadn't been rain for weeks, and everything was drying up. The townspeople were desperate. They needed rain in order to live. The situation was so bleak that the pastor of the local church called everyone together for a special prayer meeting. The whole town showed up.

While they were praying fervently a traveling evangelist happened to pass through. During a break in the meeting he asked what they were praying for. "Rain," a villager replied.

"Rain?" the evangelist asked, puzzled. "You're praying for rain, and not one of you brought an umbrella? Where's your faith?"

It's easy to go through the motions of praying. It's easy to pray after we've tried everything else or when there isn't anything else we can do. But we need to have the faith Paul had.

Paul wanted to join his friends, so they all prayed about it. Then he sent them a letter telling them to fix the guest room because he hoped to join them soon in answer to all of their prayers. If Paul had asked for rain, he would have put up his umbrella. We should, too.

■ ■ ■ ■

And one thing more: Prepare a guest room for me, because I hope to be restored to you in answer to your prayers. Philemon 22.

Penny for Your Thoughts

ome people seem to wear their thoughts on their faces. You know what they're thinking just by looking at them. These are the kind of people you don't want on your team when you're playing card games that involve bluffing. But most people's thoughts are a mystery to others until they are shared.

Some people think that every thought that crosses their mind should be blurted out no matter what. With these people you have to sift through a lot of information to find the important stuff. Others release their thoughts slowly, like teeth being pulled by a dentist. This can make it difficult to have a deep relationship.

But God is awesome when it comes to sharing His thoughts. Not only did He share His thoughts with the people who wrote them down in the Bible and the Spirit of Prophecy, but His thoughts are carried to you and me through the Holy Spirit whenever we want them to be. If you want to know God's thoughts, just ask Him. And then don't forget to listen.

For who among men knows the thoughts of a man except the man's spirit within him? In the same way no one knows the thoughts of God except the Spirit of God. 1 Corinthians 2:11.

First and Last

 oesn't it always seem that no matter which line you choose to stand in at the checkout counter it will always seem to move slower than any other line? And if they suddenly open another line and you dart over to get ahead of the people behind you, they will always check out before you do? "Many that are first shall be last; and the last shall be first," remember? (Matthew 19:30, KJV).

Of course, when you put it that way it sounds great. But waiting for our turn at anything is hard to put into actual practice. After all, who wants to be last in real time? Let's face it. Thinking about others first just isn't something that we do naturally, but it is something that God does.

So one thing that can help us to develop this "last shall be first" attitude is to practice being last. Let someone go ahead of you out a crowded doorway. Volunteer to take the last turn in a game. Find other ways to put others ahead of yourself. Go ahead. Be last. You'll be first with God.

■ ■ ■ ■

Each of you should look not only to your own interests,
but also to the interests of others. Philippians 2:4.

Making Amends

aria swallowed hard and then made her way to the front of the room as the other kids shuffled out. Mr. Stanley, her history teacher, looked up when she approached his desk.

"Hello, Maria. What can I do for you?"

"Mr. Stanley, I've already talked to my parents about this, and they said I should tell my teachers when I was ready. I'm sorry, but up until a couple months ago I was cheating in your class."

Mr. Stanley was quiet for a long time. "I'm sorry that you felt you had to cheat," he said finally. "I want you to know that you could have asked for help."

Maria swallowed hard. She could have avoided so much pain if only she had asked for help instead of taking the easy way out. "Thank you, Mr. Stanley. Is there anything I can do to make it up to you?"

"I appreciate your honesty, Maria, and I will let you know what you need to do to make up for it. I'm not the one you hurt by cheating. You cheated yourself. Next time you need help, don't hesitate to ask for it."

"I won't, Mr. Stanley. Thank you."

■ ■ ■ ■

Fools mock at making amends for sin,
but goodwill is found among the upright. Proverbs 14:9.

Boundary Stones

ur new home in the country included a log cabin and 10 acres of land. The boundary markers were listed on the deed. "From the large maple in a westerly direction to the stream. This is the northern boundary of the property."

The boundaries told us where our property ended and where someone else's property began. They reminded us that we didn't own all the land we could see.

We, as individuals, also have boundaries that define where we begin and end. We have physical boundaries that should prevent anybody from touching our bodies without our permission. We have spiritual boundaries, summed up in the two greatest commandments to love God and to love our neighbor as ourselves. We also have emotional boundaries that define how much we can handle.

It's important to know what our boundaries are and how to enforce them. Ask a parent or pastor to discuss your boundaries with you. We are responsible for our own bodies and emotions, and God will help us to protect them.

■ ■ ■ ■

So Jacob took a stone and set it up as a pillar. He said to his relatives, "Gather some stones." So they took stones and piled them in a heap, and they ate there by the heap. . . . Laban said, "This heap is a witness between you and me today." Genesis 31:45-48.

Be Careful, Little Mouth

It's a major crisis. You're desperate. You try to bargain with God. "Please, God, if You do this for me, I'll never ask You for anything again. I'll eat all my vegetables for the rest of my life. I'll never complain about another thing as long as I live. I'll even be nice to that horrid Joey at school. I'll give away all my video games. Please, God, *I promise.*"

Sound familiar? Then you get what you wanted (not because you pleaded for it), and you can't possibly keep all your promises to God. Instead you feel guilty for the rest of your life, and every time something bad happens you have the vague feeling that it has something to do with your broken promise.

Our promises can get us into trouble. A promise, or vow, is an important agreement that shouldn't be made lightly. In fact, the Bible says that unless you intend to keep your promise, you'd better not make one.

Promises are also important to God. He never backs down on a promise. We can be sure that whatever He says, He will do. Claim one of His promises today and every day.

It is better not to vow than to make a vow and not fulfill it. Do not let your mouth lead you into sin. Ecclesiastes 5:5, 6.

Two for the Price of One

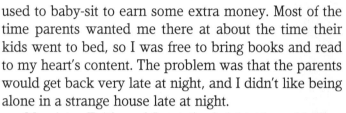

I used to baby-sit to earn some extra money. Most of the time parents wanted me there at about the time their kids went to bed, so I was free to bring books and read to my heart's content. The problem was that the parents would get back very late at night, and I didn't like being alone in a strange house late at night.

My sister Faith and I got the bright idea of billing ourselves as two baby-sitters for the price of one. We'd split the money, or sometimes one of us would just tag along for company. The parents thought they were getting great value for their money, and we were less lonely.

Most things are better when you do them with someone else. For example, work gets done more quickly. Meals are more interesting. And you get another view of a shared experience.

Having a prayer partner or a friend to study with will help you keep going when the going gets tough. If you fall, you'll get up much faster if you have someone to help you.

■ ■ ■ ■

Two are better than one, because they have a good return for their work: if one falls down his friend can help him up. But pity the man who falls and has no one to help him up! Ecclesiastes 4:9, 10.

The Good Stuff

I love to read and quilt and walk and paint and, well, you get the picture. There are hundreds of things I love to do. I could do them continuously for years without getting sick of them. But my kids would never see me, my husband wouldn't have clean socks, and my pets would probably starve.

It's easy to look at activities as "good" and "bad," but it's more complex than that. Some good activities can be bad if we do them too much. For example, some video games might even be educational. But if you play them every free minute, they are bad because they keep you from other things that will help you grow up properly.

When you wonder if an activity is good or bad, think first about how much you plan to do that activity. Set limits for yourself. Check your schedule and see if something in your life is taking up too much time. Adjust your limits. The good stuff is good only if it doesn't run your life.

■ ■ ■ ■

I can do anything I want to if Christ has not said no, but some of these things aren't good for me. Even if I am allowed to do them, I'll refuse to if I think they might get such a grip on me that I can't easily stop when I want to. 1 Corinthians 6:12, TLB.

5 OCTOBER

Work for Joy

I love to write. I would write even if it wasn't my job. I wrote long before I ever had anything published, filling notebook after notebook with words. Now writing pays for the groceries and other necessities.

One day I was grumbling to a friend about all I had to write. I had work coming out my ears. She said, "Be sure and find the joy in what you're doing, because if you don't enjoy it, why do it at all?"

And she was absolutely right, of course. It's important to enjoy the jobs we do, not so much because they are fun, but because everything we do gives us the opportunity to work for Jesus. Think about it. What if Jesus asked you to do the dishes? It'd be an honor, wouldn't it? What if He asked you to wash the car? make a batch of muffins? sort the laundry?

Well, of course, if *Jesus* asked, you'd be thrilled to do whatever job He had in mind. If we maintain that attitude toward the work that comes our way, whatever it is, it will be a joy to do.

■ ■ ■ ■

So I saw that there is nothing better for a man than to enjoy his work, because that is his lot. For who can bring him to see what will happen after him? Ecclesiastes 3:22.

Missionary at Home

ave you ever wanted a ministry of your very own? Well, you have one! Everyone has a ministry. Yours might be smiling to cheer up a weary bus driver or helping a student with a disability. It might be speaking kindly to your little sister and her friends, even though you *really* want to lock yourself in your room.

Sure, none of these things are glamorous. They probably won't make you more popular, and you might not get to travel to a foreign mission field. But we are called to be missionaries where we live, work, and go to school.

Jesus spent most of His life doing ordinary things. In fact, for all but the last few years He worked in His dad's carpenter shop. But Jesus had a ministry. There's a saying, "Your actions are talking so loud I can't hear what you're saying." It applies to all of us. Our actions, large and small, can show Jesus to others. Whom do you want to showcase today?

■ ■ ■ ■

Therefore, since through God's mercy we have this ministry, we do not lose heart. 2 Corinthians 4:1.

Look, Ma! No Hands!

This is the year my son learns how to ride his bicycle without training wheels. Do you remember when you learned? I do. I sat on the bike, and my mom placed me in the yard heading down a small slope to the neighbor's yard. I rode neatly down to their backyard and fell splash into their small pool. Talk about a wake-up call!

I tried over and over and over. Finally I was ready for the road. My mom sent me wobbling and weaving down the dead-end road on my own. It was exhilarating! I could ride. That night when my dad got home, I couldn't wait to show him I could ride a bike.

God helps us through all our trials. Sometimes we crash and have to get up and try again, but God is always there to help us. He's not like our training wheels that come off when we can ride alone. He is like our bike, always with us, carrying us on to new things, and supporting us all the way.

■ ■ ■ ■

Not only so, but we also rejoice in our sufferings, because we know that suffering produces perseverance; perseverance, character; and character, hope. And hope does not disappoint us, because God has poured out his love into our hearts by the Holy Spirit, whom he has given us. Romans 5:3-5.

Bear in the Woods

I was in my sleeping bag when I heard it. *Crash! Crunch! Crash!* My dog was still snoring, but I sat bolt upright in my tent. I was two miles from civilization, alone on the side of a mountain. *And there was a bear outside my tent.*

I was sure it was a bear. I tried to make myself believe it was just a large, friendly deer, but no self-respecting deer would plow through the woods making such a racket. It was pitch-black. The sun wouldn't be up for hours. Finally, finally I heard the bear go away. I couldn't wait for it to get light outside.

We spend so much of our spiritual life in darkness with bears prowling all around us. But we can have light any time we want it. God gave us the Bible to light the way for us. We also have prayer. And we have the writings of Ellen White to help us too. If we expect to see where we are going, we need to turn on the light and let the Morning Star rise in our hearts.

■ ■ ■ ■

And we have the word of the prophets made more certain, and you will do well to pay attention to it, as to a light shining in a dark place, until the day dawns and the morning star rises in your hearts. 2 Peter 1:19.

True Love

I'm gonna love you till the end of time," the singer croons. "Baby, this feelin' I got ain't never gonna die . . ."

The Bible tells us that love is a whole lot different than the stuff you hear about on the radio or see on TV or in the movies. Love is more than a "feeling" (warm, gushy, tingly—those are feelings); love is an action. We apply love when we act in a loving way, not when we feel loving. Satan tries real hard to mix us up about love.

Jesus loved us, so He *came* and *died* for us. His actions show us His love for us. He didn't sit up in heaven and shout down, "Hey, I love you guys!" To find love we have to understand what it is. It's an *action,* not a *feeling.* The surprise is that when we act loving, our feelings will follow our actions. Try it and see for yourself. Discover what love is really all about.

■ ■ ■ ■

Love is patient, love is kind. It does not envy, it does not boast, it is not proud. It is not rude, it is not self-seeking, it is not easily angered, it keeps no record of wrongs. Love does not delight in evil but rejoices with the truth. It always protects, always trusts, always hopes, always perseveres. 1 Corinthians 13:4-7.

On the Rock

ou know that song, "The wise man was gonna build his house upon a rock, house upon a rock, house upon a rock. The wise man was gonna build his house upon a rock, but the first week he had too much homework, and the second week was vacation, and the third week he had a soccer game, and the fourth week the rain came down and the floods came up, but since God knew he planned to build his house on the rock, God saved his house anyway."

That's not the way the song goes when we sing it, but sometimes we wish it sounded that way when we *live* it. When we build our house on the rock (Jesus), our house will stand firm against any storm Satan can dream up. But it has to be built *before* the storm. Having the building materials (Bible, devotional, Sabbath School quarterly) in a neat pile beside the rock when the storm hits isn't going to do any good.

Build your house so you don't get swept out to sea. When the rains come down and the floods come up, your house on the rock will stand firm.

And I tell you that you are Peter, and on this rock
I will build my church, and the gates of Hades
will not overcome it. Matthew 16:18.

Signals

The Bible tells us not to get angry. True or False.

Actually, the Bible tells us not to sin when we get angry. Anger is an emotion like any other emotion God gave us. Emotions tell us things about ourselves. For example, anger might be a signal to us that someone is taking advantage of us. If we use the anger signal to treat someone else badly, we sin. But if we use the anger signal to figure out what the problem is and to fix it, we have used our anger correctly.

Ignoring the anger signal is like a ship ignoring the flashing beacon of a lighthouse. It will result in trouble later on. Buried anger often turns to resentment and bitterness.

That's why it's important to deal with our anger every day. Ask God to show you how to deal with this powerful emotion so that you are using your anger signal the way He wants you to.

■ ■ ■ ■

Look after each other so that not one of you will fail to find God's best blessings. Watch out that no bitterness takes root among you, for as it springs up it causes deep trouble, hurting many in their spiritual lives. Hebrews 12:15, TLB.

And Behind Door Number Two . . .

I n a game show called *Let's Make a Deal* contestants got to choose to open a door and get the prizes behind the door or to keep the prizes they had already collected. There were three doors to pick from, but they didn't know what was behind them. It could be nothing, or it could be lots of money. They could choose the unknown or stick with the known.

What a choice, huh? I'm sure many people went home very disappointed and empty-handed. We have a choice to make too, but we don't have to deal with the unknown. We can choose to live God's way, a lifestyle that is full of blessings and life. Or we can choose one of Satan's doors of life, which leads to death and curses. Doesn't sound too appealing, does it?

It shouldn't, but Satan can make death and curses look deceptively appealing. Don't walk away from the game of life empty-handed. Hang on tight to God's blessings and the eternal life He offers us. Tell Satan he can keep his death and curses.

■ ■ ■ ■

This day I call heaven and earth as witnesses against you that I have set before you life and death, blessings and curses. Now choose life, so that you and your children may live and that you may love the Lord your God, listen to his voice, and hold fast to him. Deuteronomy 30:19, 20.

God's Umbrella

Are you joyful all the time? Do you give thanks in everything? Even when Mrs. Schnee hands back your science test with the big red F on it? Even when your puppy gets run over by a car? Even when your parents seem unreasonable?

Now, hold on a minute. Are all these bad things part of God's will for us? No, but He does want us to *give thanks in all things.* Because when we give Him thanks, we are stepping under His umbrella of protection. We can choose to have joy no matter what happens. It is a gift from God.

Joy is different than happiness, which is controlled by our five senses. It would be a little hard, say, to stand in the rain when you are hungry and tired and be happy, wouldn't it? But we can go through any number of hard times on earth and still be full of God-given joy.

Joy is Job saying, "Though he slay me, yet will I hope in him" (Job 13:15). Job certainly didn't have much to be happy about. But he put himself under God's umbrella and found joy despite his circumstances.

Be joyful always; pray continually; give thanks in all circumstances, for this is God's will for you in Christ Jesus. 1 Thessalonians 5:16-18.

The Territory Beyond

I f there's one question we ask more than any other, it is this: Why do bad things happen to good people?

How about another: Why do bad things happen to bad people?

God gave man a choice, and Adam and Eve (speaking for the rest of us) decided to let Satan rule the world. The problem is that Satan's idea of ruling the world includes such things as death and fear and violence. Satan likes nothing better than to attend a funeral in the morning, a war just before lunch, some persecution after dinner, and have a soothing sleep full of nightmares.

When God gave Adam authority over the earth, in essence, He said, "Here are the keys, son. Drive carefully." But Adam picked up a hitchhiker along the way. If God had taken the keys back after that, the universe would have cried, "Foul play!"

That doesn't mean we are powerless here on earth. We can be like police officers. We have God's authority to pull over anyone who gives Satan a ride. Claim the driver for Christ! Arrest Satan! Kick him out of the car. He can walk where he's going.

■ ■ ■ ■

God blessed them and said to them, "Be fruitful and
increase in number; fill the earth and subdue it. Rule
over the fish of the sea and the birds of the air and over
every living creature that moves on the ground." Genesis 1:28.

Training Versus Trying

ould you get up from your chair and go run a marathon right now? this minute? Do you think you would win? If exercise for you has been made up mostly of playing street hockey with some friends and walking to the bus stop, you probably wouldn't win your first competition. At least, not without some training first.

There is a big difference between trying to be an athlete and training to be an athlete. Running for miles, lifting weights, and practicing technique sounds like the hard way to become an athlete, doesn't it? Actually, it would be harder to be in your first competition without any training at all.

We train to be godly by doing things that help us to become godly people. For instance, practicing kindness even when we don't feel kind, or serving when we are too proud to want to. These things, when practiced, will help us eventually to become the kind of people who do these things automatically—the same way practicing hitting a ball will help a ballplayer hit a home run during the game.

■ ■ ■ ■

Have nothing to do with godless myths and old wives' tales; rather, train yourself to be godly. For physical training is of some value, but godliness has value for all things, holding promise for both the present life and the life to come. 1 Timothy 4:7, 8.

Building Faith

ow can we make our faith stronger? Can we exercise it like a muscle? Can we do faithups or run laps of faith to build our endurance? Is there some kind of vitamin or supplement we could take to boost our faith? *Now, multivitamins containing extra "faithin" to make your faith healthy and strong.*

No, faith isn't something we can strengthen or improve with vitamins. In fact, we can't even see our faith. If something went wrong with it, no doctor would be able to operate and fix the problem. Faith is simply believing in things we can't see with our eyes or test with our senses.

Faith can be pretty fragile. It is born in us and grows stronger when we read God's Word. Paul says that "faith comes from hearing the message, and the message is heard through the word of Christ." Daily "supplements" from the Bible will help build our faith. And just as skipping meals will make us physically weak, skipping our daily Bible study will weaken our faith.

We need good healthy portions of God's Word to help our faith grow strong and healthy. Then we'll be able to hold up under the pressure of life. Have you read your Bible today?

■ ■ ■ ■

Consequently, faith comes from hearing the message, and the message is heard through the word of Christ. Romans 10:17.

Copycat

y sister Faith was the worst copycat when we were growing up. I was older by 16 months, which isn't much, I'll admit, but it meant that I was *older*. I got to do things *first*. I grew up before she did. But no matter what I did, she wanted to do the same thing! It was annoying.

I like to think of myself as a unique individual, and even when I became an adult, it bothered me when people dressed the way I dressed or did the things I did. And then I read that imitation is the sincerest form of flattery. And it finally dawned on me that people copy others because *they want to be like them.*

We copy others because we want to be like them. And if we want to be like Jesus, we should copy Him. How many ways can you think of today to copy Jesus? Decide on just one, for now, and try it for a week. And then add another. Pretty soon you'll be just like Jesus.

■ ■ ■ ■

To this you were called, because Christ suffered for you, leaving you an example, that you should follow in his steps. 1 Peter 2:21.

Before and After

 am certain that every one of you reading this book is an angelic kid, but I sure wasn't. I was horrid. When I look back at the way I acted, I shudder. I hate running into people who "knew me when" because they always remember how wild and unruly I was. I didn't rob banks or anything like that, but I'm still ashamed of the way I acted. The good news is that no matter how bad we are, Jesus can make us brand-new.

There's a story about a girl who got into some really bad stuff. Later she became a Christian and started going to church. The pastor's son fell in love with her, and they decided to get married. But there were people in the church who weren't comfortable with their pastor's son marrying someone like her.

At a meeting he stood up to defend her, saying, "This isn't about what my fiancé has done or not done. This is about whether or not Jesus' blood can cover her sins or not. I believe it can."

Jesus' blood is the greatest stain remover on earth. Ask Him to remove *your* sin stains today.

But you were washed, you were sanctified, you were justified in the name of the Lord Jesus Christ and by the Spirit of our God. 1 Corinthians 6:11.

At the Cross

I don't know if this is a true story or not, but I think it shows what a powerful symbol the cross is. The Romans used it to humiliate their victims, but God uses it to save everyone who believes.

A young man was training to be an Olympic diver. He was an atheist, but his Christian friend kept telling him about Jesus and His love. The young man didn't pay any attention.

One night he decided to go to the indoor pool and practice diving. The lights weren't on, but there were big skylights and the moon was bright enough to see by. He climbed up to the highest diving board, turned his back to the pool, and held his arms out. When he did, he saw his shadow on the wall—it looked like a man hanging on a cross.

The man immediately knelt down on the diving board and asked God to come into his life. When he stood up, a maintenance man came in and turned on the lights. The young man looked down and saw that the pool had been drained for repairs. The cross had saved him.

For God was pleased to have all his fullness dwell in him, and through him to reconcile to himself all things, whether things on earth or things in heaven, by making peace through his blood, shed on the cross. Colossians 1:19, 20.

In the Mirror

y absolutely favorite mirror is at Ben & Jerry's ice-cream store. It's one of those circus mirrors that makes you look tall and thin. It's very flattering, and I can look thin no matter how much ice cream I eat.

But mirrors that don't accurately reflect us aren't much good, are they? I mean, I'd love to think I was tall and thin, but who am I kidding? Only me. On the other hand, if I see my defects, I can try to improve. If I need to step up my exercise program, I can do that. If my hair needs to be cut, I can make an appointment. If the mirror shows that I haven't been getting enough sleep, I can take some time to rest.

When we want to know how we're doing spiritually, we can ask God to show us what we look like. Not only will He do that, but He'll also help us to do whatever we need to in order to change. We may never be tall and thin, but we can all look more like Jesus on the inside.

Anyone who listens to the word but does not do what it says is like a man who looks at his face in a mirror and, after looking at himself, goes away and immediately forgets what he looks like. James 1:23, 24.

Pass or Fail

For years I really thought that Jesus tested our faith to see if we would pass or fail. And then I realized how silly that was. Jesus knows me better than anyone else. He doesn't need to make me take a spiritual test to see how I'm measuring up. He can see all of my heart. It's no secret to Him.

Let's say I have a problem with anger (let's just say I do); Jesus doesn't make things go badly for me to see if I'll get mad about it. If I fail, He doesn't check it off on some list and say, "That's too bad. You'll have to take that one again."

No, Jesus *helps* us to reach higher than we can by ourselves. He doesn't test us to trip us up. He's not out to get us, lurking around corners waiting for us to do something wrong. He loves us more than we'll ever be able to understand. Nothing we can do can make Him love us more or less than He does right now. And He wants to help us to be good.

■ ■ ■ ■

When tempted, no one should say, "God is tempting me."
For God cannot be tempted by evil, nor does he tempt
anyone; but each one is tempted when, by his own evil
desire, he is dragged away and enticed. James 1:13, 14.

The War Within

ave you ever been in a tug-of-war? In some of them the losers end up in a mud pit in the middle of the playing field. Ick. It's fun to watch, though. First one team is winning, and then the other, both sides struggling to pull the other across the center line.

It sometimes feels like that inside us, doesn't it? When we have choices to make, we are tugged both ways. Part of us wants to do what God wants, and part would rather take the easy way out and follow Satan. It creates a tug-of-war inside us. We grit our teeth and think that if we just put our mind to it and pull hard enough, we can be kind and loving and joyful.

But we've got it all wrong. The fruit of the Spirit is *fruit*. In other words, God grows it in us. We can't make it pop out on the tree because we want to.

Our job is to stay connected to God. It's the Holy Spirit's job to grow fruit in our lives.

■ ■ ■ ■

For the sinful nature desires what is contrary to the Spirit,
and the Spirit what is contrary to the sinful nature.
They are in conflict with each other, so that you
do not do what you want. Galatians 5:17.

Little Shields

I t's time for the battle! Quick, put on your armor! Here's your big, thick helmet, your *(umph!)* very heavy breastplate, and the chain mail to protect your arms and legs. And don't forget your shield, which is about the size of a dinner plate, and you'd . . .

What? You want a bigger shield? You want a shield the size of Manhattan? Or at least bigger than your body? Maybe something the size of a bicycle tire? I don't blame you. It would be pretty hard defending yourself with a small shield, wouldn't it?

Of course, that's what we often try to do. We have the entire Bible, thousands of words with which to defend ourselves when Satan attacks us. But if we memorize only a few of those verses it's like going into a raging battle with only a tiny little shield for protection. You have to be pretty good to defend yourself with a tiny shield.

Fortunately, there is a way to make our shields bigger, much bigger. Begin by memorizing Bible verses. Try to memorize one a week at first. As you memorize, your shield will get bigger and bigger. Don't forget to take it into battle with you!

■ ■ ■ ■

But you are a shield around me, O Lord;
you bestow glory on me and lift up my head. Psalm 3:3.

Fight the Good Fight

nything that is worth having is worth fighting for. Ever heard that expression? When the going gets tough, it can be tempting to get going, but giving up isn't the answer. Our whole life is a fight to stay true to what we believe. That's a tiring fight. We can easily get discouraged the same way a soldier does.

Slogging through the mud, eating yucky food, seeing death all around. These are discouraging things. Soldiers live in tents (when they are lucky), endure drafts and interrupted sleeping hours, have few possessions, and are at the beck and call of their commanding officer. And that's just the beginning.

In the same way, we are soldiers for Jesus. There's a battle going on, and we have to deal with the yucky stuff too. The good news is that our side has already won! The battle might be tough, but we need to stay in and fight to the end. We'll receive more than a Purple Heart; we'll receive a brand-new body and live forever. That's worth fighting for, isn't it?

Endure hardships with us like a good soldier of Christ Jesus. No one serving as a soldier gets involved in civilian affairs—he wants to please his commanding officer. 2 Timothy 2:3, 4.

Spread What You Read

My husband, Rob, and I read a lot. We read to ourselves and out loud to each other. Sometimes when we're reading different things in the same room, we'll keep interrupting each other to read bits and pieces out loud. We can hardly wait to share what we've read because we think it will interest the other person.

That's what witnessing is, isn't it? Sharing? But it's easy to get a bit terrified of witnessing. I picture standing on the street corner handing out tracts or forcing myself to ask someone if they know about God in hopes that they'll want to hear. But witnessing doesn't have to be anything like that. Witnessing is just telling someone else about the great things God is doing for you.

Of course, there is a catch to witnessing. God has to be doing something in your life in order for you to tell other people about it. That's why it's so important to have a relationship with God. When you do, witnessing won't seem as scary. It'll be like sharing what you read with someone else. The only difference is that sharing Jesus is a lot more important.

He himself was not the light; he came only as a
witness to the light. The true light that gives light
to every man was coming into the world. John 1:8, 9.

God's Ticket

ouldn't it be nice if God gave you a ticket you could use whenever you were anxious about anything? You could ask God for an A on a test or safety when you fly to England for the exchange student program. Whatever you did, you could do it on God's ticket to safety and happiness so that everything would be sure to come out OK.

The trouble is that Christianity and prayer aren't tickets. They don't automatically protect us from bad stuff. If it were possible, everyone would do it. Christians would be the happiest and safest people on earth. But we all know that bad things happen to good people too. What matters more than what happens to us is what we make of it.

We can't put ourselves on God's ticket, because there isn't one. Instead we can put ourselves in God's will. That means that we are happy to let God decide where we will be and what we will be doing. If we do that, we'll be happy knowing that no matter where we are God is right there with us, no matter if it's sitting out a soccer game with a twisted ankle or receiving an award for helping other students.

For where two or three come together in
my name, there am I with them. Matthew 18:20.

Never Afraid

I wasn't always afraid of flying. I rode in very small planes a couple times when I was about your age. And when I was in high school, our drama club flew to New York City. After I realized that planes could crash, I started to be afraid of flying. Well, actually, afraid of crashing.

Most of the time during takeoff you can find me sitting bolt upright, my knuckles white, and my lips moving. "I will never be afraid; God is my rock . . ." Reminding myself that God is in control always makes me feel better. Once the plane is airborne I feel like I am riding in the palm of His hand.

Seeing the earth so far below with nothing but thin air between me and the ground, I get an awesome sense of what our earth looks like to God. I can understand how astronauts looking back on our earth, which seems to be the size of a large marble, are awestruck at the magnitude of our "little" universe.

One thing I know for sure: riding in the palm of God's hand, on earth or in the friendly skies above, is the safest place on earth to be. In God there is no fear.

Therefore we will not fear, though the earth give way and the mountains fall into the heart of the sea. Psalm 46:2.

Again and Again and Again

I watched Dan Jansen, the speed skater, when he competed at the 1994 Winter Olympics. I was sitting on the edge of my chair. This wasn't Dan Jansen's first trip to the Olympics. It was his fourth!

He was a top speed skater for years, but he failed to win a gold medal at his first Olympics. Or his second Olympics. I think the whole world cried with him when he had to skate only hours after hearing that his sister Jane had lost her battle with leukemia.

Dan Jansen didn't get a medal at his third Olympics either, but that didn't discourage him too badly. He tried again in the 1994 Winter Olympics. His best race was the 500 meters, but he didn't get the gold in that race. His last shot was the 1,000 meters. *This time he won the gold medal!* Dan Jansen finally triumphed. I don't think it mattered what nationality you were, you *had* to be happy for Dan Jansen.

God roots for us like that too. And when we fail He doesn't hold it against us. No matter how many times we confess the same sin, He always wants us to win the next time. He tosses our sins into oblivion, because all that really counts is our victories.

■ ■ ■ ■

As far as the east is from the west, so far has he removed our transgressions from us. Psalm 103:12.

Caged Birds and Other Captives

I read a story recently about a preacher who came to church one morning with an old, empty birdcage. He told his congregation that he had met a young boy the day before who had three frightened birds in a cage. The preacher asked the boy what he planned to do with the birds. "I'm going to play with them, pull out their feathers, and then I'm going to feed them to my cat."

When the preacher offered to buy the birds, the boy replied, "Aw, you don't want these old things. They can't even sing."

"How much?"

"Fifty bucks."

The preacher gave the money to the boy and promptly let the birds out of the cage.

The preacher told the congregation that morning, "One day Satan came out of the Garden of Eden, and he was tickled pink. 'I caught me a whole world of people,' he said.

"When Jesus asked him what he was going to do with them, Satan replied, 'I'll teach them how to hate and hurt and kill.'

"Jesus asked how much Satan wanted for them. 'You don't want them,' Satan said. 'They'd just hate you anyway.'

"Jesus asked again.

"'I want your whole life.'

"Jesus paid the price, opened the door, and set us free."

You are not your own; you were bought at a price. Therefore honor God with your body. 1 Corinthians 6:19, 20.

The Potatoes of Forgiveness

**A** woman told me how one of her teachers taught her how important it is to forgive people. The teacher asked her students to bring a clear plastic bag and some potatoes. For each person they felt they could not forgive, they were to take a potato, write the person's name on it, and put it in the bag. When they were done they had to carry the bag around with them wherever they went for a week—to school, to bed, at the dinner table, everywhere.

The woman said that the inconvenience of carrying around the heavy bag with her everywhere made her realize how much spiritual "weight" she was carrying around by not forgiving people. Also, the potatoes eventually became an icky, nasty, slimy mess. Pretty graphic description of unforgiveness, isn't it?

When we don't forgive someone, we hurt ourselves. We are the ones who have to carry it around with us. It gets nasty, and it's heavy. We spend a lot of energy watching over it if we refuse to let it go. Ask God today to show you if you are carrying around any potatoes you need to get rid of.

Be kind and compassionate to one another, forgiving each other, just as in Christ God forgave you. Ephesians 4:32.

Honest Scales

aria followed Julie through the lunch line. Her tray was loaded with great stuff. It was lasagna day in the cafeteria, and the chefs really knew how to cook. She held her tray out for some carrots and chose a dessert. She took out the $5 bill her mother had given her to pay for her lunch.

Maria handed the money to the woman at the checkout. The woman was distracted by some boys who were horsing around with their trays. "You boys, stop that now, or you'll end up in the principal's office."

The boys slunk away with guilty looks, and the woman at the checkout handed Maria $6 as change. Maria immediately realized that it was too much money. For a second she was tempted to keep it. *But,* she thought, *that wouldn't be honest.*

"You gave me too much change," she said, handing it back.

The woman's eyes widened. "Did I? Well, thank you, young lady. I appreciate your honesty."

Maria walked out of the line feeling much richer than if she had kept the money.

If I have walked in falsehood or my foot has hurried after deceit—let God weigh me in honest scales and he will know that I am blameless. Job 31:5, 6.

Hiding Out

avid knew a thing or two about battles. He had fought enough of them. He also knew something about hiding. He and his men had hidden from King Saul for a long time. It must have been pretty scary ducking around and running for their lives. I'm sure that they often felt alone and abandoned and unwanted during those hard years.

But even then God never abandoned David. He was with David, protecting him and keeping him from harm. God hid David so that Saul couldn't find him. David couldn't see God in person, and maybe he even felt as if God was nowhere to be found. But God was with him every step of the way. David hid in God. God was his refuge, something David wrote about in his psalms.

We don't have to be running from angry kings in order to hide in God. We might be tortured by insensitive kids at school, treated unfairly by stressed-out adults, or just feeling lonely. God *wants* us to come to Him for comfort. He wants to be our refuge. The hope He gives us for eternal life with Him is the ray of sunshine that will brighten any earthly day. So let the Son shine in!

■ ■ ■ ■

He said: "The Lord is my rock, my fortress and my deliverer;
my God is my rock, in whom I take refuge, my shield and
the horn of my salvation." 2 Samuel 22:2, 3.

Fashion Statement

I was a fashion disaster. I had no idea what colors matched (pink and green?). And I didn't know that stripes and plaids shouldn't be worn together. I didn't have many outfits to begin with, and the combinations I came up with got me some weird looks.

With the help of a fashion-conscious roommate I learned how to match my clothes so that I wasn't ever mistaken for a circus clown again. Eventually I even got some sense of fashion, and now, while I won't be asked to saunter down any runways, I do pretty well.

Sometimes we spend more time on what goes on the outside of us than what is on the inside. But people notice our insides too. In fact, they notice our insides more.

Have you ever met someone you thought was beautiful, but when you got to know that person you found out that he or she was rude, crude, and socially unacceptable? The person probably didn't seem so good-looking anymore. Then you met someone else who wasn't really good-looking, but who was kind, humble, and gentle. After you got to know the person, he or she seemed beautiful.

We can dress our outsides all we want. But if we don't keep the inside of us dressed nicely, we might as well wear purple plaids and orange stripes.

■ ■ ■ ■

Instead, it should be that of your inner self, the
unfading beauty of a gentle and quiet spirit, which
is of great worth in God's sight. 1 Peter 3:4.

Cake

I love the story about a little boy who hangs out in the kitchen with his grandmother. As he watches her make a cake, he complains about everything—school, his family, his health, everything. When he stops to take a breath, his grandmother asks him if he'd like a snack.

She offers him cooking oil (yuck), raw eggs (gross!), baking soda (are you kidding?), and flour. Finally the boy gives her "the look" and says, "Grandma, those things are all yucky."

His grandmother agrees with him. "By themselves, they all seem bad. But when you put them together in the right way, they make a delicious cake. God works the same way. Sometimes we wonder why He lets us go through such bad times, but even those difficult times can end up working for good. We should trust God, and in the end our lives will result in something wonderful."

■ ■ ■ ■

In this you greatly rejoice, though now for a little while you may have had to suffer grief in all kinds of trials. 1 Peter 1:6.

Flying the Plane

 was on an airplane not too long ago. After we had been in the air for a while, the pilot's voice came over the intercom. "Ladies and gentlemen, we have reached our cruising altitude of 30,000 feet. I'm going to switch over to autopilot now and take a nap. Anyone who feels qualified can come forward and take turns flying the aircraft."

Just kidding! And am I ever glad he *didn't* say that. I wouldn't want anyone unqualified flying the plane, even though it was only a short flight.

You and I are flying on the aircraft of life. And God is our pilot. He is flying the plane. Think about it. Every time we take over and start doing things our own way, we're flying the plane. Is it any wonder we have no peace?

If I decided to fly the plane, I would be a nervous wreck. I *know* I'm not qualified. I'd definitely crash. Maybe not immediately. But I *would* crash. And before I crashed, I'd be in for a really scary ride.

In the flight of your life, sit back, enjoy the ride, but leave the flying to God.

He will not let your foot slip—he who watches over you
will not slumber; indeed, he who watches over Israel
will neither slumber nor sleep. Psalm 121:3, 4.

Spiritual Vitamin

I try to take my vitamins. I know they're good for me. They keep me healthy. I feel better when I take vitamins. It's just that, well, I have a hard time swallowing them. So sometimes I "forget." And I feel guilty for a while. And then I get sick. And start taking them again.

Sometimes I treat God like a vitamin. It's hard to find time to spend with Him, even though I know I should. I know I'll feel better if I spend time with Him, and it would be easier to say no to Satan's temptations. But I get lazy, and before I know it I'm on the ground, wondering how I fell.

It's natural to turn to God when things are going badly. That's when we feel like we need Him most. But the truth is that we need God all the time. It's in the good times that He fills us up with the strength to stand up strong.

Just as I need to take my vitamins regularly, we also need to connect with God on a daily basis. And when we do so, our spiritual bodies will become healthy and strong.

■ ■ ■ ■

For in the day of trouble he will keep me safe in his dwelling; he will hide me in the shelter of his tabernacle and set me high upon a rock. Psalm 27:5.

My People

hen I was your age, the strangest hairdo a kid could have was a Mohawk—a spiky, purple, deadly looking Mohawk. Even a ponytail on a guy was considered weird. Girls were "over the top" if they had dark hair and put in dark purple highlights you could just barely see. *(And I'm not that old.)*

Things have changed a lot in the past 15 years. I know this because I was at a store the other day and saw a package of belly button tattoos. Of course, there are other huge clues. Lots of kids today could set off airport security with their piercings. You know the most interesting thing, though? Everyone who gets a tattoo or a piercing or who dyes their hair neon pink is doing it to be different. *But they're all doing the same thing!*

We're supposed to be God's people. We're supposed to be different. In the same way that tattoos and piercings will make you different but the same as everyone else, following God will make you one of His people. You can still be "different," but you will be unmistakably His. You won't even need a tattoo or flaming hair to prove it.

■ ■ ■ ■

I will put my law in their minds and write it on their hearts. I will be their God, and they will be my people. Jeremiah 31:33.

Onstage

he stage is in total darkness. Suddenly you see movement. A mime's whitened face and gloves appear. You can't see the rest of the mime because he is dressed completely in black. His body blends into the darkness of the stage, making it look as though his head and hands are floating around by themselves. A neon ball bounces onto the stage, and the white hands catch it. The mime performs tricks, takes a bow, and is gone.

It's funny onstage, but in real life and in the church, it's not so funny. Hands that aren't attached to the "body" of the church can't function as they should. A head that floats separately can think great thoughts but can't direct other body parts to get a job done.

God made each one of us unique with a special purpose in mind. But we should do our special jobs cooperating with the other members of the church "body." There we can receive the help we need to reach our potential. That's why unity is so important in the church. By working together, we demonstrate God's love and power to the world. The rest of the world is watching, offstage, the greatest drama in history.

*For we are God's workmanship, created in Christ Jesus
to do good works, which God prepared in advance
for us to do. Ephesians 2:10.*

To Will and to Do

But why can't I do that?" Josh whines.

Patiently I explain to him why he can't. Later I hear one of his friends asking him to do exactly the same thing, and Josh says, "No, I can't," and explains why. I beam with pride. Why? Because my son obeyed me, not just because I was watching, but even when he didn't think I was paying any attention.

Lots of people trust us. Parents trust us to obey them, whether we are with them or out of their sight. God trusts us to follow Him, even when things look bad and friends tease us. Law-enforcement officials trust us to obey the laws of our town and state. Teachers trust us to obey the school rules.

But trust can be broken easily. Only after it's broken can you really see how fragile it is and how hard it is to fix. By then it can be too late, and sometimes it can't be fixed at all. Trust is one of your most valuable possessions. Take good care of it.

■ ■ ■ ■

Therefore, my dear friends, as you have always obeyed—not only in my presence, but now much more in my absence—continue to work out your salvation with fear and trembling, for it is God who works in you to will and to act according to his good purpose. Philippians 2:12, 13.

The Presence of God

Frank Laubach was a missionary to the illiterate. He taught them how to read so they would be able to read the Bible. He traveled all over the world and was known in almost every land on earth while he was alive. He wrote more than 50 books and was a great teacher. The most important question Frank Laubach wanted to answer was this: Is it possible to have a conscious contact with God all the time?

He made his whole life an experiment to answer this one question. He didn't live by himself, and he was a very busy man, but his whole life was concentrated on that one question.

And do you know what? He *did* answer the question. Frank Laubach found that if he stayed in constant contact with God, it was as if an unseen hand prepared the way for him. He felt God's presence with him all the time. And sin disgusted him because he knew its power to drag him away from God's presence.

Even though Jesus was God Himself, He talked about having this same relationship with God the Father. Try Frank Laubach's experiment this week. See how long and how often you can stay in God's presence. You may never want to come away!

I am in the Father and the Father is in me. John 14:11.

MPTY-11

Grungy Grudges

Grudges are sneaky little critters. You might even forget about them until one day, *wham!* They pounce on you, and you realize you've been keeping a grudge and didn't even know it!

You might not realize it, but grudges eat a lot of your energy. They also take up room. They like dark corners and creepy spaces, so you can't let a lot of light in either. You might get some joy, but since grudges don't get along with joy, you'll have to get rid of one or the other.

You can rid your life of grudges forever. You don't have to put up with the unwanted pests. The best way to get rid of a grudge is not to let one in your house. You can do this by taking care of problems when they happen and not letting them fester and grow into grudges.

To get rid of grudges you already have, drag the little beggars into the light and tell them to take a hike. Spray them with some prayer, and soon your whole house will smell fresh. Then you'll be able to take in all the joy you want.

If anyone says, "I love God," yet hates his brother, he is a liar. For anyone who does not love his brother, whom he has seen, cannot love God, whom he has not seen. 1 John 4:20.

The King and the Servant

ne of the king's subjects stole some of the silver one day as he was walking through the royal kitchen. Eventually the king found out and called the thieving servant to the royal throne room. The servant entered with shaking knees and threw himself down in front of the king.

"I beg forgiveness from the bottom of my heart," the servant wailed. "I don't know what came over me. Please forgive me."

"You are forgiven," the king said.

A week later the king was rudely awakened. The servant he had forgiven was in his room.

"What is it?" the king asked sleepily.

"Please forgive me," the servant begged.

"I've already forgiven you," the king reminded him.

This continued week after week until the king was worn out. "Look," he said wearily. "I forgave you once for stealing the silver. That is all that was necessary. Now forgive yourself so I can have a little peace."

God's forgiveness is complete. We don't have to beg for it, and we don't have to harass Him for it. We simply have to ask and then accept. The most perfect forgiveness won't mean a thing unless we forgive ourselves.

O you who hear prayer, to you all men will come.
When we were overwhelmed by sins, you
forgave our transgressions. Psalm 65:2, 3.

Payback

aman wanted revenge. He wanted it so badly he could taste it. He'd fix that Mordecai and fix him good. Imagine! Refusing to bow down to a regal person such as himself! Haman thought long and hard about all the ways he could get even with Mordecai. In the end death seemed like the only thing good enough for Mordecai.

Haman concocted an elaborate plan to kill not only Mordecai but all of the Jews. This would have included the queen, Esther. The Jews would all die by the sword except for Mordecai. For Mordecai there was a special gallows built. Mordecai would hang, and Haman would watch.

But revenge doesn't often end up the way we plan it. It sure didn't for Haman. Instead of Mordecai hanging from the gallows, Haman was the one who was hung. In our puny human way we like to think we can make people pay when they hurt us.

But the truth is that revenge is in God's hands. It doesn't belong to us. We need to leave the job to Him. If Haman had done that, he might have lived to tell about it.

Make sure that nobody pays back wrong
for wrong, but always try to be kind to each
other and to everyone else. 1 Thessalonians 5:15.

The Whole Truth and Nothing But

Are you awake? I want to ask you a very deep question. Ready? What is truth?

In Rutland we have a beautiful old theater that has been restored. Not too long ago I got to hear Josh McDowell, a Christian leader, speak there. I sat smack dab in the middle of the balcony. It was great.

But what he said was frightening. He said that people today believe that everyone has their own truth. In other words, there is no such thing as one absolute truth. If it's true for you, then it's true.

But that isn't true!

As Christians we're lucky to have the Bible and know what the truth is. Jesus said that He is the truth. If we measure everything by Jesus, we'll know what is truth and what isn't. We won't be the way Paul described, "like children, forever changing our minds about what we believe because someone has told us something different, or has cleverly lied to us" (Ephesians 4:14, TLB).

Instead we'll be able to measure every one of Satan's lies with Jesus' truth. Satan's lies will fall short because we *have* the truth. Now all we have to do is walk with it.

Jesus answered, "I am the way and the truth and the life. No one comes to the Father except through me." John 14:6.

God's Lap

ietrich Bonhoeffer was a young German pastor who joined the resistance in World War II. He was murdered by the Nazis, hanged in the concentration camp in Flossenbürg, Bavaria, on April 9, 1945, with the Americans only miles away.

He said, "I believe that God can and wants to create good out of everything, even evil. For that He needs people who use everything for the best. I believe that God provides us with as much strength to resist in every calamity as we need. But He does not give it in advance, so that we trust Him alone. In such a trust all anxiety about the future must be overcome."

In the suffering of people we can sometimes see what is possible for Christians to achieve when they are really depending on God the way they should. You know, when life is pretty good, God is like a chair we rest on when we are tired. But when things are going bad, God is the chair we collapse on and don't want to get off.

If we are constantly resting in God, we'll be in the perfect place to handle anything. We'll be sitting on God's lap.

■ ■ ■ ■

Look to the Lord and his strength; seek his face
always. Remember the wonders he has done, his miracles,
and the judgments he pronounced. Psalm 105:4, 5.

Practice Your Patience

I admit patience is not one of my virtues. In fact, it's barely in my vocabulary. In this world of McMoments it comes in handy that almost everything I want is available drive-thru, to go, express delivered, or one click away. The only thing wrong with this is that my patience, instead of getting bigger, gets smaller and smaller.

And this is a problem. Because patience is a virtue I'd like to have, wouldn't you? Patient people are secure, happy to rest while waiting, and sure of the final outcome. They are content and peaceful. Come to think of it, they have a whole lot going for them.

You and I can have all that too. First, we should start by asking Jesus for patience. Jesus is the very definition of patience. He "is the same yesterday and today and forever" (Hebrews 13:8).

Second, we can practice patience deliberately by doing some things the hard way rather than the easy way. Stand in a long line, or walk to a friend's instead of getting a ride. There are lots of ways to practice your patience. And it'll get easier as you go along.

Better a patient man than a warrior, a man who controls his temper than one who takes a city. Proverbs 16:32.

Gross Me Out

y friend Michele told me a gross story. Are you ready for this? Her pastor was saying that you have a choice. You can grow in a healthy way that will please God or in bad ways that please yourself. You can grow one way or the other, but you can't grow both ways.

She said it's like walking along a pretty country lane as a new person in God because you're His child. Slowly you're changing into the person He wants you to be.

All of a sudden you smell this awful smell. You walk over to the ditch and see a body lying there. It's your old dead self, the person you were before you met God.

What if you jumped into the ditch and started hugging the old thing? Yuck, you say. You're right, but every time we choose to do what we want even though it's not what God wants, it's like hugging the smelly old body.

So the next time you're walking along minding your own business and you smell something funky, run in the other direction.

■ ■ ■ ■

For we know that our old self was crucified with him so that the body of sin might be done away with, that we should no longer be slaves to sin—because anyone who has died has been freed from sin. Romans 6:6, 7.

Growing Together

Every now and then I come across something in nature that is extremely bizarre. One time I saw a tree that had grown totally around a rock.

Another time it was a tree that kept growing in spite of the barbed wire someone had strung around it when it was much smaller. The tree grew right over the wire.

Of course, these didn't happen overnight. Slowly, over time, because they were so close, the two objects grew together. No matter what, you can't separate these trees from the things that have fused into them.

When we grow with Jesus, it is the same way. We might start out as two separate beings: Jesus and us. But over time we become fused together so that nothing can ever separate us. Like the rock and the tree we become a fantastic sculpture that amazes everyone. People will see us molded to Jesus. They will stop and say, "Wow, I never knew a life could look like that!"

For I am convinced that neither death nor life, neither angels nor demons, neither the present nor the future, nor any powers, neither height nor depth, nor anything else in all creation, will be able to separate us from the love of God that is in Christ Jesus our Lord. Romans 8:38, 39.

You Can Quote Me

Have you ever quoted anyone? Chances are you have.

I quote people all the time when I write. I'm not sure if anyone has ever quoted me, but I came up with a great quote just in case someone ever wants to. "If you want to know the value of skin, don't ask a model. Ask a burn patient."

The value of something is determined by what it is worth. To a model, the value of skin is in his or her ability to look great. It has nothing to do with the ability to get out of bed in the morning, go outside and enjoy life, or even touch someone else.

But to a burn patient, skin is the difference between life and death. Skin is the body's first defense against disease. Without skin there is nothing to hold muscles and organs inside the body.

And *that* is how you can tell the value of something, by how much it is worth, truly worth. Worth is based on need, not on want. There are qualities that we desire, such as straight teeth, beauty, a sense of humor, or knowledge. And then there are qualities that we need, such as honesty, patience, love, and wisdom.

Be sure you value the right things. They will never disappoint you.

■ ■ ■ ■

Kings take pleasure in honest lips; they value a man who speaks the truth. Proverbs 16:13.

Here's a Secret

Shhhhhh. Come closer. I want to tell you a secret.

Did you know that the secrets we hide away are powerful? When we have bad secrets, things about us that we don't want others to find out, we are always on our guard. We have to be constantly aware of what we say so that we don't give ourselves away. It's an agonizing struggle that takes its toll.

On the other hand, a secret can be a powerful tool for good. If we have good things hidden in our hearts, such as God's Word, we'll have the power to be strong during times of temptation. Jesus advised His followers to go away by themselves and to pray in secret. He promised that God, who sees what is done in secret, would reward them.

Our secrets will eventually show up in our lives. It will be easy to see whether they are good secrets or bad secrets. It's like planting seeds. You can plant weeds or vegetables. The seeds are hidden, but sooner or later it's going to be obvious to everyone what you planted.

Make the right choice. Be sure to plant good secrets in your heart.

But when you pray, go into your room, close the door and pray to your Father, who is unseen. Then your Father, who sees what is done in secret, will reward you. Matthew 6:6.

Pass the Potatoes, Please

OK, without cheating, being perfectly honest, how would you rate yourself in terms of popularity, looks, and personality compared to, say, your best friend? Now how about compared to that girl (or boy) that sits behind you in math class and has bad breath? Now how about compared to Britney Spears (or Leonardo DiCaprio)?

Ahhh, you see, I tricked you. How we rate is all a matter of comparison. Compared to our close friends we may do all right. Compared to the people we consider geeks we look great. But compared with movie stars, singers, and athletes we're the last thing on the menu. Whenever we start comparing ourselves to others we'll always come out on both ends of the scale.

The bad news is that we rate each other all the time: good, bad, ugly, talented, popular, dumb. The good news is that the only thing that really matters is what God thinks of us, and He cares about our insides. We can all reflect God, no matter how smart or good-looking or popular we are, and even if we feel as appealing as leftover mashed potatoes, we'll look like a million bucks in His eyes.

■ ■ ■ ■

You are the ones who justify yourselves in the eyes
of men, but God knows your hearts. What is highly
valued among men is detestable in God's sight. Luke 16:15.

It Is Well With My Soul

oratio G. Spafford's life seemed to go from bad to worse, but through it all he held on to God. He had a successful law practice in Chicago but still had an active interest in spiritual affairs. He and his wife, Anna, had four girls and a boy, but the boy died when he was very young. Later Horatio invested heavily in real estate. But Mrs. O'Leary's cow kicked over a lantern to start the great Chicago fire, and Horatio lost everything.

Booking passage on the luxury steamer S.S. *Ville du Havre,* the Spaffords planned to sail to England for a break. When Horatio was detained, his family sailed without him. In the middle of the Atlantic, the ship was rammed and sank in 12 minutes. Only 47 people were saved. Anna cabled two heartbreaking words to her husband: "Saved alone."

Horatio immediately set out to join her. As he stood at the rail looking down on the billowing waves over the spot where his daughters had drowned, he wrote the words to the hymn that has comforted so many hurting people:

> When peace, like a river, attendeth my way,
> When sorrows like sea billows roll—
> Whatever my lot, Thou hast taught me to say,
> It is well, it is well with my soul.*

---

*Horatio G. Spafford, "It Is Well," *The Seventh-day Adventist Hymnal,* No. 530.

***You will keep in perfect peace him whose mind
is steadfast, because he trusts in you. Isaiah 26:3.***

With Wings as Eagles

ot far from my house is a great spot that hang gliders like. They climb way up to the top and jump into thin air. Circling near the peak, they seem to soar effortlessly, like colorful feathers. On beautiful days there are so many hang gliders that the sky is dotted thickly.

If you look very closely, sometimes you can see that they are not alone up there. Soaring along with the hang gliders are hawks. They perform a circular airborne dance with the hang gliders, twirling around and around, coming closer and then falling away. It's fascinating to watch.

I've listened to biologists explain just how it is that the birds (and the hang gliders, for that matter) stay up in the air like that, but I'd really rather just imagine what it must feel like. It looks so effortless. The birds just spread their wings, and the wind holds them up.

We need to learn that concept in our walk with Jesus. At some point all our knowledge about Christianity is just knowledge. In the end we have to step off the cliff, spread our wings, and fly with Jesus, trusting Him to hold us up.

But those who hope in the Lord will renew their strength.
They will soar on wings like eagles; they will run and
not grow weary, they will walk and not be faint. Isaiah 40:31.

Joy Juice

I haven't had a cat for very long. Mittens came to us as a barn cat and by mutual agreement decided to stay on indefinitely. Cats are, well, they're different than dogs. A dog wants to be with you all the time, sleeping at your feet, if possible, and drooling into your slippers. A cat, on the other hand, can take you or leave you.

But what strikes me most about cats is their purr. When I pet a cat, a rumble starts up. After we had Mittens for a while, we thought we should have named him Evinrude (after the outboard motor). Even though cats don't purr all the time, you always *know* the purr is in there, just waiting to come out.

Joy is like that. We have joy in us because we belong to Jesus. He is coming for us soon. He loves us. He saved us. That makes the joy that's in us that will never go away. Happiness brings out the purr, but even when we aren't happy, we need to remember that the joy Jesus gave us isn't gone. It's like a purr, waiting for something to bring it out again.

■ ■ ■ ■

I am coming to you now, but I say these things while I am still in the world, so that they may have the full measure of my joy within them. John 17:13.

Believe It or Not

Every now and then I am asked to have the children's story in church. It's great. All those serious little eyes, staring at you as if you are about to snatch a rabbit out of a hat. One of my favorite stories is one that I read to them from a picture book.

It's a great story in itself, but the point I am making is that you can't believe everything you read. For instance, in this story the author is portraying Jesus as an artist who made the earth and everything in it. Neat concept, huh? Until she gets to the part about how Jesus makes two people and then a third.

Hello? In my Bible it says He made two people period.

Before I tell the story, I warn the kids that I'm going to ask them to point out the mistake, and they usually can. But if we had never read the Bible, we wouldn't know that the story was wrong.

Now, that particular story isn't going to hurt too much if I believed every word. But Satan has plenty of other lies that can hurt very much. Only if we know the truth will we know when someone is trying to pass off a mistake.

Test everything. Hold on to the good. Avoid
every kind of evil. 1 Thessalonians 5:21, 22.

You're History

One of the things I like to do for fun is dress up like a French woman who lived in the eighteenth century. I have to wear "jumps," a bodice which is laced up so tightly that it is hard to bend over to pick things up. Then there are petticoats (skirts) and lots of them! They go down to my ankles, and they're heavy to carry around and hot during the summer.

Everything was different in the eighteenth century. People cooked differently, dressed differently, wrote differently, and worked differently. Learning about this stuff from a history book is very different from pretending to live it now. You understand it a lot better when you live it yourself.

That's one reason it's so important for us to have tolerance for others. Because we don't know all the circumstances, we can't judge them. And if we have been in their circumstances, we should be the first to help, because we've been there too. Our history can give them a future. This is what the Bible calls compassion. And it's timeless.

This is what the Lord Almighty says: "Administer true justice; show mercy and compassion to one another. Do not oppress the widow or the fatherless, the alien or the poor. In your hearts do not think evil of each other." Zechariah 7:9, 10.

Say Cheese!

I decided that I wanted to learn how to develop pictures, so I took a class in photography and darkroom techniques. It was held at a high school in the evenings. I went after work. The instructor gave us loads of hand-rolled film, taught us how to load it, tried to teach us how to shoot it, and set us loose on the unsuspecting world.

My friend Susan and I shot roll after roll, but the part we couldn't wait for was learning how to develop the pictures we had shot. Finally the big day came, and we were allowed into the darkroom to process our film. We exposed the paper and put it in the chemical bath to process. Nothing happened. Then slowly, slowly, an image began to form on the paper. It seemed to take forever, but finally it was a fully formed picture.

Sometimes it seems like it's taking an awfully long time for us to reflect the image of God. But just like processing pictures in a darkroom, it takes time. In the beginning it even seems too incredible to happen. Then slowly God's image will appear in us, and everyone will gather around to see it.

And just as we have borne the likeness of the earthly man, so shall we bear the likeness of the man from heaven. 1 Corinthians 15:49.

Into the Light

hen I was in academy I got to go on a field trip because I wrote for the school newspaper. The trip was to a college.

My friend Diane and I decided to go to bed early, and we headed out across the campus toward our dorm room. It was pitch black. We couldn't see our hands if we held them in front of our faces.

Clutching each other, we tried to stagger up the road. We went crashing off the road, got slapped by bushes, and finally managed to scramble back onto the road. We were terrified that we would get lost and not be able to find our way back. There wasn't a light anywhere. Somehow we made it back to the dorm.

I don't remember anything else about the trip, but I remember that very clearly because it scared me so much. If your life is in the dark, ask for light. God will flood your life with it. The bushes can't slap you across the face if you know where they are.

■ ■ ■ ■

Everyone who does evil hates the light, and will not come into the light for fear that his deeds will be exposed. But whoever lives by the truth comes into the light, so that it may be seen plainly that what he has done has been done through God. John 3:20, 21.

Rules of the Game

Let's say that the day you picked up this devotional you read a list of rules I posted at the beginning:

1. Send me $10 a month.
2. Write an essay about what you learn from each devotional.
3. Whistle "Jesu, Joy of Man's Desiring" before you read a devotional.

You'd say to yourself, "I don't have to do them if I don't want to."

But let's say that you and I were good friends. And I explained that I was going to send the $10 to feed starving children, that your essays were going to be entered into a contest for a big prize, and that "Jesu, Joy of Man's Desiring" is my favorite tune. Would you be more willing to obey my rules?

It goes like this: Rules – Relationship = Rebellion.

It works that way with God too. If we don't have a relationship with Him, we aren't going to want to obey His commands. We have to fall in love with God first. Then we'll want to do whatever will make Him happy.

■ ■ ■ ■

If you fear the Lord and serve and obey him and do not rebel against his commands, and if both you and the king who reigns over you follow the Lord your God—good! 1 Samuel 12:14.

Thinking About Vacation

eadlines are hard. I have to deal with them all the time. You probably do too. You have deadlines for assignments (maybe you call them due dates) and deadlines for signing up for things. Everything has a time limit attached to it. Do it before, or else. The pressure can be hard to take.

When I get really stressed out, I think about vacation. This will be the second year I take a vacation with my family. We spend a whole week at a cabin in the Adirondack Mountains.

If I concentrate hard enough, I can smell the balsam in the air and hear the loons calling. I feel the canoe rocking gently beneath me, and I feel the water stirring as a big muskie rises to the surface. Yep, I almost believe that if I open my eyes, I'll be there.

Even better than vacation is concentrating on heaven and on Jesus. We're always going to have worries and problems, but we don't need to focus on them. We can think about spiritual things instead. When we do that, the earthly problems can't grab onto us. If your problems are more than you can take, think about heaven and earthly annoyances will go slip-sliding away.

Set your minds on things above,
not on earthly things. Colossians 3:2.

Search Me

he alarm buzzed fiercely, and Maria groaned in her sleep. Morning already. She reached over and slapped the alarm off. Before she could talk herself into a few more winks, she rolled out of bed and rubbed her eyes. She sat at her desk and swallowed a yawn.

Bowing her head, she prayed, "Lord, thank You for giving me another day of life. Please help me to understand Your words. Thank You for loving me and for helping me with my problems. Please keep me strong, and help me to resist the desires I still have sometimes to cheat. Show me what Your will is for my life, and help me to do it. Thank You. Amen."

It was the fifth morning that week that Maria had gotten up early to study her Bible, do her Sabbath school lesson, and read her devotional. She felt as though it was her special time with God when He could tell her what He wanted for her life. The more she met with Him, the more she wanted to. She opened her Bible, eager to see what He wanted to say to her that morning.

Search me, O God, and know my heart; test me and know
my anxious thoughts. See if there is any offensive way
in me, and lead me in the way everlasting. Psalm 139:23, 24.

Thrills, Chills, and Spills

his winter we had a couple feet of snow. We took the kids outside to slide in the dark. At night when the ground is covered with snow, it's surprisingly light. Rachel wanted to ride with me, and since I'd never learned how to steer properly, we careened down the hill at great speeds, shrieking and laughing. At the bottom we'd spill out of the sled and trek back to the top to do it again. I hope my kids never forget our nighttime sledding.

It's important for us, as Christians, to have fun. One of Satan's most powerful tricks is to get us to believe that nothing should be fun and that we should never, under any circumstances, enjoy ourselves.

The crazy thing is that all the wonderful things we enjoy (sunsets, friends, nature, singing) were created for us by God. Satan didn't invent one fun thing (death? war? sickness?). If he can't get us to believe all fun is wrong, then he tries to get us to have so much fun that it becomes wrong because we overdo it.

In life God is the host, and Satan is a party crasher. Don't let him rain on your parade.

Shout with joy to God, all the earth! Sing the glory of his name; make his praise glorious! Psalm 66:1, 2.

Mission Possible

OK, so maybe you don't hear their chains clinking around when they walk, but each of us knows someone who isn't a Christian. In fact, we probably know several someones. They could be people in our own families, friends at school, or people we meet every day in whatever we do. They have one thing in common: they're prisoners.

What are you going to do about it? Yes, you. If all those people were walking around with *real* chains that you could see, wouldn't you want to help them out if you could? If you had a key, wouldn't you set them all free? You can! You have the key to unlock their chains and give them freedom. You know Jesus, and you can share Him with them.

I'm not talking about preaching at them. Most people would rather see a sermon than hear one. Not all sermons have words; the best ones have kind actions. Being a Christian is more than something that you talk about; it's something that you live. Make sure your actions speak loud and clear.

The Spirit of the Sovereign Lord is on me, because the Lord has anointed me to preach good news to the poor. He has sent me to bind up the brokenhearted, to proclaim freedom for the captives and release from darkness for the prisoners. Isaiah 61:1.

Knowing God

fter reading this book you probably know a little bit about me, even though you never knew me before. You wouldn't make airplane noises around me or scare a horse I was riding. You know about my family and pets. You even know that I don't like to let people borrow my books. How do you know? Because I told you.

But what if you hadn't read this book and someone had told you about me? Would you believe them? How would you know they were telling the truth? They might tell you that not only do I fly, but I jump out of airplanes for fun. They might tell you I have four dogs because they don't know my wolf dog passed away.

Knowing God is important. But we need to get our information directly from the source. I can tell you about God. Your parents can tell you about God. Your pastor can tell you about God. And we might all be 100 percent accurate. But *you'll* never know for sure until *you* get to know Him personally.

■ ■ ■ ■

"No longer will a man teach his neighbor, or a man his brother, saying, 'Know the Lord,' because they will all know me, from the least of them to the greatest," declares the Lord. Jeremiah 31:34.

Had Your Hug?

y friend Ginger likes hugs. In fact, she believes she needs them to keep her healthy. She carries buttons around with her when she travels, and if you hug her, she'll give you a button.

Experts agree with her. The standard rule of thumb is that you need four hugs a day for survival, eight hugs a day just to keep you feeling good, and 12 a day if you want to grow. That's a lot of hugging!

On the cross Jesus stretched out His arms to hug the whole human race. When we follow His example of giving ourselves for others, we might just find out that we get back as much or more than we give. After all, you can't give a hug without getting a hug. But remember always to ask permission before you give someone a hug, and to respect his or her wishes.

Before you do anything today, give your parents a hug. Now get started on the rest of the 12 you need!

■ ■ ■ ■

But while he was still a long way off, his father saw him and was filled with compassion for him; he ran to his son, threw his arms around him and kissed him. Luke 15:20.

The Story of Us

You have a story. I have a story. We all have stories about how we became Christians. Maybe you don't think your story is spectacular. Maybe God didn't save you from a horrible death, or you weren't saved by an obscure missionary in the jungles of Africa. But your story, no matter how thrilling or how dull, is a slice of the gospel. It can help someone who is struggling to break free from their chains.

Maybe your story is about why you are still a Christian or about your walk with God and what He's doing in your life. Whatever it is, it is your story to tell. And stories are meant to be shared. That's how they change people.

Jesus was a great storyteller. He grabbed people's attention with His stories. By telling stories to the people, He changed their lives.

Share your story, and watch what God can do with it. You will be amazed at how He can change lives if you are willing to tell people how He has walked with you and what He has taught you.

He said to them, "Go into all the world and preach the good news to all creation. Whoever believes and is baptized will be saved, but whoever does not believe will be condemned." Mark 16:15, 16.

No Bananas

here is an old song I like called "Yes, We Have No Bananas."

Short history lesson: before CDs there were cassette tapes; before cassette tapes, vinyl records (and eight-track tapes); and before *that* there were thick records played on record players called a Victrola that you had to crank up. (Before that there was singing.)

It took me years, but I finally found a record of the "No Bananas" song. Every now and then I dig it out and play it on my Victrola. We even named our canoe *No Bananas.*

Not that we have anything against bananas, you understand; it's just a cute joke. We really like bananas (really we do). But you have to be careful with them.

Have you ever noticed that if one banana in a bunch starts to go, the rest will rot quickly? All the good bananas aren't enough to stop the rotting process. It's the same way with any bad influence. If we get too close to it, we can be sure it will affect us. Don't let a rotten banana ruin your bunch.

Your boasting is not good. Don't you know that a little yeast works through the whole batch of dough? Get rid of the old yeast that you may be a new batch without yeast—as you really are. 1 Corinthians 5:6, 7.

Barkis Is Willin'

ttitude is everything. Your attitude affects your whole life. If you go around convinced that everyone is out to get you and nothing will go right, then that's what you'll find. But if you expect the best from people and you believe that all things are possible, opportunities will open up for you that you can only dream about right now.

It can be hard to keep a good attitude when we don't feel very cheerful or optimistic. God is willing to help us to rely on Him and to tap into the joy we have inside us if we want Him to. We just have to be willing.

In Charles Dickens' story about David Copperfield, one of the characters, Mr. Barkis, decides he wants to marry the lovely Peggotty. He sends a message by young David to let her know. The message is simple: "Barkis is willin'." And his attitude earns him a fine wife.

Ellen White says, "Of ourselves, we are not able to bring the purposes and desires and inclinations into harmony with the will of God; but if we are 'willing to be made willing,' the Saviour will accomplish this for us."*

Barkis was "willin'"; are you?

---

*The Acts of the Apostles, p. 482.

■ ■ ■ ■

*Restore to me the joy of your salvation and grant
me a willing spirit, to sustain me. Psalm 51:12.*

The Rest of the Story

A magazine I write for publishes the most embarrassing moments of famous people. Because I often get to interview celebrities, I always ask them what their most embarrassing moment was in case it's good enough to be published.

I hear stories like when Carman accidentally brushed his teeth with muscle rub just before a meet-and-greet after a concert. Talk about minty fresh!

And then there was the time Cammi Granato (captain of the women's hockey team at the Olympics) skated to the middle of the rink and fell flat on her face in front of celebrities, professional hockey players, and 7,000 screaming (and laughing) fans.

We smile at these things and are glad they never happened to us, but we don't think much about the rest of the story. There's always more. These people learned to laugh at themselves and didn't let a mistake ruin their life.

We all make mistakes, and they can be very embarrassing. If we let them keep us from trying something new, the story ends there. But remember what they say: "Laughter is the best medicine." Even when you are laughing at yourself.

■ ■ ■ ■

But the Lord provided a great fish to swallow Jonah, and Jonah was inside the fish three days and three nights. Jonah 1:17.

Beach Glass

A couple weeks ago we went to the banks of Lake Champlain, not far from where I grew up. Maybe you've heard of our monster? He's called Champ. No joke.

Cryptozoologists believe the "creature" might be a plesiosaur, a type of underwater reptile from prehistoric times. Others think it might be a large lake sturgeon. Champ has been sighted since 1609 when Samuel de Champlain, the explorer the lake is named for, wrote about a creature he described as a 20-foot serpent as thick as a barrel with a head like a horse.

We didn't see Champ, but we did find beach glass. We love this stuff. You've probably seen it. At the ocean it's called sea glass. Small shards of glass, rubbed against the rocks and sand, are buffed. Their sharp edges are made smooth, and people collect them for their unique beauty.

It takes time for the glass to become smooth, just as it takes time for God to smooth our characters. But when He's done, we will look like colorful treasures on the beach of life.

■ ■ ■ ■

Prepare the way for the Lord, make straight paths for him.
Every valley shall be filled in, every mountain and hill made
low. The crooked roads shall become straight, the rough ways
smooth. And all mankind will see God's salvation. Luke 3:4-6.

Burden Bearers

hen my husband, Rob, and I need to move our 14-foot canoe, we do it together. He can lift it alone if he wants to, but it's easier for him if we share the load. I can't move the canoe by myself, so working together makes it possible for me to move the canoe from the truck to the water and back again.

Any burden is easier to carry when we share it with someone else. Whether they hold onto part of it or just support us as we carry it, either way it will be lighter. We will go farther with help than we can possibly go by ourselves.

You can help carry other people's burdens. Sometimes all it takes is being willing to listen to them talk about their problems. You don't have to offer advice. Just listen. If there is something you can do to help, offer to do what you can. And instead of just telling your friend you will pray for them, do it. Pray for them *with* them.

Everyone has burdens. You can help this time. Next time it might be you who needs someone to lean on. If we all help each other, we'll be able to get through anything.

■ ■ ■ ■

Carry each other's burdens, and in this way
you will fulfill the law of Christ. Galatians 6:2.

Pigeon and the Blackbirds

I t was my birthday. My sister Faith and I were walking on Church Street in Burlington. As we headed into Banana Republic we saw a baby pigeon. It was so small that it didn't have its flight feathers. All it could do was waddle away from us.

We immediately thought, *It's fallen from its nest and will starve to death!* Later I found out that a baby bird's parents will continue to feed it after it falls out of the nest, but at the time I was ignorant.

So I caught it, brought it home, and raised it. Eventually it flew away and joined a flock of blackbirds because there were no pigeons near our house. Talk about strange. Here was a flock of blackbirds and one pigeon.

The pigeon (we called him Pigeon) acted like a blackbird. He did all the things blackbirds do, even though he wasn't a blackbird. I guess even birds want to be accepted by their peers.

The trick is to make good decisions about which peers to hang out with. Be picky about it. Choose people who act the way you want to act, because you *will* act like them eventually.

He who walks with the wise grows wise,
but a companion of fools suffers harm. Proverbs 13:20.

Mission Statement

I might have made this up, but one of my favorite sayings is "If you don't know where you're going, that's exactly where you're going to end up."

Going through life without goals is like trying to hit a target when you are blindfolded. How can you hit something you can't see? You can't assume that if you just live, you will automatically live in a way that pleases God. First, you have to know what would please God. And then you have to plan your life around that.

A mission statement puts into writing what you intend to do. It lists your goals and what steps you plan to take to achieve them. For example, if you had a mission statement, part of it might be to know more scriptures, and your plan could be to memorize a verse every week.

This week, write your own mission statement. With goals in front of you, it will be easier to stay on God's track all the way to the finish line.

Make it your ambition to lead a quiet life, to mind your own business and to work with your hands, just as we told you, so that your daily life may win the respect of outsiders and so that you will not be dependent on anybody. 1 Thessalonians 4:11, 12.

Let Us Pray

I love fall, when the leaves turn beautiful shades of red, orange, and yellow. In the back of my mind I know that they are dying, but they certainly are beautiful.

I love snow too, even though it is so cold. You really have to respect it because it can be deadly. These are probably not things that Adam would have enjoyed. The death of the leaves to him was probably devastating, and the bitter cold was probably like a slap in the face when he remembered Eden.

Things aren't always as we see them. I look at the leaves, and I see beauty. God looks at them and sees beauty and death.

It's the same when we pray. We don't always know what to pray for. Sometimes we pray for the wrong things. Selfishly we feel that if we get what we want, it won't hurt anyone else. But only God knows what is best for *everyone*.

That's why when we pray, it's important for us to put ourselves in His will. He will tell us what to pray for. He can see it like it is.

■ ■ ■ ■

In the same way, the Spirit helps us in our weakness. We do not know what we ought to pray for, but the Spirit himself intercedes for us with groans that words cannot express. Romans 8:26.

Who, Me?

What happens when you listen to the Holy Spirit? Lots of things. When Philip listened, he ended up hitching a ride on a chariot and explaining the Scripture to an Ethiopian eunuch. This would be like you accepting a ride from, say, Michael Jordan, in his limo. Imagine trying to get past your shock and saying something, *anything*.

Philip did. But first he listened, and then he started where the eunuch was at. Philip told him the story of Jesus so that the eunuch could understand it.

We might know staggering amounts of information about Jesus and be able to recite pages of Scripture, but if we don't listen to people and try to help them with the problems they have, everything we know is going to do them no good.

Everyone who has a relationship with Jesus should help those who don't. From my 6-year-old son telling his friend that he has to obey his mom, to the person who helps in a soup kitchen.

Ask yourself: How can I help? What can I do? And listen, because the Holy Spirit will tell you. After that, the possibilities are endless.

So he started out, and on his way he met an Ethiopian eunuch, an important official in charge of all the treasure of Candace, queen of the Ethiopians. Acts 8:27.

Step Aside

he first time I spoke, it was in front of hundreds of kids. I was paralyzed with fear. I had two options: speak or faint. I decided to speak. I could always faint later. Somehow I got through the weekend and lived long enough to be asked to speak again. And again. And again.

Eventually I figured out that writing is different than speaking, and if I ever wanted to succeed in front of an audience, I had to give up control (which for me meant not reading my speech). I had to get out of the way and let God control what came out of my mouth in the same way I let Him control what my fingers type when I write. This is scary for me, but I did it, and my speaking improved.

When you have to do something that scares you, remember this: you might fail, but God will never fail. If you step aside and let God work through you, what He wants to accomplish will be done.

■ ■ ■ ■

In all my prayers for all of you, I always pray with joy because of your partnership in the gospel from the first day until now, being confident of this, that he who began a good work in you will carry it on to completion until the day of Christ Jesus. Philippians 1:4-6.

Flaming Arrows

I f I had to go into battle, I'd want a shield like the kind the Romans carried. It was big enough to cover your whole body, which made it hard for anyone to hit you with anything. Also, they had this great trick of standing shoulder to shoulder and putting their shields up to make a wall that protected all of them at the same time. Smart move. In that way they could advance on the enemy, and any arrows shot at them would bounce harmlessly off their shields.

Being a lone soldier offers some protection, but being with a group of other soldiers offers more. It's the same with Christianity. In our spiritual battles God will protect us, even if we are alone. But if we stand with other Christians, we will have not only their support, but their protection, too.

That's why it's important to stick close to your Christian friends and the people at your church. You may not always agree with them on everything, but we're all in the same war together, fighting a common enemy. We need all the protection we can get. Take your stand with the people on your side.

■ ■ ■ ■

In addition to all this, take up the shield of faith, with which you can extinguish all the flaming arrows of the evil one. Ephesians 6:16.

Blind Side

Shortly after I got my license I had a fire-engine-red motor scooter, which is a cross between a motorcycle and a moped. I rode that thing everywhere.

One night when I was riding down a major road in Essex, I decided to make a left-hand turn. I glanced in my rearview mirror, didn't see anything near me, stuck my arm out, and zipped into the left lane.

The next thing I heard was a squeal of tires. I looked down, and there was a car fender uncomfortably close to my knee. I had almost been hit.

When I looked in the mirror before making the turn, I didn't see the car behind me. It was in my blind spot, the place behind you that you can't see in the mirror.

We have blind spots in our lives, too. They are the spots where we think we couldn't possibly fall down. Satan takes advantage by letting us get real smug about them. Then he attacks, and *blam!* down we go.

The best way to avoid being hit on your blind side is to let Jesus watch your back. Then you won't have to worry about being blind-sided by Satan.

■ ■ ■ ■

Be self-controlled and alert. Your enemy the devil prowls around like a roaring lion looking for someone to devour. 1 Peter 5:8.

Under Pressure

man was walking along the beach. He saw a figure up ahead of him. The figure would stoop, straighten, and then toss something into the waves. The person repeated this behavior over and over.

The man couldn't imagine what the person was doing. He began walking more quickly so he could solve the mystery.

As he got closer he saw that it was a woman. When he got close enough to speak he said, "Excuse me, ma'am, but I couldn't help wondering what you are doing."

She smiled at him and said, "I'm tossing stones into the water."

The man chuckled. "Ma'am, you'll never clear the beach that way."

"Oh, I'm not trying to clear the beach," she replied. "I'm clearing my soul. I've been asking the Lord to help me with things that are troubling me. Every time I think of something, I name a rock after the trouble, and then I throw it into the sea. Then it doesn't belong to me anymore. It's God's responsibility."

This week, try naming your problems, and then give them to God. Your problems will no longer belong to you. They will become God's responsibility.

■ ■ ■ ■

Humble yourselves, therefore, under God's mighty hand, that he may lift you up in due time. Cast all your anxiety on him because he cares for you. 1 Peter 5:6, 7.

Setting an Example

ince I'm older than my three sisters, my mom always told me that I was supposed to be an example to them. It was up to me to show them how they should behave. I'm sure I didn't always do a great job, but I tried to take my responsibility seriously.

You don't have to be the oldest to set an example, though. Every Christian should set an example for others. Maybe you're not older than your friends or your siblings. You might even be the youngest person at your church or in your class. But you can still be a good influence. There are many examples of young people serving as leaders, not only in the Bible, but also in our church history.

Age isn't nearly as important as willingness. What if young Samuel hadn't been willing to listen to God? What if Jesus had thought He wasn't old enough to teach in the Temple? What if Paul had turned Timothy away because he was too young? Instead, these people made a greater impression because of their age. You can too. Set an example that won't soon be forgotten.

■ ■ ■ ■

Don't let anyone look down on you because you are young,
but set an example for the believers in speech, in life,
in love, in faith and in purity. 1 Timothy 4:12.

Rejoice and Weep

ing David had a terribly confusing day. His troops won a great victory and saved him and his family, but his son Absalom was killed. Instead of rejoicing that he was safe, David wept for Absalom.

This made his troops feel terrible. They had risked their lives to save him, and here he was crying for his son. They slunk back into the city, their heads hung low.

The Bible tells us to rejoice with those who rejoice and weep with those who mourn. People like to share their feelings. When they're happy they want to tell someone why. And when they're sad they want a shoulder to cry on. They want someone to agree with them. "Yes, this is wonderful," or "What a tragedy."

Imagine that you just told your mom about the perfect score you got on a test. What if she says, "Yes, but don't forget that the next one will be even harder." Or what if you tell your friend about failing a test, and she says, "Yeah, but your hair looks great today!"

Don't you wish someone would listen to you and share your moment of victory or consolation? You can be that kind of listener for someone else. Rejoice with those who rejoice, and weep with those who mourn.

Rejoice with those who rejoice;
mourn with those who mourn. Romans 12:15.

The Race Before Us

he Olympics are the granddaddy of all races. In the very first ones the athletes wore long flowing robes. They had to take off their robes for the race so that they wouldn't get tripped up by their own clothes. The Bible talks about our sins being like the athletes' robes. We need to take them off so they don't trip us up in the race for life.

Even though athletes train for a long time, they still get tired before they finish the race. That's why it's important for them to pace themselves so they don't get too tired.

We need to pace ourselves too. Running a good race is never easy. And if we don't pace ourselves, we'll get tired and quit before we reach the finish line.

Athletes who get medals stand on the podium while their national anthem is played and a medal is put around their neck. If we do well in *our* spiritual race, our name will be listed with others in the hall of faith, and we will be given golden crowns as the angels sing "Hallelujah."

Therefore, since we are surrounded by such a great cloud of witnesses, let us throw off everything that hinders and the sin that so easily entangles, and let us run with perseverance the race marked out for us. Hebrews 12:1.

Two Rich Fools

ast night I listened to two millionaires bragging about who was richer. One said he lived in a castle; the other lived in Europe. The first flew in private jets; the second owned a jet and flew it himself. This went on for an hour while we stood in line waiting to get into a *rummage sale.*

The two men had probably not been born as wealthy as they are today, but they had certainly forgotten where they had come from. All they could see was their present wealth and status.

We have the same problem sometimes. We see someone doing wrong, and we think, *I would never do that,* as if it's beneath us. We completely forget that the only thing between us and evil is the Holy Spirit living in our hearts.

Without God we aren't any better or any worse than anyone else. We're all capable of the same bad behavior. If we remember that, our compassion might be the lifeline that leads others back to God.

At one time we too were foolish, disobedient, deceived and enslaved by all kinds of passions and pleasures. We lived in malice and envy, being hated and hating one another. But when the kindness and love of God our Savior appeared, he saved us, not because of righteous things we had done, but because of his mercy. Titus 3:3-5.

Everybody's Doing It

ut, Mom, all my friends are doing it!" Have you ever said that in a whining voice? I have. I used to say it all the time. It seemed as if everyone in school were wearing the same kinds of clothes, listening to the same kinds of music, and watching the same kinds of TV programs. Everyone except me, that is.

Mom never listened, though. She would just say, "If all your friends were going to jump off a bridge, would you do that, too?" And she had a point. Mom was awfully clever. Because, of course, if my friends were going to do something that dangerous, I wouldn't be right there behind them wanting to join the fun.

A lot of the things my friends were doing weren't a whole lot safer than jumping off a bridge. I just couldn't see it at the time.

The question to ask about what your friends are doing isn't "How will this hurt me?"

The question to ask is "How will this help me?"

If it won't help you, why do it? Instead of being a follower, be a leader. Chances are your friends will be right behind you.

In everything set them an example
by doing what is good. Titus 2:7.

The Gift That Keeps On Giving

I love to watch my kids open presents. They can't wait to rip the pretty paper off the boxes and see what's inside.

It's interesting to see what happens when they find out. If it's a toy, they might squeal and play with it for a few minutes before moving on to the next present. If it's something practical, like socks, they toss it over their shoulder and go on to the next present.

Even though the practical gifts are the ones they are least interested in, those are the ones they will use the most. The presents they were so excited about get lost, broken, and forgotten about.

So when God asked Solomon what he wanted for a present, Solomon asked for wisdom, which was like asking for socks. He wanted something useful. He could have asked for anything he wanted, but he wanted a gift that would help others.

I like to think of Solomon's example when I pray. His story reminds me not to ask God for flashy things I won't appreciate later on. Instead, I ask God for peace, kindness, patience—gifts that will keep on giving.

When all Israel heard the verdict the king had given,
they held the king in awe, because they saw that
he had wisdom from God to administer justice. 1 Kings 3:28.

A Child Is Born

hen you were born, your parents probably sent out birth announcements. They proudly told everyone they knew that you had been born into their family. They might have included a picture of you, all red and wrinkled. The announcement probably told when you were born and how much you weighed and, of course, your name.

When Jesus was born, God sent birth announcements too. He sent the most incredible birth announcement the world has ever known. He sent millions of angels with a singing babygram. A new Person had been born, and God the Father was so proud He wanted everyone to know about the Baby. This special Baby was unlike any the world had ever known.

Today is the day we celebrate Jesus' birthday. Spend some time thanking God for giving us such a wonderful gift.

Further reading: You can find the Christmas story in Luke 1-2:20.

■ ■ ■ ■

"I bring you good news of great joy that will be for all the people. Today in the town of David a Savior has been born to you; he is Christ the Lord. This will be a sign to you: You will find a baby wrapped in cloths and lying in a manger." Sudden a great company of the heavenly host appeared with the angel, praising God and saying, "Glory to God in the highest, and on earth peace to men on whom his favor rests." Luke 2:10-14.

Discipline

I f your life was perfect, what would it be like? Would you make pop quizzes illegal? Would you lower the standards for passing high school to saying the ABCs and being able to eat a whole bag of chips at one sitting? Would you give teachers a permanent vacation? Would you make it a law that everyone had to be nice to you? Would you turn your parents into a chauffeur and a maid?

If your life was perfect, then you wouldn't be a Christian. Being a Christian means growing in character. We can't grow in character if we have perfect lives, if everything always goes our way, and if everyone loves us. Character grows through hard times, mean people, and challenges that are way beyond us. At those times God is able to work with us and make our character like His.

So you've got problems? Bad days? People are mean to you? Dogs bite your ankles? Teachers flunk you? Rejoice! God loves you, and He's working with you. No matter what happens, it's gonna be a great day!

Endure hardship as discipline; God is treating you as sons. For what son is not disciplined by his father? If you are not disciplined (and everyone undergoes discipline), then you are illegitimate children and not true sons. Hebrews 12:7, 8.

Preach It!

I'll admit I never thought much about my hair. It was on top of my head. It was blond. It was straight. When it was in the way I pulled it back into a ponytail or tucked it behind my ears. Most of the time I wore it straight and very long. Not because I thought about it, but because I wasn't thinking about it at all.

It became painfully obvious how little I thought about my hair when my sister Faith and I went to Camp Lawroweld. All the girls *did stuff* to their hair. They curled it. They *styled* it. It was like I woke up that day and realized it was time to change. I watched the other girls and learned new things to do with my hair.

In the same way our actions can show people what they're missing out on. For example, when our friends see us enjoying the Sabbath with our families, they might realize they're missing out. Not because we told them, but because of how we live our lives. If we are always positive, even in negative circumstances, they know we've got something they don't.

Every day in everything you do, your actions preach a sermon. Make it a good one.

I have set you an example that you
should do as I have done for you. John 13:15.

Real Friends

s I hiked up Mount Mansfield with some of my friends, I did a very stupid thing. We had all climbed up onto a rocky precipice. From this cliff there was a gangplank of rock about 12 feet long, two feet wide, and a long way down. Everyone was taking turns walking out on it. So I did too. But because I'm afraid of heights, when I got out there I froze.

As you can probably guess, the others got me down. And nothing could ever convince me to try that again. Not even if they laughed at me and called me a chicken.

My friends would probably understand and respect my decision later on. But some people I know wouldn't.

You might know some people like that. If you don't join the crowd, they think something is wrong with you. And they tease you to see if pressure will make you change your mind.

It's important to make a firm stand with these types of people. Say no, and simply stick with your decision. If they keep pressuring you to do something dangerous or wrong, you've made a very important discovery. They aren't really your friends after all.

Of course, your former friends will be very surprised when you don't eagerly join them any more in the wicked things they do, and they will laugh at you in contempt and scorn. 1 Peter 4:4, TLB.

Ebenezer

ast year we went on a vacation to Wells, New York. I think that area has the largest deposit of garnets anywhere. They are only industrial quality, but chances are if you pick up a rock, there are garnets in it.

When we were canoeing, we found a huge black stone studded with them. I made my husband lug it home for me. Every time I see it I am reminded of the wonderful week we spent on vacation.

All along your life are memories. Certain things remind you vividly of them. It might be a shirt, a person, a rock, a pair of shoes, or a photograph. I call these things "memory markers." They are reminders that we can see and feel, which help us to remember important things that have happened. In the Bible we also read about people setting up stones or markers of great events.

As you look back over this past year, no doubt you have added many markers. Set up another one today that will remind you of a renewed commitment to Jesus as you prepare for the new year. Every time you see it you'll be reminded of your commitment.

■ ■ ■ ■

Then Samuel took a stone and set it up between Mizpah and Shen. He named it Ebenezer, saying, "Thus far has the Lord helped us." 1 Samuel 7:12.

Carry On

Maria brought her test paper up to the front of the room and laid it on the teacher's desk. Returning to her seat, she noticed the studied casualness of a new girl sitting next to her. The girl seemed too unconcerned.

Glancing sideways, Maria caught the new girl copying the answers off the paper next to her. She was cheating. Maria said nothing as she slid into her seat. But as soon as class was over she approached the new girl as everyone walked out of the room.

"I can help you," Maria offered.

The girl jumped a little. "Help me do what?" she asked, blushing.

"I can help you study so that you don't have to cheat."

"I didn't," the girl began. Then she stopped. "So what if I cheat?"

"Wouldn't you rather not?" Maria asked.

"Yes," the girl admitted. "I don't like cheating. But I was getting good grades in the school I came from. And if my grades drop, my parents won't be happy."

"Let's study together. I'm sure you'll get good grades."

The girl smiled and stuck out her hand. "It's a deal."

■ ■ ■ ■

You are living a brand new kind of life that is continually learning more and more of what is right, and trying constantly to be more and more like Christ who created this new life within you. Colossians 3:10, TLB.

New Beginnings

ere we are, at the close of another year. Looking back, we can see the mistakes we made and the victories we had. Looking forward, we see a new year stretching ahead like a big, empty canvas waiting for our lives to be painted on. What kind of picture are you going to paint?

When I was a kid, I used to make New Year's resolutions. I listed a page of them every year. Sometimes I reached them, sometimes I didn't. But every year I would make new ones and start all over again. I still make New Year's resolutions, but my list is shorter now.

Since the new year is a time for new things, I'd like to make a suggestion for you. A friend of mine does this, and I think it's a great idea. Every new year she starts a different version of the Bible. Personally I have enjoyed the Message version. There's something about reading the familiar Bible stories in a slightly different language that helps us to see them in slightly different ways. Who knows, you may see something you never saw before.

Thanks for spending the year with me. Go with God, and have a happy new year!

And whatever you do, whether in word or deed,
do it all in the name of the Lord Jesus,
giving thanks to God the Father through him. Colossians 3:17.